A CHRONOLOGY OF POST WAR
BRITISH POLITICS

A
CHRONOLOGY
OF
POST WAR
BRITISH POLITICS

GEOFFREY FOOTE

CROOM HELM
London • New York • Sydney

© 1988 G. Foote
Croom Helm Ltd, Provident House,
Burrell Row, Beckenham, Kent, BR3 1AT

Croom Helm Australia, 44–50 Waterloo Road,
North Ryde, 2113, New South Wales

Published in the USA by
Croom Helm
in association with Methuen, Inc.
29 West 35th Street,
New York, NY 10001

British Library Cataloguing in Publication Data

Foote, Geoffrey
    A chronology of post war British politics.
    1. Great Britain — Politics and
    government — 1945–
    I. Title
    320.941   JN231
    ISBN 0-7099-4922-7

Library of Congress Cataloging-in-Publication Data

ISBN 0-7099-4922-7

January 1945 — June 1987

1945

January

3   A White Paper on local government in England and Wales decides not to interfere with the existing structure of local government.

6   Labour refuses to allow Common Wealth, an egalitarian socialist party which had won several wartime by-elections, to affiliate.

12   The Red Army opens its final offensive on Nazi Germany.

18   Winston Churchill, Prime Minister in the coalition government, is severely criticised by Labour backbenchers in the Commons after defending the suppression of a Greek leftist insurrection by British troops.

23   Two corporations are created to supply and direct capital; the Industrial and Commercial Finance Corporation for small and medium businesses, and the Finance Corporation for Industry Ltd for the rehabilitation and development of industrial businesses.

February

1-3   The Liberal Party Assembly in London pledges itself to a 'liberal policy of radical reform' and, declaring the state's primary aim to be the achievement of full employment, demands a long-term programme of state expenditure on social services.

4-11   Churchill meets with President Roosevelt and Stalin in Yalta to discuss the problems of German surrender, Poland and the establishment of a United Nations.

13   A world trade union conference, organised by the British Trades Union Congress (TUC), brings together United States and Soviet trade union delegates in London.

15   The Representation of the People Bill is enacted, integrating the local and parliamentary franchise, reducing the business franchise, and allowing postal voting for the armed forces.

28   Sir Stafford Cripps, the former leader of the Labour left, is readmitted to the Labour Party six years after his expulsion.

March

14-15   The Conservative Party annual conference in London calls for the abolition of wartime controls and the restoration of private enterprise to the greatest degree possible; R.A. Butler becomes Chairman of the Conservative Central Council.

22   Henry Willink, Minister of Health, announces that emergency measures will be needed for housing in the next two years.

23   British forces under Field-Marshall Montgomery cross the Rhine.

28   After Churchill's refusal to repeal the 1927 Trades Dispute Act, the TUC General Council appeals to the Labour Party and organises a campaign to persuade the electorate that the Act is wrong.

The last V-rocket falls on Britain.

April

12   President Franklin Roosevelt dies suddenly; Harry Truman becomes the new United States President.

In the Motherwell by-election, Dr McIntyre wins the seat for the Scottish National Party (SNP).

21   The Labour Party publishes *Let Us Face the Future*, promising the nationalisation of basic industries, economic planning and increased social security.

24   Sir John Anderson, Chancellor of the Exchequer, refuses to change the existing level of taxation in his budget, and increases borrowing to meet the deficit of £2,300 million.

25   The UN conference opens in San Francisco.

26   Common Wealth gains its third by-election victory at Chelmsford from the Conservatives, indicating a swing to the left and a desire for an end to the wartime electoral truce.

28   Mussolini, the Italian Fascist leader, is killed by partisans.

30   Hitler commits suicide in Berlin.

May

8   VE Day is celebrated throughout Britain as German

forces surrender.

18   Churchill writes to the coalition leaders to call for a continuation of the coalition until the defeat of Japan, and proposes a referendum on the prolongation of Parliament's life.

21-5   The Labour Party conference is held at Blackpool; Clement Attlee, the Labour leader, rejects Churchill's proposals for continuing the coalition (and, in a letter, describes the referendum proposal as alien to British political traditions); *Let Us Face the Future* is endorsed, and Herbert Morrison, Home Secretary and deputy leader, proposes public ownership for each industry on its merits.

23   Churchill ends the coalition government, and forms a 'caretaker' Conservative ministry; a general election is announced for *5 July*.

June

5   The Allied Control Commission assumes control throughout Germany, which is divided into four occupation zones.
        In a radio broadcast, Churchill declares that Labour would have to introduce a Gestapo to enforce socialism.

11   Churchill issues a manifesto proposing a Four-Year Plan of mutual co-operation between state and industry to maintain high employment.

15   The Family Allowances Bill, providing for the payment of five shillings per week for each child after the first, is enacted.
        The Distribution of Industry Bill is enacted, giving the government new peacetime powers to control the location of industry.
        Parliament is dissolved.

17   The Liberal manifesto announces a pragmatic approach to public ownership and support for a Welfare State.

26   The UN Charter is signed by the representatives of 50 nations in an attempt to create an international organisation which could use force against aggressor nations; this aim is virtually negated by the right of permanent members of the Security Council to veto all but procedural questions, and by the permission of 'regional' agreements and agencies.

30   Churchill accuses Harold Laski, Chairman of Labour's National Executive Committee (NEC) of being the real Labour leader.

July

4   In his reply to Churchill, Attlee reasserts the constitutional independence of the Parliamentary Labour Party (PLP) from the NEC.

5   Polling day, with a 72.8 per cent turnout (25,095,195 votes); polling is delayed in 22 constituencies until *12 July* and in one constituency until *19 July* to take local holidays into account; the result is delayed to *26 July* in order to count the vote of the armed services.

17-   Churchill, accompanied by Attlee, goes to Potsdam to dis-
Aug 2 cuss the occupation of Germany with Truman and Stalin.

26   The general election results are announced, showing a Labour landslide victory with an overall majority of 146; 393 Labour MPs are elected, 210 Conservatives, 12 Liberals, 2 Communists, and 22 others; Labour has 11,967,746 votes (48.0 per cent), Conservatives 9,972,010 (39.6 per cent), Liberals 2,252, 430 (9.0 per cent); 13 cabinet ministers are defeated, including Harold Macmillan, Leo Amery and Brendan Bracken; Sir Archibald Sinclair, the Liberal leader, is also defeated.

Attlee becomes Prime Minister of the first majority Labour government, with Hugh Dalton as Chancellor of the Exchequer, Ernest Bevin as Foreign Secretary, Chuter Ede as Home Secretary, and Herbert Morrison as Lord President of the Council in charge of the nationalisation programme.

August

1   Labour MPs sing *The Red Flag* as Parliament reassembles. Clement Davies is elected Liberal leader.

6   The United States drops an atomic bomb on Hiroshima.

9   The United States drops a second atomic bomb on Nagasaki.

15   VJ Day is celebrated as Japan's surrender marks the end of the Second World War.

16   In the Debate on the Address, Attlee points to the country's economic problems and states the need to continue wartime controls on the economy.

20   Bevin announces the British government's support for the Greek Royalist government until conditions of stability are restored.

24   Lend-lease is ended by the United States, causing alarm in the government and ending the hope of a rapid return to economic recovery.

September

10-14   The TUC Annual Congress at Blackpool is mainly concerned with the need to accelerate demobilisation; the United States delegate makes a bitter attack on Soviet trade unions.

11   Bevin attends the Allied foreign ministers' conference in London, which seeks to draft a peace settlement for Germany.

20   The All-India Congress Committee, led by Mahatma Gandhi and Jawaharlal Nehru, rejects the British proposals for self-government within the Empire and demands that Britain quit India.

23   Egypt demands the end of British military occupation.

25-Nov 2   A dock strike at Birkenhead over a demand for more wages spreads quickly to the major ports, in defiance of the union leaders, and troops are called in.

October

15   Sir Stafford Cripps, President of the Board of Trade, announces that tripartite working parties of representatives of state, industry and labour are to be the principal body governing most major industries.

17   Aneurin Bevan, Minister of Health and Housing, makes a statement of intent on housing, proposing to use local authorities to solve the problems of lower income groups by building housing for let.

27   Dalton introduces a supplementary budget abolishing post-war credits and reducing income tax from one shilling to nine pence.

29   Dalton introduces a Bill to nationalise the Bank of England; no change is to be made to the Board, though the Governor is now to be appointed by the Crown; Conservative opposition is purely formal.

November

1   Labour makes sweeping gains in the municipal elections.
Lord Winster, Civil Aviation Minister, announces that public ownership is to be the guiding principle in air transport.

7   In a Commons debate on the atomic bomb, Bevin warns scientists that they are the servants of the state, bound by the official Secrets Act, and calls on the Soviet Union 'to lay her cards on the table' about her international intentions.

14   Harold Macmillan returns to the Commons after winning a by-election at Bromley.

15   After the report of the Select Committee on Procedure, it is agreed to send all bills to five Standing Committees, each with a core membership of 20.

19   Morrison warns that compensation may be affected if industries selected for nationalisation attempt to delay the time of transfer.

23   Arthur Deakin, a tough follower of Bevin, is elected General Secretary of the Transport and General Workers' Union (TGWU).

28   The Conservative Central Council, a conference of activists, calls for the adoption of a vigorous anti-socialist policy, though the leadership is intent on accepting the Welfare State.

December

7   An agreement with the United States, for a loan to Britain of US$3.75 billion, is signed.

12   Conservative discontent with the conditions of the United States loan forces Churchill to abstain on the motion to accept; 98 MPs vote against (71 Conservatives and 23 Labour).

20   The Coal Industry Nationalisation Bill is published, setting up a National Coal Board (NCB) on the lines of a corporation, but disappointing left-wingers who had hoped for workers' control.

General

George Orwell's fable, *Animal Farm*, attacks the Soviet Union as a betrayal of socialism.

1946

January

23   James Griffiths, Minister of National Insurance, introduces the National Insurance Bill, providing state benefits for unemployment, illness and old age in return for weekly insurance payments.

25   Lord Wavell, the Indian Viceroy, tells the Central Legislative Assembly in New Delhi that the government is to establish an all-India constitutional conference.

30   The PLP suspends Standing Orders for two years, freeing Labour MPs from disciplinary procedures.

February

5   Bevan introduces the Housing Bill, increasing Treasury subsidies for local authority housing in England and Wales.

12   In the debate on the repeal of the 1927 Trades Disputes Act, Bevin states that he regards the measure as a personal stigma, in that it unjustly assumes unions to be enemies of the state.

14   The Bank of England Bill is enacted.

19   Attlee announces that a Cabinet mission comprising Sir Stafford Cripps, A.V. Alexander, and Lord Pethick-Lawrence is to go to India.

19-23   A mutiny in the Royal Indian Navy sets off rioting against British rule in Bombay and Karachi.

20   The Federation of British Industries (FBI) asks the government not to proceed with its nationalisation measures too hastily, and to restrict them to individual industries.

March

4   Churchill, in a speech at Fulton, Missouri, in the presence of President Truman, calls on Britain and the United States to stand up to the Soviet Union, which had imposed an 'iron curtain' across Europe; Attlee refuses to dissociate the government from its sentiments.

6   In response to an appeal by Attlee and Bevin, trade union executives pledge themselves to increased productivity.

7   Labour retains control of the London County Council (LCC), with 90 Labour members against 28 Conservatives, two Liberals and two Communists.

24   The Cabinet mission arrives in India.

29   Britain grants the Gold Coast a new constitution, making it the first British African colony with a majority of Africans in the legislature; this fails to satisfy the nationalists, led by Kwame Nkrumah, who want independence.

April

9   Dalton's budget gives only minor tax reliefs because of the danger of inflation.

17   John Wilmot, Minister of Supply, announces the government's intention to nationalise iron and steel, arousing strong opposition from the Conservatives and the steel employers.

29   An Anglo-American committee advises against the partition of Palestine as a solution to Zionist demands for a separate Jewish state.

May

2   The National Health Service Bill, setting up a free health service for all on the basis of a nationally centralised hospital service, is given a second reading by 359 to 172 votes; the Conservatives oppose the Bill on the grounds that it involves the extinction of private hospitals and the substitution of fees for salaries for general practitioners.

9-11   The Liberal Party Assembly meets in London amidst warnings of the eclipse of British Liberalism.

12   The FBI opposes the nationalisation of iron and steel, arguing that it will cause instability and uncertainty throughout industry.

22   The 1927 Trades Disputes Act, outlawing certain strikes and making political funding more difficult, is repealed.

June

10-14   The Labour Party annual conference meets at Bournemouth; Bevin is forced to defend himself against criticisms that he is following a Conservative, not a Socialist, foreign policy, especially with regard to his opposition to Communism and Zionism.

23   Negotiations on the nature of a post-Independence India finally break down with the Congress Party demanding that India remain unified while the Moslem League demands a separate Moslem state; the Cabinet mission leaves India having failed in its task.

27   John Strachey, Minister of Food, announces the rationing of bread and flour in response to a world wheat shortage; in Northern Ireland emergency bread distribution centres are set up in Belfast and Derry.

July

1   Lord Woolton becomes Conservative Party Chairman.
12   The Coal Nationalisation Bill is enacted.
15   President Truman signs a bill of credit for US$3.75 billion.
22   The Irgun, a Zionist guerrilla group, bombs the King David Hotel in Jerusalem, killing 91 people: British, Arabs and Jews; this highlights the increasingly violent attacks on British troops and Arabs in Palestine and intensifies the revival of anti-Semitism in Britain.

August

1   The National Insurance Bill is enacted.
16   In India the Moslem League holds a 'day of action' to call for a separate Moslem state; widespread communal violence results, with 5,000 killed in Calcutta.
22   Arthur Horner, a Communist, is elected General Secretary of the National Union of Mineworkers (NUM) and pledges full co-operation with the state.

A squatting movement begins and rapidly spreads throughout the country as homeless families move into empty army camps.

September

2   An interim government led by Nehru is set up in India, but the Moslem League boycotts it and calls for a separate state.

8   Under Communist leadership, 300 homeless families occupy vacant luxury flats and mansions.

14   Five Communist leaders are arrested on trespass charges, and the London squatters are put under eviction threats.

October

3-5   The Conservative Party annual conference at Blackpool urges the leadership to put forward positive policies to win back the party's electoral support; Lord Woolton opens a major recruiting campaign.

4   The Defence White Paper recommends a Defence Committee under a new Ministry of Defence as spokesman for the three services.

14   Attlee refuses Welsh Labour demands for a separate Secretary for Wales on the grounds that there would be duplication of officials in London and Cardiff.

21-5   The TUC Annual Congress, Brighton, endorses calls for higher productivity and an end to 'restrictive practices', and calls for a 40-hour week; on foreign affairs, a large minority is critical of the government's anti-Soviet stance; Vincent Tewson replaces Sir Walter Citrine as TUC General Secretary.

21   Bevan defends his policy of encouraging local authorities to build houses against Conservative calls to give private enterprise the task.

27   Cripps, in a speech at Bristol, says that he does not believe many workers are capable of running industry.

30   In a free vote, the Commons agrees to set up a Royal Commission to investigate the control and ownership of the press.

November

6   The National Health Service Bill and the Cable and

Wireless Bill are enacted.

The Report of the Royal Commission on Equal Pay (under Lord Justice Asquith) accepts the principle of equal pay for men and women in non-industrial employment, but points to difficulties of applying the principle in industry given the opposition of the unions.

8 The Select Committee on Parliamentary Procedure rejects reform of procedure as an infringement of private Members' rights, but admits the overwhelming pressure on parliamentary time.

13 Morrison as Leader of the Commons rejects the rights of private Members to any time and announces that the whole of the next session should be public business.

18 Richard Crossman moves a critical amendment to the Address calling for a democratic socialist foreign policy, but withdraws after Attlee makes it an issue of confidence; nevertheless, 100 MPs abstain in the vote.

52 Labour MPs vote against the continuation of conscription.

28 The Transport Bill is published, providing for the nationalisation of road and rail transport, inland waterways, docks and harbours; Conservatives and Liberals oppose on the grounds that it creates an inefficient monopoly.

At a PLP meeting, calls for the restoration of Standing Orders to discipline further backbench rebellions are unsuccessful.

December

2 Bevin and the United States Secretary of State Byrnes agree to the economic fusion of the British and American zones in Germany.

9 A Constituent Assembly in India calls for independence, but it is boycotted by the Moslem League, which is calling for its own nation.

10 The FBI and the British Employers' Confederation (BEC) agree in principle to merge; the merger does not take place until 1964.

12 Dr Guy Dain, Chairman of the British Medical Association (BMA), refuses to enter into negotiations with Bevan after a poll of his members opposes the new

National Health Service (NHS).

A Liaison Committee of Transport and Industry is formed by employers threatened by nationalisation to organise protests against public ownership.

20   Churchill denounces the government's policy of 'scuttle' from India as Cabinet opinion moves towards an early withdrawal.

Coal shortages begin to hit industry badly.

General

Michael Polanyi's *Full Employment and Free Trade* develops the Keynesian analysis of the economy.

Terence Rattigan's play, *The Winslow Boy*, celebrates the courage of the upper classes in the face of bureaucracy.

1947

January

1   As the NCB begins operation, Attlee foresees 'great possibilities of social advance for the workers and, indeed, for the whole nation', but Horner stresses the independence of the NUM as well as its opposition to unofficial strikes.

2   Attlee privately rebukes Bevin for his opposition to an early withdrawal from India, and points out that the government can no longer command the Indian Army's full obedience.

7   A strike of road haulage workers opens a period of industrial strife, especially in transport, shipbuilding and engineering.

8   The Town and Country Planning Bill is introduced, subordinating property development to planning needs.

10   The Electricity Bill is introduced, nationalising the electricity industry.

12   Churchill heads the United Europe Committee to further the cause of European unity.

13   The Cripps plan rations coal to industry and consumers, as coal shortages coincide with the coldest weather for 66 years, followed by floods.

15   The BMA decides to reopen negotiations on its participation in the NHS after a conciliatory letter from Bevan.

21   Attlee states that the regulation of wages and salaries is to be voluntary.

26   Egypt breaks off negotiations with Britain over withdrawal from the Canal Zone in protest at the British plans to give the Sudan self-government.

31   Churchill calls for the relinquishment of the Palestine mandate.

February

6   Ellen Wilkinson, the Minister of Education, dies, possibly by suicide.

7   As Britain suffers a major fuel shortage, Emmanuel

Shinwell, the Minister of Fuel and Power, forecasts complete disaster within ten days and announces the cessation of electricity supply for industrial consumers in London and parts of England.

A British proposal to divide Palestine into Arab and Jewish zones is rejected by both sides in the conflict.

10   Shinwell announces a complete cessation of the domestic supply of electricity to industry, and coal is to be requisitioned under the regulations of the Defence of the Realm Act (DORA); 1,800,000 workers are laid off as a result of the new orders.

20   Attlee informs the Commons that Wavell is to be replaced as Indian Viceroy and that independence must be given to the sub-continent no later than *1 June 1948*.

22   The *Economic Survey for 1947* is published, outlining the principles of democratic planning.

March

4   The fuel crisis begins to ease.

6   Churchill, in a Commons debate on the decision to transfer power to India, states that 'it is with deep regret that I have watched the clattering down of the British Empire with all its glories'.

A limited number of party political broadcasts is to be transmitted over radio after agreement between the BBC and the leading parties.

11   The Exchange Control Bill is enacted, making the existing controls on the movement of capital permanent.

12   The Truman Doctrine, outlined by President Truman in a speech to Congress, announces the replacement of British by United States support for the governments of Greece and Turkey.

23   Lord Mountbatten becomes Viceroy of India, with a mandate to negotiate an early independence.

26   Attlee announces the composition of a Royal Commission on the Press under Sir David Ross, provoking accusations of political prejudice in its composition.

31   The National Service Bill, providing for the continuation of conscription, has its second reading and 72 Labour MPs vote against.

April

2	Britain refers the Palestine mandate to the UN.
15	Dalton's budget offers greater income tax relief but higher indirect taxes, and worries are expressed over the deteriorating balance of payments situation.
17	Pethick-Lawrence resigns as India Secretary, and is succeeded by Lord Listowel.
24	The Moscow conference of foreign ministers fails after divisions emerge between the Soviet Union and the Western powers over Germany.
24-6	The Liberal Party Assembly at Bournemouth, calls for a true industrial democracy based on co-partnership and profit-sharing.

May

1	*Keep Left* is issued, written by Michael Foot, Richard Crossman and Ian Mikardo; it calls for a Socialist foreign policy separate from both the Soviet Union and the United States.
	Morrison says that unofficial strikes are strikes against trade union democracy.
7	The period of full-time National Service is reduced from 18 months to twelve months.
11	The Conservatives publish the *Industrial Charter*, written by the Conservative Industrial Policy Committee, chaired by Butler; it accepts the nationalisation measures and proposes a Workers' Charter guaranteeing employment security and individual status.
14	The United Europe Committee holds its inaugural meeting in the Albert Hall; Churchill, as chairman, calls for a United States of Europe.
22	*Cards on the Table* is issued by the Labour Party, accusing the Soviet Union of trying to eliminate Britain as a power in Europe and the Middle East.
26-30	The Labour Party annual conference meets at Margate; Morrison, rejecting too rapid an advance towards socialism, looks to the middle classes as 'our partners in the great social enterprise', though Shinwell declares that Labour represents the working class, and the rest 'did not matter two hoots'; the NEC rejects demands for equal pay for women.

27   The Cabinet finally endorses the decision to partition India, with the two territories on India's eastern and western flanks becoming Pakistan.

June

2   The various communal leaders in India accept the 'balkanisation of India', as Nehru describes the proposed partition.

4   Mountbatten announces that India is to obtain its independence on *15 August*, nearly a year earlier than envisaged.

5   The United States Secretary of State, George Marshall, calls for a European Recovery Programme to aid the crisis-ridden European economies.

13   Bevin applauds the Marshall speech as 'one of the greatest speeches in world history'.

30   Dalton announces drastic cuts in tobacco, petrol and newsprint quantities in the face of a growing exchange crisis.

July

2   The Dominions Office becomes the Commonwealth Relations Office.

7   An Economic Planning Board with Sir Edwin Plowden as Chairman is established to act as 'the eyes and ears of the government' (Morrison).

15   The convertibility clause leads to a disastrous drain of dollars from Britain.

At the TGWU conference, Deakin calls for the partial direction of labour, arguing that 'it is our standard of life that is at stake', and he is supported in this by the TUC General Council.

18   The Government of India Bill is enacted.

19   Bevan threatens the House of Lords at a miners' rally in Morpeth.

22   George Isaacs, Minister of Labour, imposes 'staggered hours' on industry.

30   The PLP discusses the economic crisis as the Attlee Must Go (AMGO) movement grows.

Churchill addresses a demonstration of 60,000 in Blenheim Park and accuses the government of over-planning and extravagance.

August

1   Anti-Semitic demonstrations in Liverpool and Manchester, after the hanging of two British sergeants in Palestine, degenerate into violence.

6   Attlee announces an austerity plan.
     The Agriculture Bill is enacted.

8   The Transitional Powers Bill and Orders in Council give the government drastic powers to use defence regulations in order to increase production and redress the trade imbalance.

12–   An unofficial miners' strike at Grimethorpe Colliery
Sept 11 sparks off widespread unofficial action, especially in Yorkshire, highlighting the growing animosity between the NCB and the miners, especially as the Board prosecutes persistent absentees.

15   The proclamation of Indian Independence; India is partitioned, with Nehru as Indian Premier and Liaquat Ali Khan as Premier of a Moslem Pakistan; a mass slaughter of Hindus and Moslems caught on the wrong side of the borders follows.

20   Dalton announces the suspension of sterling convertibility.

September

1-5   The TUC Annual Congress at Southport supports government plans for the direction of labour; Bevin advocates an Empire Customs Union and calls for increased production as a necessary basis for Britain's political independence, leading to United States complaints.

9   Cripps sees Attlee to discuss the formation of a new government under Bevin, but Attlee explains that he has no wish to resign, thereby ending a potential threat to his leadership.

11   Labour does badly at the Liverpool Edge Hill by-election,

where its majority is reduced from 6,039 to 1,953.

18   The London Trades Council expresses concern at the revival of Fascist and anti-Semitic activity in east London.

29   In a government reshuffle, Cripps becomes Minister of Economic Affairs, while Harold Wilson at 31 becomes the youngest Cabinet minister as President of the Board of Trade.

October

2-4   The Conservative Party annual conference, Brighton, adopts the *Industrial Charter*; Eden asks the party to 'think Imperially' in trade and defence matters, and Lord Woolton calls for a £1,000,000 'fighting fund' and a major expansion of the Young Conservatives.

5   The Communist Information Bureau, or Cominform, is established in Warsaw to co-ordinate the activities of European Communist parties.

6   The Control of Engagement Order is in force, providing for the direction of labour.

21   The King's Speech announces that a Bill will be introduced to amend the 1911 Parliament Act by reducing the Lords' veto to one year, instead of three; Churchill denounces the proposals as an 'act of social aggression'.

23   Cripps reduces capital expenditure by £200 million, temporarily ending the construction of new houses and factories. Churchill supports the measures while denouncing the policy of state planning.

30   Gary Allighan, a Labour MP, is expelled from the Commons by 187 to 175 votes for 'dishonourable conduct' in alleging that inebriated MPs gave confidential information to the press for money.

November

1   Municipal elections show a Conservative revival, especially in the north-west of England.

12   Dalton announces some details of his autumn budget of increased taxes to a reporter from the *Star* before he tells the Commons.

13   Dalton resigns over the budget leak; Cripps succeeds him as Chancellor of the Exchequer.

18   Lord Addison, Lord Privy Seal, rejects an appeal for an all-party conference on the role and composition of the Lords.

23   Sir Oswald Mosley announces a new Union Movement in place of the old British Union of Fascists.

26   The Liberals reject a fusion with the Conservatives, after leading Conservatives call for an anti-socialist front.

29   The UN announces a plan for the partition of Palestine, with Jerusalem under UN Trusteeship.

The Gallup poll gives the Conservatives 50.5 per cent, Labour 38 per cent, and the Liberals 9 per cent.

December

12   The report of the Boundary Commission envisages a complete redistribution of seats throughout the country, the first general redistribution since 1918; all two-member constituencies are to be divided into single constituencies.

21   Morgan Phillips, Labour General Secretary, calls for a campaign against Communist infiltration of the trade union movement.

General

Labour Party membership is 5,040,000; TUC membership is 7,540,000; Communist Party membership is 43,000.

R.B. McCallum and Alison Readman produce a pioneering study, *The British General Election of 1945*, beginning the series of Nuffield election studies.

1948

January

1   The nationalisation of the railways is in force.

3   Attlee, in a radio broadcast, warns of the Communist danger to democracy and claims for a socialist Britain a different system than either the United States or the Soviet Union, combining social justice with democracy.

4   Burma becomes independent as a republic.

8   The BMA calls for the absolute rejection of the NHS.

22   In a Commons debate on foreign policy, Bevin calls for a Western European Union to promote co-operation against Soviet domination.

February

4   A White Paper on Incomes, Costs and Prices denounces the wage-price spiral and calls for voluntary collective agreements to regulate incomes (approved by the TUC General Council on *18 February*).

        Ceylon becomes a self-governing dominion.

9   Bevan denounces the BMA opposition to the NHS as 'a squalid political conspiracy'.

12   Cripps asks the FBI to work out a voluntary plan on reducing profits and prices.

        The BMA votes overwhelmingly against participation in the NHS.

19   All-party discussions begin on the powers and composition of the upper chamber.

21-3   The Communist Party Congress, meeting in London, condemns the TUC General Council for accepting wage restraint and calls on the left to oppose the present Labour government.

25   A Communist *coup* in Czechoslovakia helps to facilitate the passage of the Marshall Aid proposals through the United States Congress.

March

6   In a letter to the Croydon North constituency, Churchill envisages 'a progressive Conservative administration, reinforced by the best men of good will and ability outside the Conservative ranks'.

8   The Labour Party publishes *Public Ownership: the Next Step* which accepts the mixed economy but calls for partial nationalisation on the principles of opposing monopoly and inefficiency; no specific industries are mentioned.

11   The Conservatives retain the Croydon North by-election, increasing their majority from 607 to 11,664.

15   The government bans Communists and Fascists from work vital to state security.

Cripps accepts the FBI proposals for voluntary price controls and limitation of dividends.

17   Britain signs the Brussels Treaty with France, Belgium, the Netherlands and Luxembourg for a 50-year alliance, and economic and military co-operation.

24   All-party discussions on the Parliament Bill break down over the question of the Lords' delaying power, though there is general agreement on the introduction of a non-hereditary element.

A TUC delegate conference supports voluntary wage restraint against strong left-wing opposition by 5.4 million to 2 million votes.

April

1   The electricity industry comes under public ownership.

6   Cripps's first budget institutes a capital levy on investment income, and increases indirect taxes.

7   A conciliatory Bevan wins over the doctors to participate in the NHS after making concessions on the retention of paybeds and fees.

9   The Local Government Boundary Commission proposes the reshaping of the local government system in England and Wales into three types of local authority — county, county borough and county district.

14   The Commons votes for the suspension of the death penalty by 245 to 222 votes.

19   Eden launches a campaign to double Conservative membership after Woolton announces the achievement of the £1,000,000 'fighting fund'.

21   Churchill, at the Albert Hall, calls for a Europe united on Christian principles against the 'Asiatic imperialism' of Communist rule.

22-4   The Liberal Party Assembly, Blackpool, calls for a Council of Western Europe to increase European unity, and eventually for a democratic European Federation based on a Charter of Human Rights.

28   John Platts-Mills is expelled from the Labour Party for supporting the Italian socialist, Pietro Nenni (then in alliance with the Communists), and 21 other Labour MPs are warned off pro-Communist activities by the NEC; Alfred Edwards is also expelled for his strong criticisms of steel nationalisation.

A Standing Committee on Scottish Bills is established as a measure of devolution and to save parliamentary time; it is to debate Scottish legislation before returning them to the House for a formal second reading.

May

2   Shinwell, the War Secretary, calls for the introduction of an element of democracy into the nationalised industries to prevent disillusionment with socialism.

13   Sir Charles Reid resigns as NCB chairman, having no confidence in its 'uninspiring and cumbersome organisation'; Hugh Gaitskell, Minister of Fuel and Power, refuses to answer a question on Reid's resignation in the Commons.

14   The British mandate in Palestine ends; a Zionist government is formed in the new state of Israel, which is forced to fight Arab states for its existence.

17-21   The Labour Party annual conference, Scarborough, supports government policies on wage restraint; Morrison calls for a consolidation of the government's achievements and a more gradual tempo for any new public ownership.

31   Hugh Dalton comes back to the Cabinet as Chancellor of the Duchy of Lancaster.

June

9   The Parliament Bill is defeated in the Lords by 177 to 81 votes, leading Morrison to call a special parliamentary session in September to overcome the Lords' veto.

12   At the first Young Conservative rally in the Albert Hall, Churchill claims that British youth are in revolt against the equality of poverty.

14-30   The London and Liverpool dockers' strike leads to the declaration of a State of Emergency; the strike ends after Attlee personally appeals to the workers' loyalty to their official union.

19   The Malay Communist party issues a call to arms against the British forces, inaugurating 'the emergency', as the guerrilla war is to be called.

25   Bread and flour rationing is ended.

26   The Conservatives issue the Agricultural Charter, drawn up by Butler's committee, accepting minimum rates for agricultural workers and giving guarantees of prices and markets for farmers.

July

5   The NHS is inaugurated.

The National Insurance Act is in force.

Bevan, in a Manchester speech, says that he has a 'deep, burning hatred for the Tory party' and describes Conservatives as 'lower than vermin'.

20   The Lords vote to retain the death penalty by 99 to 19 votes.

24   The Soviet Union stops road and rail traffic between Berlin and the West; to prevent West Berlin from being starved, the Western Powers organise the Berlin Airlift of food and other supplies.

30   The Representation of the People Bill is enacted, abolishing the business and university franchise and reducing the number of MPs from 640 to 625.

The British Nationality Bill is enacted, restoring nationality to women who marry aliens and conferring the status of British subjects on all Commonwealth citizens.

The Gas Bill is enacted, taking the gas industry into public ownership.

September

3   The TUC and FBI agree to co-ordinate action for higher productivity.

Evan Durbin, a Labour junior minister and early revisionist theoretician, is drowned in a bathing accident in Cornwall.

6-10   The TUC Annual Congress, Margate, supports government policy on wage restraint; Deakin attacks the World Federation of Trades Unions (WFTU) as a Russian instrument, and several unions like the Amalgamated Engineering Union (AEU) and the Electrical Trades Union (ETU) are accused of being under Communist influence.

7   Sean Costello, the Irish Premier, announces that his government intends to repeal the External Relations Act; tension between Unionist and Nationalist in Northern Ireland increases as a consequence.

23   The Parliament Bill is rejected by the Lords a second time by 204 to 34 votes.

October

7-9   The Conservative Party annual conference meets at Llandudno; Churchill says that 'nothing stands between Europe today and complete subjugation to Communist tyranny but the atomic bomb in American possession'.

15   The Liberal's issue *Programme for Britain* which calls for proportional representation, home rule for Scotland and Wales, and ownership for all through profit-sharing and co-partnership.

27   Attlee establishes the Lynskey Tribunal to investigate allegations of corruption in the Board of Trade.

28   Attlee pledges that 'no change should be made in the constitutional status of Northern Ireland' without her free agreement, angering the 'Friends of Ireland' group of Labour MPs.

The NUM National Executive repudiates the support

for striking French miners given by Horner, its Communist General Secretary.

29   The Iron and Steel Bill is published, provoking a major anti-nationalisation campaign by employers and the Conservatives.

November

1   Cripps points to the success of the prices and incomes policy in ending a period of economic crisis.

5   Harold Wilson, President of the Board of Trade, abolishes a large number of economic restrictions on business in his 'bonfire of controls'.

14   The Edmonton by-election, caused by Durbin's death, shows the sharpest drop yet in Labour support, as the Labour majority falls from 19,069 to 3,327.

24   The TUC General Council issues advice to its constituent unions to eliminate Communists from office.

December

1   The National Service Bill, which restores the length of national service to 18 months, has its second reading and 40 Labour MPs vote against.

2   The TGWU agrees to ban Communists from holding office in the union.

19   The Labour Party announces closer co-operation with the Northern Ireland Labour Party, leading to a schism in the latter party over its implied support for partition.

General

John Jewkes, in *Ordeal by Planning*, attacks socialist controls and calls for an untrammelled market economy.

1949

January

13 Cripps, at a press conference, says that Britain is heading towards a surplus in its balance of payments.

18 Morrison as Leader of the Commons relaxes government time to allow the first private Members' bill since 1939.

19 The TUC withdraws from WFTU, as it contains Communist unions.

25 The Lynskey Tribunal reports, finding justification for some of the allegations of financial dealings, but declaring rumours of large sums of money involved to be baseless.

February

1 Clothes rationing ends.

3 John Belcher resigns as a junior minister at the Board of Trade after the findings of the Lynskey Tribunal.

10 The Unionists easily win the elections to the Northern Ireland Parliament at Stormont on a partitionist platform.

16 The British Council of the European Movement is constituted on an all-party basis.

21 The Northern Ireland Labour Party formally dissociates itself from the Irish Labour Party.

24 The Conservatives fail to win the South Hammersmith by-election, where the Labour majority only falls from 3,458 to 1,613; recriminations break out in Conservative ranks as a result.

26-7 The Labour NEC meets ministers at Shanklin, the Isle of Wight, to formulate an election programme.

March

22 Wilson removes the need for 900,000 licences (mainly rations of clothes and textiles) a year in a major relaxation of controls.

24-6 The Liberal Party Assembly, Hastings, demands equal rights for women in terms of pay and for easier divorce and separation rules; it also calls for the abolition of the hereditary element in the upper chamber, and Home Rule for Scotland and Wales.

31   Churchill, in a speech at the Convocation of the Massachusetts Institute of Technology, Boston, declares that the 14 men in the Kremlin are 'as wicked as, but in some ways more formidable than, Hitler'.

April

4   Britain signs the North Atlantic Treaty in Washington with the United States, Canada, France, Belgium, the Netherlands, Italy, Portugal, Denmark, Iceland and Norway, setting up NATO as a defensive organisation.

4-9   The Conservatives make sweeping gains in the county council elections.

6   Cripps, in his budget, warns of the growing dollar deficit and says that government spending on defence and social services necessitates an effective reduction in food subsidies and increases in indirect taxes.

8   Labour loses overall control of the LCC.

12   Labour publishes *Labour Believes in Britain* as an election programme, containing concessions to the left, including a major extension of public ownership and the introduction of equal pay for women; it sparks off a major anti-nationalisation campaign by the insurance, cement and sugar industries, including the invention of Mr Cube by Tate and Lyle.

18   The Republic of Ireland is formally proclaimed in Dublin.

26   The Council of Wales is established to inform the government of Welsh interests, but is subject to widespread Welsh criticism because of its lack of power.

May

9   The Iron and Steel Bill is given its third reading by 333 to 203 votes amidst pandemonium caused by the Opposition.

12   The Berlin blockade is ended, with the Russians defeated by the airlift.

The North Atlantic Treaty is approved by the Commons by 333 to 6 votes.

17   Discontent is expressed at the Conservative Central Council over the leftward drift of party policies.

18   Konni Zilliacus and Leslie Solley are expelled from the Labour Party for their consistent opposition to the government's foreign policy, while a stern warning is given to 66 Labour MPs who oppose the Ireland Bill.

23   The Federal Republic of Germany is proclaimed, with its capital at Bonn formally sealing the division of the two Germanies.

June

2   The Ireland Bill is enacted despite strong criticism from within the Labour Party, giving constitutional guarantees to Northern Ireland, while giving citizens of the Irish Republic the same rights as British citizens.

6-10   The Labour Party annual conference, Blackpool, sees discontent with the wage restraint policy and with the lack of industrial democracy in the nationalised industries, but no critical motions are passed.

7   Troops are sent to Liverpool and Bristol docks to break the strikes there.

21   The Royal Commission on the Press reports, calling for a General Council of the Press by the profession itself and warning of the increasing monopolisation of the local press.

July

6   Cripps announces a major fall in the gold and dollar reserves in the Sterling Area and, while ruling out devaluation, orders a temporary standstill in new dollar purchases.

7   Troops are sent to the London docks as a State of Emergency is declared.

11   The Conservatives issue *Imperial Policy*, calling for Imperial Preference in tariffs to encourage imperial unity, and accepting self-government within the Empire 'as soon as colonial peoples are ready for it'; this completes their series of special policy studies.

14 Cripps announces a £100 million a year cut in Britain's dollar imports.

16 The gold and dollar reserves have fallen by US$39 million in the past week to US$1,525 million.

19 A Conciliation Board is appointed for the first time to arbitrate on a rail dispute.

22 In a controversial speech at Wolverhampton, Churchill says that Socialism and Communism are intimately connected.

23 The Conservatives issue *The Right Road for Britain* as their election document, arguing for the retention of economic controls until the trade gap is closed, but an eventual partnership of capital and labour under the guidance rather than the control of the state.

26 Eden points to a loss of confidence in their union leaders by the dockers as a cause of strikes, and says that the government should stop constantly blaming Communist sabotage.

August

19 The Cabinet finally decides that a devaluation is necessary in the face of the continuing fall of the gold and dollar reserves (the announcement is not made until mid-September after Cripps and Bevin had visited Washington).

September

3 The gold and dollar reserves reach a low point of US$1,410 million.

5-9 The TUC Annual Congress meets at Bridlington; in a message, Attlee rejects pay differentials as 'bad economics and bad social morality', and says that wage increases cannot be justified without productivity increases.

12 Cripps and Bevin, after talks in Washington with the United States and Canadian governments, announce an increase in United States investment in Europe and the liberalisation of trade between European countries.

18 Cripps announces the devaluation of the pound from US$4.03 to US$2.80.

October

1   The Chinese Communists, led by Mao Tse-Tung, proclaim a People's Republic at Peking, signifying their final victory in the long civil war with the Nationalists, who flee to Taiwan.

10   Lord Beaverbrook, in the *Daily Express*, issues an election policy for the Conservatives of Empire Free Trade combined with lower taxes and a national minimum wage (rejected by Churchill on the next day).

12-14 At the Conservative Party annual conference, London, Churchill admits that as far as the existing nationalisation measures are concerned, 'it is physically impossible to undo much that has been done'.

13   Attlee announces that there will be no autumn election.

24   Attlee announces government economies of £250 million to control inflation.

29   The Scottish Covenant is launched by a Scottish National Assembly, comprising local authorities, trade unions and churches, to secure a separate parliament for Scotland within the United Kingdom.

The Gallup poll shows 45 per cent Labour, 39 per cent Conservative, and 12 per cent Liberal support.

November

1   The Overseas Food Corporation, handling a scheme to grow groundnuts in Tanganyika, announces a loss of £23 million in its first year.

16   George Strauss, Minister of Supply, announces concessions on the Iron and Steel Bill postponing the vesting date until after the next election.

21   In the Commons debate on the 'groundnuts' scheme, John Strachey, the Minister of Food, is severely criticised by Conservatives for the profligate waste involved in a plan which had not been based on any real analysis of the rainfall or the soil in East Africa.

23   The TUC General Council recommends continued wage restraint as a result of the new economic crisis, but only on condition that prices remain stable.

The Labour NEC agrees to drop industrial insurance

from its nationalisation list after intense opposition from the Co-operative movement.

24   The Iron and Steel Bill is enacted.

29   The Lords reject the Parliament Bill for the third time by 110 to 37 votes, though this cannot prevent the Bill from becoming law.

December

7   The International Confederation of Free Trade Unions (ICFTU) is established with TUC participation.

16   The Parliament Bill is enacted.

General

George Orwell's novel, *1984*, is taken up as a frightening picture of Communist rule, though the author's intentions were more subtle.

1950

January

6   Britain recognises Communist China, despite United States displeasure.

11   A general election is announced for 23 February.

12   A meeting of trade union executive committees agree to support the TUC General Council plan for wage stabilisation by only a small majority.

Keeping Left attacks the wage restraint policy.

A State of Emergency is proclaimed in the Gold Coast after communal riots in Accra.

18   Labour issues its election manifesto, *Let Us Win Through Together*, listing the cement, chemical, and sugar refining and manufacturing industries for public ownership.

20   The Communist election manifesto calls for the ending of United States control of Britain's economy and foreign policy.

25   The Conservative Party election manifesto, *This is the Road*, calls for 'a true property owning democracy' and promises the Scotland Office Cabinet status.

27-8   At an emergency Liberal conference at Caxton Hall, Westminster, Clement Davies declares that Liberals have high hopes of emerging from the election stronger than for two generations.

The expulsion of Communists from trades councils begins.

February

3   Parliament is dissolved.

5   The Liberals issue their manifesto, *No Easy Way*, claiming to be the only party free of class conflict.

9   In the United States, Senator Joseph McCarthy's attack on Communists in the State Department intensifies the crusade against radicals, giving it the name 'McCarthyism'.

14   Churchill, speaking in Edinburgh, hints that he would organise a summit meeting with the Soviet Union; Bevin

dismisses this as a stunt.

23   Polling Day with an 83.9 per cent turnout (28,771,124 votes); the election results show the Labour lead reduced to only five; 315 Labour MPs are elected, 298 Conservatives, nine Liberals and three others; Labour has 13,266,176 votes (46.1 per cent), Conservatives 12,492,404 (43.5 per cent), Liberals 2,621,487 (9.1 per cent), and Communists 91,765 (0.3 per cent); it is a disaster for the Liberals and Communists, who lose 319 and 97 deposits respectively.

28   Attlee reconstructs his government, with Gaitskell as Minister of Economic Affairs to aid the ailing Cripps, and Shinwell as Defence Minister.

March

1   Klaus Fuchs is found guilty of betraying atomic secrets to Soviet agents.

7   In a conciliatory gesture to the Liberals, Churchill suggests a committee of inquiry into the possibility of proportional representation, but this is rejected by Morrison as Leader of the Commons on the grounds that a mandate for electoral reform had not been given by the voters.

28   In a foreign affairs debate, Churchill pleads for West Germany to join in the system of European defence against Communism, but Bevin rejects his plea in an anti-German speech.

29   The government suffers its first Commons defeat, when it is decided to adjourn the fuel and power debate by 283 to 257 votes; Attlee refuses to resign on the grounds that the defeat was not serious.

April

18   Cripps presents a cautious budget, with a reduction in income tax balanced by increased taxes on petrol.

19–
May 1   There is a new outbreak of strikes in the London docks, and troops are called in.

29   Woolton calls for joint co-operation between the Conservative and Liberal parties.

May

9   Churchill announces a Conservative study group on relations with the Liberals.

19   Clement Davies, in a rebuff for Conservative hopes of unification, says that neither the Liberal Party nor its faith are up for sale.

20-1   The Labour Cabinet and NEC meet with representatives of the trade unions and the Co-operative Party at Dorking, and reach a close understanding on the need to win the middle-class vote and to consolidate the government's gains.

26   Petrol rationing ends.

June

13   The Labour NEC publishes *European Policy* (written by Denis Healey), which strongly criticises European economic unity; Attlee dissociates himself from the pamphlet.

25   The Korean War begins, as Communist troops from North Korea invade the South; the UN Security Council, boycotted at that time by the Soviet Union, condemns the North and calls for a withdrawal of its forces.

27   President Truman orders United States forces to support the South Korean army.

         Attlee denounces North Korea, declaring that 'this is naked aggression, and must be checked'.

July

5   The government's action in opposing North Korea is approved by the Commons unanimously.

26-7   In a two-day debate on defence, Shinwell announces that British troops will be sent to Korea.

27   Hector McNeill, the Secretary for Scotland, rejects a plebiscite on Home Rule for Scotland, preferring 'the normal process of our parliamentary democracy'.

30   Attlee calls for vigilance against 'the enemy within', especially in the trade unions.

August

11   Churchill carries a motion at the Strasbourg congress of the European Movement calling for the creation of a European army.

21   In *Labour and the New Society*, only water is mentioned as a candidate for nationalisation.

September

4-8   The TUC Annual Congress, Brighton, rejects wage restraint by a small majority and calls for statutory control of profits; it also supports the UN forces in Korea after a furious attack on 'red Fascism' by Deakin.

6   Attlee rejects the suggestion of Quentin Hogg, who had just become Lord Hailsham, that legislation be introduced to enable him to retain his seat in the Commons.

13   In the defence debate, Gaitskell stresses that the burden of rearmament must fall upon the domestic consumer.

15   UN forces land at Inchon in a military manoeuvre that forces North Korea to withdraw its forces from the South.

    The National Service Bill, extending conscription to two years, is passed by the Commons without a division.

16   As unofficial strikes increase, Deakin calls for the Communist Party to be made illegal, as it was 'not a political party . . . but a conspiracy against the country'.

16-Oct 5   The London gasworkers' strike ends after ten strikers are imprisoned for a month.

27   George Isaacs, Minister of Labour, says that there are Communist plans to cause chaos in British industry.

29   Oliver Stanley, the Conservative Treasury spokesman, argues for a floating rate for sterling rather than the artificial setting of lower rates as in the 1949 devaluation.

29-30   At the Liberal Party Assembly, Scarborough, Clement Davies warns of the dangers of the destruction of an independent force standing between the two great parties, and stresses Liberal independence in a further rebuff to Conservative gestures of alliance.

October

1	UN forces, confident of victory, invade North Korea.
2-6	The Labour Party annual conference, Margate, accepts *Labour and the New Society*, and supports government policy on Korea, with Bevin stressing that 'I do not believe the United States will ever be aggressors'.
7	Richard Crossman warns in the *New Statesman* of the dangerous gap between government policies and the hopes of Labour supporters.
12-14	The Conservative annual conference, Blackpool, calls for 300,000 houses a year to be built; Churchill looks to a 'growing association of Tory democracy with the trade unions'.
15	Attlee appeals for volunteers for civil defence.
19	Cripps retires from the government, and is succeeded as Chancellor of the Exchequer by Hugh Gaitskell.
	The Rev J.G. MacManaway, an Ulster Conservative MP, is debarred from the Commons under the House of Commons (Clergy Disqualification) Act, 1801.
29	Morgan Phillips warns Labour members to stay away from the Communist-inspired World Peace Congress to be held at Sheffield.

November

6	In the debate on the Address, Bevan describes the Conservative 300,000 house target as 'impractical and dishonest'.
8	The 'ten minute' rule for private Members' bills is reintroduced by 235 to 229 votes.
10	Lady Megan Lloyd George and two other Liberals refuse to support their party in harassing the government by continual divisions in the Commons.
13	The World Peace Congress transfers from Sheffield to Warsaw after the government, against protests from its backbenchers, bans prominent delegates such as the poet Louis Aragon and the musician Dmitri Shostakovitch from entering the country.
26	The UN forces are overwhelmed by 1,000,000 Chinese troops, and are pushed back into South Korea.

December

4   Attlee visits Washington to argue with President Truman against the use of nuclear weapons in Korea; he succeeds, probably because Truman had already decided against their use.

10   Oliver Stanley, the Conservative Treasury spokesman, dies.

13   It is announced by the British and United States governments that Marshall Aid to Britain is to cease from the New Year.

18   The FBI demands the right of its member companies to decide on dividend limitation without government interference.

25   The 'Stone of Destiny' is stolen from Westminster Abbey by Scottish nationalists.

1951

January

17   In a Cabinet reshuffle, Bevan becomes Minister of Labour, while the responsibility for housing is transferred from the Health Ministry to the Local Government and Planning Ministry.

18   The report of the Broadcasting Committee to parliament rejects the idea of a commercial channel as a degrading competition for listeners, but calls for more controversial programmes on television.

26   In a speech at Forest Hill, Attlee warns that the resistance to Soviet domination would entail sacrifice from all sections of the community.

29   Attlee announces a three-year defence programme of £4,700 million.

February

2   A dockers' strike begins in Liverpool.

7   Seven dockers are charged with conspiracy, leading dockers in London to strike as calls grow for the repeal of the wartime Order 1305 banning strikes (the strikes in London and Liverpool end by *22 February*).

14-15   In a defence debate in the Commons, the new defence estimates are hailed by Macmillan as a substantial advance on the government's earlier vacillation, but Churchill moves a vote of no confidence in the government's ability to defend the country, which is defeated by 308 to 287 votes.

15   The Iron and Steel industry passes into public ownership, a move described by Churchill as 'an act of party aggression'.

    The Executive Committee of the British Communist Party issues *The British Road to Socialism*, with Stalin's blessing, abandoning the Marxist call for a dictatorship of the proletariat.

March

9   Bevin is moved from the Foreign Office as a result of illness to become Lord Privy Seal, while Herbert Morrison succeeds him as Foreign Secretary.

16   Nearly 10,000 dockers hold a 24-hour strike when seven dockers are committed for trial under Order 1305.

17   In a radio broadcast, Churchill announces that the Conservatives had decided, in the national interest, to use to the full their parliamentary and constitutional power to force an early election.

April

3   Bevan warns, in a speech at Bermondsey, that he 'will never be a member of a government which makes charges on the National Health Service'.

10   Gaitskell presents his budget, increasing taxes and imposing prescription charges for false teeth and spectacles in order to pay for rearmament.

11   General MacArthur is dismissed by President Truman after openly defying the President in calling for an extension of the war in Korea to China.

13   The 'Stone of Destiny' is returned to Westminster Abbey.

14   Ernest Bevin dies.

17   The case against the seven dockers accused of conspiring to strike is withdrawn while Order 1305 is under consideration, and they are released.

21   Bevan resigns as Minister of Labour in protest at the prescription charges.

23   Wilson resigns as President of the Board of Trade on the grounds that the economy could not bear the level of rearmament which the government had set, and is followed by John Freeman, a junior minister.

26   A private meeting of 15 Labour MPs, including Bevan and Wilson, inaugurate the 'Bevanite' grouping as the successor to *Keep Left* and proceed to launch a left-wing revolt against the government's foreign and defence policy.

May

2   Dr Musaddiq, the Iranian Prime Minister, announces the nationalisation of British oil assets in Iran.

10   The Cabinet considers military intervention in Iran, with Morrison and Shinwell particularly favourable.

June

7   Guy Burgess and Donald Maclean, two diplomats who mysteriously disappeared, flee to the Soviet Union.

15   Sir Hartley Shawcross, the new President of the Board of Trade, says that Resale Price Maintenance is to be made illegal.

July

2   The Cabinet decides against military intervention in Iran, which it is felt would severely damage British status in Asia.

5   The International Court rules against Iran in the dispute with Britain over oil nationalisation.

14   The *Tribune* group publishes *One Way Only*, by Bevan and Wilson. It calls for a reorientation of foreign policy to support colonial liberation movements and reduced armaments.

        At the TGWU conference, Deakin warns against further nationalisation.

26   Gaitskell announces an anti-inflationary policy of price and dividend controls in the autumn.

August

2   Alfred Robens, the new Minister of Labour, with Conservative agreement, replaces Order 1305 with a new and looser Industrial Disputes Order providing the machinery to settle disputes.

September

3-7   The TUC Annual Congress, Blackpool, sanctions demands for all-round wage increases while supporting the government's rearmament policy; it also demands equal pay for equal work.

19   A general election is announced for *25 October*.

25   The *Tribune* group publishes *Going Our Way*, which includes a strong attack on trade union leaders.

28   The Conservative election manifesto is published, written by Churchill, calling for a stable government and promising the denationalisation of steel and the construction of 300,000 houses a year.

30   The Labour manifesto is published, making no new public ownership proposals and calling for peace and full employment.

October

1-3   At the Labour Party annual conference, Scarborough, Bevan emphasises party unity in the election.

3   The Liberal manifesto is published, calling for national unity and the ending of party and class strife.

5   Parliament is dissolved.

6   Henry Gurney, the British High Commissioner in Malaya, is assassinated by Communist guerrillas.

25   Polling day with an 82.6 per cent turnout (28,596,594 votes); the Conservatives win the election with an overall majority of 17 while obtaining fewer votes than Labour; 321 Conservatives are elected, 295 Labour, six Liberals, and three others; Labour has 13,948,883 votes (48.8 per cent), the Conservatives 13,718,199 votes (48.0 per cent), and the Liberals 730,546 votes (2.6 per cent).

27   Churchill becomes Prime Minister, and forms a Conservative government with Sir Anthony Eden as Foreign Secretary, R.A. Butler as Chancellor of the Exchequer, David Maxwell-Fyffe as Home Secretary and Lord Woolton as Lord President of the Council.

Egypt abrogates the 1936 Treaty with Britain in protest at the granting of self-government to the Sudan.

31   W.S. Morrison is elected Speaker of the Commons in the first contested election for 56 years.

The TUC General Council pledges full co-operation with the new government.

November

6   The King's Speech pledges the government to denationalise iron and steel, and road haulage.

7   In a statement on the deteriorating balance of payments situation, Butler warns that the nation is in danger of being 'bankrupt, idle and hungry', and announces economies of £350 million per year.

13   Harold Macmillan, the Minister of Housing, regrets that the 300,000 housing target could not be reached in the next year.

December

6   In the defence debate, Churchill says that the government is unable to carry out the full programme of rearmament expenditure, and admits that Bevan 'by accident, perhaps not from the best of motives, happened to be right'.

General

In the election, the first television political broadcasts are made, though the parties are generally coy with regard to the new medium.

1952

January

9   Churchill and Truman agree that the use of United States bases in Britain is 'a matter for joint decision'.

15   General Sir Gerald Templer becomes the British High Commissioner in Malaya.

15-21   The Commonwealth Finance Ministers agree to defend the Sterling Area by reductions in imports and government expenditure.

24   British troops kill 41 Egyptians during a riot at Ismailia, setting off further anti-British rioting.

29   To meet the continuing balance of payments crisis, Butler announces further prescription charges for the NHS and cuts in imports; Gaitskell, the Labour Treasury spokesman, attacks the proposals as 'inadequate, inappropriate and unjust'.

February

6   King George VI dies, and is succeeded by his daughter as Queen Elizabeth II.

20   The NATO Council, meeting in Lisbon, approves the project for a European Defence Community (EDC).

21   Identity cards are abolished.

26   In a Commons debate, Churchill announces that Britain has produced her own atomic bomb.

March

5-6   In the Commons defence debate, the Opposition accept the defence programme, but abstain on the grounds of no confidence in the government's ability to implement it; 57 'Bevanite' MPs vote against the programme, however.

11   Butler's budget reduces food subsidies, but also reduces income tax and raises allowances to benefit about 2,000,000 wage-earners; Bank Rate is raised to 4 per cent.

Standing Orders are reimposed by the PLP in order to prevent further Bevanite revolts.

19   General Templer tells the Malay Legislative Council that the Communist insurgency must be ended by political, social and economic as well as military measures; he begins a successful campaign which is to serve as a model for other 'anti-insurgency' campaigns.

April

3   Labour recaptures overall control of the LCC.
15   Eden announces that Britain will sign a mutual defence treaty with the EDC.

May

7   Ian Macleod becomes Minister of Health.
8   Labour makes big gains in municipal elections.
15   A White Paper on the BBC calls for an independent broadcasting service.
      Butler warns of inflation if the unions do not moderate their wage demands.
15-17   At the Liberal Assembly, Hastings, Clement Davies attacks the swing of policies between the two parties as bringing democracy into disrepute; the reorganisation of the party is confirmed, with paid organisers in more manageable constituencies.
27-31   The EDC Treaty is signed in Paris, with reciprocal NATO-EDC guarantees.

June

11   In a speech to the Press Association, Churchill sounds alarm over the economic situation.
      Herbert Morrison expresses regret over the proposal to set up an independent television channel.
26   In a debate in the Commons over the bombing of a Yalu River power station by United States aircraft, Eden admits that problems of consultation with the United States had

been causing concern in the Cabinet.

July

8   Dr Hewlett Johnson, the 'Red Dean' of Canterbury, accuses the United States of using germ warfare in Korea, and is condemned by the government and the church; the Archbishop of Canterbury calls him a public nuisance who must be endured unless he became a real danger to the state.

9   The Transport Bill is published, returning road haulage to private enterprise.

23   General Neguib seizes power in Egypt, where a republic is proclaimed.

25   The European Coal and Steel Community is established.

29-30   In the debate on the economic situation, Churchill stresses that the present rearmament programme is 'utterly beyond our economic capacity to bear'.

September

1-5   The TUC Annual Congress, Margate, approves the policy of rearmament, but tempers its support for wage restraint by pointing to the unequal burden of government policies on the poorest members of the community.

29-
Oct 3   The Labour Party annual conference, Morecambe, asks for a list of 'key and major' industries to be taken into public ownership; the Bevanites win six of the seven constituency seats on the NEC, leading Deakin to ask for an anti-Bevanite campaign in the trade union movement.

October

5   At Stalybridge, Gaitskell attacks the Bevanites as 'a group of frustrated journalists', and says that a sixth of the constituency delegates were either Communist or Communist-inspired.

7   In a speech at the Mansion House, Butler reports on the general improvements in the economy.

9-11   At the Conservative Party annual conference, Scarborough, Butler attacks those Conservatives who were calling for more cuts in government spending as advocating 'radically unsound, cruel or unnecessary policies'; a new recruiting campaign is launched by Woolton based on house-to house canvassing.

20   A State of Emergency is proclaimed in Kenya after the Mau Mau disturbances, and Kenyan nationalist leaders are arrested by the British authorities.

23   The PLP votes by 188 to 51 to disband all unofficial groups within the party in a move aimed at the *Tribune* group.

In the Cleveland by-election, the Conservatives retain the seat with a small swing away from Labour.

28   The left-wing *Tribune* group of MPs dissolves itself in accordance with PLP instructions.

November

11   Bevan challenges Morrison for the deputy leadership, but loses by 194 to 82 votes.

24   Woolton retires from the Cabinet because of illness; Lord Salisbury succeeds him as Lord President of the Council.

27   Bevan is elected to the 'shadow Cabinet' in the lowest place.

December

4   Churchill announces a curtailment of defence spending.

General

Labour Party membership is 6,108,000; TUC membership is 8,020,000. Bevan's *In Place of Fear* presents Labour as the party of poverty against property.

New Fabian Essays, edited by Richard Crossman is published, marking a major attempt to revise Labour Party thinking away from traditional socialist policies.

1953

January

5 Churchill has discussions with President-elect Eisenhower.

20 Dwight D. Eisenhower is inaugurated as United States President.

27 Sidney Silverman, a Labour MP, fails in an attempt to stop the hanging of a 19-year-old accomplice to murder.

February

3 Eden expresses concern in the Commons on the unilateral nature of United States belligerence in encouraging Taiwan to attack China.

4 The rationing of sweets is ended.

5 After a visit by United States Secretary of State Dulles, Eden reassures the Commons that United States foreign policy is not aggressive, and that collaboration between the United States and Britain was as close as it had been with Truman.

12 Britain and Egypt finally reach agreement on the Sudan, recognising the right of the Sudanese people to self-determination.

13 A backbench Conservative attempt to restore birching fails by 159 to 63 votes.

16 The Transport Bill is passed through the Commons against little opposition.

March

5 Stalin dies; a collective leadership for the Soviet Union gradually emerges, centred around Malenkov, Bulganin, and Khruschev.

Attlee averts a Bevanite revolt on the Defence White Paper by asking for it to be reviewed annually with the intention of eventually reducing national service.

17   The Iron and Steel Bill denationalising the industry passes the Commons.

The Gallup poll shows 46 per cent Conservative, 44 per cent Labour and 8 per cent Liberal support.

April

8   Jomo Kenyatta, a Kenyan Nationalist leader, is convicted of managing the Mau Mau insurrection.

9-11   The Liberal Party Assembly, Ilfracombe, presents a programme of electoral reform to Churchill (who rejects it for the present parliament).

14   Butler's budget reduces income and purchase taxes, and abolishes the levy on excess profits; Butler and Gaitskell appear on television to broadcast on the budget for the first time.

May

11   In a review of foreign affairs in the Commons, Churchill points to the importance of developments in the Soviet Union since the death of Stalin, and asks for a high-level conference to attempt to resolve differences.

13   The Conservatives win the Sunderland South by-election, turning a Labour majority of 306 into a Conservative majority of 1,175.

14   The Iron and Steel Bill, denationalising the industry, is enacted.

21   Sir Lincoln Evans, of the Steelworkers Union, becomes a member of the new Steel Board in the face of left-wing criticism from *Tribune* and the *Daily Worker*.

June

2   The coronation of Queen Elizabeth is broadcast on television, an event seen as cementing national unity above class divisions.

11   The Bevanites attack Oliver Lyttleton, the Colonial Secretary, for a statement linking the Kenyan Nationalists with Mau Mau.

14   Attlee warns that a future Labour government would end independent television.

16   Labour issues *Challenge to Britain*, which concentrates on secondary education, demanding the abolition of grammar schools; it also calls for the renationalisation of steel and road transport.

24   The TUC General Council votes by 20 to six to accept that responsible trade unionists could sit on the new Iron and Steel Board.

27   Churchill lightens his prime ministerial duties for a month after suffering a stroke (though this is kept secret); he does not resign because Eden, his natural successor, is also ill, and Lord Salisbury becomes acting Foreign Secretary.

July

27   An armistice is signed at Panmunjom which ends the Korean War.

August

16   A royalist *coup* in Iran, supported by the United States intelligence service, the Central Intelligence Agency (CIA), leads to the overthrow of Musaddiq.

24   A month-long electricians' strike causes considerable disruption and increases the government's worries of Communist influence in the labour movement.

         An all-party movement for a Welsh Parliament is launched.

September

7-11   The TUC Annual Congress, the Isle of Man, endorses the General Council's interim report opposing any extension of public ownership for the moment.

28-   The Labour Party annual conference, Margate, rejects
Oct 2 the call to abolish grammar schools in favour of a milder resolution expressing preference for comprehensive education; to prevent a damaging contest for Treasurer, Morrison

becomes an *ex officio* member of the NEC as deputy leader.

October

6   British troops are sent to British Guiana to prevent the pro-Soviet People's Progressive Party from gaining power.

8-10   At the Conservative annual conference, Margate, Churchill calls for German rearmament if France rejected the EDC.

20   Churchill abandons the attempt to restore the university franchise.

22   James Griffiths for Labour supports the government's policy in British Guiana as preventing an anti-British *coup*, although he is cautious on the suspension of the constitution there.

23   The Central African Federation is established, connecting Northern and Southern Rhodesia and Nyasaland against African wishes.

28   Morrison is re-elected as Labour's deputy leader against Bevan by 181 to 76 votes.

November

13   A White Paper on television is published, proposing to establish a new public corporation to control sponsored television.

16   The National Service Act extends conscription for five years; the Opposition call for an annual review is defeated by 304 to 261 votes.

December

4   Churchill meets Eisenhower and the French Premier Laniel in Bermuda.

16   The Opposition move a vote of censure on the government's African policy.

17   Eden defuses a right-wing revolt of 41 Conservatives by announcing the suspension of negotiations with Egypt on the future of the Canal Zone.

General

Conservative Party membership reaches a record of 2,805,832.

1954

January

8-15   The Commonwealth finance ministers meet in Sydney, Australia, to consolidate the economic progress of the Sterling Area.

25   Eden meets the foreign ministers of France, the Soviet Union and the United States in Berlin in an attempt to reduce Cold War tensions, but proposals by the Western powers to reunify Germany by free elections are rejected by the Soviet Union.

February

18   The Defence White Paper shifts the emphasis of defence away from the army to the Royal Air Force.

23   A meeting of the PLP decides to support German rearmament by 113 to 104 votes.

24   Eden affirms the need for German rearmament in a debate in the Commons and is supported by Morrison on the grounds that an outcast Germany would become a Germany with dangerous grievances.

25   Gamal Abdel Nasser, an Arab nationalist, seizes power in Egypt and, after a period of manoeuvring, edges Neguib out.

March

2   In the defence debate, the Opposition divides the House on the length of national service, but is defeated by 295 to 270 votes.

5   The Television Bill is published, with a strong emphasis on governmental control of the Independent Broadcasting Authority (IBA).

25   Labour opposes the Television Bill on its second reading, but is defeated by 296 to 269 votes.

April

5   In a debate on the thermonuclear bomb, Labour's call for an international summit to defuse international tensions is accepted by Churchill.

6   Butler's budget is presented with very few changes in the national structure of taxation.

13   Attlee supports Eden's proposal for the South-East Asia Treaty Organisation (SEATO) on being assured that the new organisation would not be a bolster for maintaining an obsolete colonialism.

14   Bevan resigns from the 'shadow Cabinet' in protest at Labour's support for SEATO, which he regards as designed to defeat national liberation movements; Wilson breaks Bevanite ranks to take his place on the 'shadow Cabinet'.

22-4   The Liberal Party Assembly, Buxton, adopts (against the Executive's wishes) a policy enforcing compulsory co-ownership upon all limited liability companies.

26   The foreign ministers of Britain, France, the United States and the Soviet Union meet again in Geneva.

May

7   The French fortress of Dien Bien Phu falls to the Communist Vietminh forces in Indo-China.

13   Bank Rate is reduced to 3 per cent as confidence in the economy grows.

19   The PLP reaffirms Standing Orders, but refuses to discipline Morrison for making a personal attack on Bevan in the May issue of *Socialist Commentary*.

June

19   Labour issues *In Defence of Europe*, which supports German rearmament within the structure of the EDC.

20   Bevan condemns the BBC broadcast of a discussion on German rearmament as an unwarranted intrusion into the internal affairs of the Labour Party.

29   Churchill and Eisenhower issue the Potomac Charter, a six-point declaration stressing the special relationship

between Britain and the United States.

July

13   The Suez group of about 40 Conservative MPs under Captain Waterhouse announces that it will vote against any withdrawal of British troops from the Canal Zone.

14   Attlee's criticisms of United States foreign policy, especially its refusal to admit Communist China to the UN, are dismissed by Churchill as 'one long whine of criticism'.

20   An armistice for Indo-China is signed by France at Geneva by which Vietnam is 'temporarily' divided into a Communist North and a pro-Western South, while Cambodia and Laos are recognised by France as independent states; Britain and the Soviet Union are co-signatories, but the United States refuses to recognise the agreement.

Sir Thomas Dugdale resigns as Minister of Agriculture over the Crichel Down affair, in which the Ministry of Agriculture had sold land requisitioned during the war to a relative of one of the civil servants.

23   *Tribune* publishes *It Need Not Happen*, arguing against German rearmament as threatening European peace; the pamphlet criticises the chauvinism of the 'No Guns for the Huns' campaign being carried on in the Labour movement, however.

27   The report of the Royal Commission on Scottish Affairs recommends more powers for the Scottish Office to overcome Scottish frustration at the general English tactlessness about the Scottish national identity.

28   Oliver Lyttelton resigns as Colonial Secretary, and is succeeded by Alan Lennox-Boyd.

29   The agreement to withdraw troops from the Canal Zone is approved by the Commons by 257 to 26 votes; Captain Waterhouse and the Suez group vote against, arguing that the agreement is a surrender of 80 years of British endeavour in Egypt.

30   The Television Bill is enacted.

August

22   The EDC Treaty project collapses after France refuses to join.

September

6-10   The TUC Annual Congress, Brighton, accepts German rearmament by a narrow majority of 4 million to 3.6 million votes.

8   Britain signs the South-East Asia defence treaty in Manila with the United States, Australia, New Zealand, Pakistan, Thailand and the Phillipines.

27-   The Labour Party annual conference meets at Scar-
Oct 1 borough; German rearmament is narrowly supported by 3.2 million to 3 million votes; Gaitskell is elected Treasurer by 4.3 million to 2 million votes for Bevan, signifying the emergence of Gaitskell as the favourite of the union leaders instead of Morrison.

29   Bevan launches a furious attack on the Labour leadership, and makes an apparently veiled reference to Gaitskell as 'a desiccated calculating machine' unmoved by human suffering.

October

7-9   At the Conservative Party annual conference, Blackpool, Butler prophesies that living standards will double in the next quarter century.

16   In a Cabinet reshuffle, Maxwell-Fyffe becomes Lord Chancellor as Lord Kilmuir, Gwilym Lloyd George succeeds him as Home Secretary, and Macmillan becomes Minister of Defence.

19   Britain agrees to withdraw its troops from the Canal Zone.

November

19   The Boundary Commission proposes a readjustment of constituency boundaries to raise the number of seats in the Commons from 625 to 630.

23   The Opposition move a censure motion on the offer, made by the Independent Broadcasting Authority (IBA), of contracts to newspaper companies, which Labour argues would undermine the new television channel's political impartiality; the censure is defeated by 320 to 268 votes.

In a speech at Woodford, Churchill reveals that he had advised General Montgomery in the closing days of the war to leave German soldiers with their arms so that they could help to fight against a Soviet advance should it prove necessary; the speech causes consternation among his supporters.

December

16   Peter Baker, a Conservative MP, is expelled from the Commons and imprisoned for forgery, the first time this has occurred since Horatio Bottomley was imprisoned in 1922.

General

The *Daily Worker's* circulation since 1951 has fallen from 185,000 to 87,000.

There are now 3.5 million television licences in Britain.

1955

January

25 Butler announces the introduction of equal pay for women in the Civil Service.

27 The Boundary Commission changes are approved by the Commons against Labour opposition.
Bank Rate is raised to 3½ per cent.

February

8 Malenkov resigns as Soviet Premier and is succeeded by Bulganin.

10 Sidney Silverman's motion to suspend capital punishment is defeated in the Commons by 245 to 214 votes.

March

1 In the Commons defence debate, Churchill argues for the hydrogen bomb on the grounds of its deterrent effect.

3 Attlee agrees with Churchill that 'deterrence, by the possession of the thermonuclear weapon, is the best way of preventing another war'; Bevan, though careful not to endorse a unilateralist position, intervenes in the defence debate to criticise Attlee's lack of leadership, and leads 62 MPs in abstaining from a Labour amendment.

4 A private bill by S.O. Davies providing for a 72-member Senate for Wales is defeated by 48 to 14 votes.

15 The *Times* points to the worrying ease with which large demands for increased wages are being granted by short-sighted employers.

16 The PLP agrees by 141 to 112 votes to withdraw the whip from Bevan, a move regarded with general surprise with an election in the offing.

23 The Labour NEC agrees by 14 to 13 votes not to expel Bevan from the Labour Party after Attlee asks for assurances from Bevan on his future conduct.

26- A printworkers' unofficial strike in Fleet Street ensures
Apr 21 that there is no political reporting for four weeks.
30 The NEC calls on the government to develop the
hydrogen bomb in order to consolidate British independence.

April

5 Churchill retires from the government; Eden becomes
Prime Minister, with Macmillan succeeding him as Foreign
Secretary.
14-16 The Liberal Party Assembly, Llandudno, specifically
refers to the Crichel Down affair in calling for increased civil
liberties for the individual against the state.
15 A General Election is called for *26 May*.
19 Butler presents an election budget, reducing income tax
and halving the purchase tax on cotton, rayon and linen.
25 Lady Megan Lloyd George leaves the Liberals to join the
Labour Party.
26 Lord Stansgate's Bill to enable his son, Anthony
Wedgewood Benn, eventually to renounce the peerage is
rejected by the Lords by 52 to 24 votes.
28 Bevan is readmitted into the PLP.
29 The Conservatives issue their election manifesto, *United
for Peace and Progress*, offering a chance to double living
standards within 25 years.

Labour issues its election manifesto, *Forward With Labour*,
calling for a summit to deal with international problems and
promising the renationalisation of steel.

May

1 Arthur Deakin of the TGWU dies suddenly.
6 Parliament is dissolved.

The Liberals issue their manifesto, *Crisis Unresolved*,
offering a defence of the 'fundamental freedoms' against
tyranny.
11 Attlee, in a television appearance, suggests the possibility
of reducing the length of national service.
14 The Warsaw Pact is signed by the Soviet Union and
seven East European states as a defensive alliance and

counterpart to NATO.

23-
July 4 The outbreak of a dockers' strike over an inter-union dispute is believed to harm further Labour's electoral prospects.

26 Polling day in the general election, with a 76.8 per cent turnout (26,759,729 votes); the Conservatives increase their majority to 60, with 345 Conservative MPs elected, 277 Labour, six Liberals and two Sinn Fein (both in prison); the Conservatives obtain 13,310,891 votes (49.7 per cent), Labour 12,405,254 votes (46.4 per cent) and the Liberals 722,402 votes (2.7 per cent).

28-
Jun 14 The outbreak of a rail strike, combined with the print and dock strikes, highlights the increase in unofficial strike activity.

June

4 In a move aimed at Morrison's leadership chances, Hugh Dalton resigns from the 'shadow Cabinet' because of his age, and calls on others over 65 (with the exception of Attlee and Morrison) to do so as well.

15 'Jock' Tiffin, a supporter of Deakin, is elected TGWU General Secretary.

22 The NEC appoints a sub-committee under Harold Wilson to investigate the organisation of the Labour Party.

30 Lord Woolton retires as Conservative Party Chairman and is succeeded by Oliver Poole.

July

4 Britain agrees with the South African government to return the Simonstown naval base while retaining the right to use it for strategic purposes.

5 BBC research indicates that only 5 ½ million people had heard or seen the recent party election broadcasts, compared with 13 million in 1951.

13 The execution of Ruth Ellis for murdering her lover, together with new evidence in the Evans-Christie murders of 1950, strengthen the movement for the abolition of capital punishment.

18-23   Eden meets President Eisenhower, Soviet Premier Bulganin and French Premier Faure at the Geneva summit, where he proposes the reunification of Germany; the proclaimed and apparently sincere desire for peace on both sides fails to find practical expression, however.

25   Butler presents a set of deflationary measures to the Commons, increasing hire-purchase deposits and reducing both bank loans and the capital requirements of the nationalised industries.

26   Gaitskell attacks Butler for creating inflation as a result of his blatant electioneering earlier in the year.

27   The Postmaster General, Dr Charles Hill, imposes, against the wishes of the BBC, a '14-day rule', by which the BBC would not be able to discuss controversial matters in the fortnight before Parliament debated them.

August

13   The Irish Republican Army (IRA) raids an army training centre at Arborfield, Berkshire, indicating the resurgence of an organisation thought defunct since the war.

28   At a Warwickshire garden party, Eden warns local Conservatives of economic difficulties ahead, saying 'we are trying to do too many things at once'.

30   The London conference of the foreign ministers of Britain, Greece and Turkey fails to reach agreement on Cyprus, where tension between the Greek and Turkish communities is increasing.

September

5-9   At the TUC Annual Congress, Southport, the General Council is given powers to intervene at an early stage in industrial disputes by 4.8 million to 3 million votes.

October

5   The Wilson sub-committee reports that the Labour Party organisation was the cause of the recent election defeat, declaring that Labour is 'still at the penny farthing stage in a jet-propelled era', and calls for a nucleus of full-time agents to be sent to marginal constituencies.

6-8   At the Conservative Party annual conference, Bournemouth, Eden announces a gradual raising of the call-up age for national service and a reduction in the strength of the armed forces by 100,000.

10-14   At the Labour Party annual conference, Margate, Gaitskell is re-elected Treasurer against Bevan by 5.4 million to 1.2 million votes; the Labour League of Youth is abolished in favour of youth sections.

25   Two Ulster Unionists take the Sinn Fein seats in the Commons.

26   Butler presents a supplementary budget which increases purchase tax by a fifth and checks government lending to local authorities; Gaitskell virulently attacks it as the natural result of the earlier electioneering policies.

November

26   A State of Emergency is proclaimed in Cyprus.

30   In a parliamentary discussion of the 14-day rule on broadcasting of controversial issues, the government decision is upheld by 271 to 126 votes.

December

1   Martin Luther King begins a non-violent campaign of civil disobedience after the arrest of a woman in Montgomery, Alabama, for sitting in the white section of a bus.

5   Macmillan makes a statement to Parliament on the increasingly serious situation in Cyprus.

7   Attlee announces his retirement as Labour Party leader after 20 years.

14   Gaitskell wins the first ballot for the Labour leadership outright with 157 votes; there are 70 votes for Bevan and 40 votes for Morrison; a disappointed Morrison resigns as deputy.

20   In a Cabinet reshuffle Butler becomes Lord Privy Seal
and is succeeded as Chancellor of the Exchequer by Macmillan, himself succeeded as Foreign Secretary by Selwyn
Lloyd.

1956

January

1   The Sudan becomes an independent republic.

7   Eden takes the unprecedented step of denying that he plans to resign after a growing number of press reports that Butler is ready to succeed him.

25   The Guillebaud Committee finds the NHS satisfactory as a public service and does not recommend any major changes.

February

1   Eden and Eisenhower produce the Declaration of Washington, affirming a joint Anglo-American policy in the Middle East.

2   James Griffiths is elected Labour deputy leader against Bevan by 141 to 111 votes.

14   Khruschev denounces Stalin's policies and record in a secret speech to the 20th Soviet Communist Party Congress; the speech causes a major crisis in the world Communist movement.

Bevan is appointed Colonial spokesman by Gaitskell in an attempt to end the split in Labour's ranks.

16   Bank Rate increases to 5½ per cent, the highest since 1931.

A Labour amendment calling for the abolition of the death penalty passes the Commons on a free vote by 293 to 262.

17   Macmillan announces deflationary measures, cutting food subsidies and imposing more hire-purchase restrictions.

23   Eden announces that the government is giving priority to a private Member's Bill to abolish capital punishment.

28   In the Commons defence debate, Walter Monckton, the Minister of Defence, announces plans for the evacuation of 12 million people in Britain in the event of war.

March

2   General John Glubb, the British commander of the Arab Legion, is dismissed by King Hussein of Jordan.

5   Britain begins to jam radio broadcasts to the Greek Cypriot community from Athens.

7   In the Commons debate on the Middle East after Glubb's dismissal, Gaitskell condemns the government's use of the Baghdad Pact as an agency of Middle Eastern policy.

9   Archbishop Makarios, the Greek Cypriot leader, is deported to the Seychelles by the British.

14   In the Commons debate on the Cyprus situation, Bevan condemns the government's inability to understand, despite the past experience of Ireland and India, that it is necessary to negotiate with people they may regard as seditionists or terrorists.

30- The British Communist Party Congress holds a secret
Apr 2 discussion of the anti-Stalin revelations of Khruschev; the party now has 33,959 members.

April

17   Macmillan's budget, which he describes as a 'savings budget', introduces Premium Bonds; they are described by Wilson, the Labour Treasury spokesman, as a 'squalid raffle'.

18-28 Bulganin and Khruschev visit Britain.

May

10   Frank Cousins, a left-wing socialist, is elected TGWU General Secretary.

13   Harry Pollitt resigns as British Communist Party General Secretary on the grounds of ill-health and is succeeded by John Gollan; the Communist Executive condemns the 'abuses and injustices' of the Stalin era in the Soviet Union, especially the execution of 'devoted patriots and Communists'.

June

4	Egypt declares that she will not extend the Suez Canal Company's concessions after they expire in 1968.
7	The Conservatives retain the Tonbridge by-election, but their majority falls from 10,196 to 1,602.
13	The last British troops leave the Suez Canal Zone.
26	Macmillan announces major savings in defence spending.
27	William Carron, an autocratic Catholic, is elected President of the AEU.
28	Silverman's bill abolishing capital punishment passes the Commons by 286 to 262 on a free vote, and is then sent to the Lords.

July

10	The Lords reject the bill abolishing capital punishment by 238 to 95 votes.
19	Britain joins the United States in refusing to help to finance the Egyptian government's Aswan High Dam project.
26	Nasser nationalises the Suez Canal.
30	The Egypt Committee of Cabinet ministers decides to seek ways of overthrowing Nasser.

August

2	In a Commons debate on Suez, Eden announces that precautionary military measures have been taken; Gaitskell compares Nasser with Hitler and Mussolini, but warns against the use of military force to resolve the dispute.
	At the Egypt Committee of the Cabinet, Macmillan emerges as a leading advocate of force, and the desirability of an Israeli attack is discussed.
3	The Gold Coast League Assembly demands independence from Britain.
9	British families are airlifted from the Suez Canal Zone.
16	The first London conference on Suez takes place, but is boycotted by Nasser.
29	Macmillan issues an appeal for wage restraint.

September

3-7   The TUC Annual Congress, Brighton, rejects the Chancellor's appeal for wage restraint and warns the government against the use of force in Suez.

9   Nasser rejects the 18-nation proposals to solve the Suez crisis.

12-13   In a special parliamentary session on Suez, Eden warns against 'abject appeasement'; Gaitskell strongly criticises any use of force without UN support, and calls on the government to take the issue to the Security Council.

18   Britain agrees to grant independence to the Gold Coast.

19   The second London conference on Suez meets.

21   The London conference establishes a Canal Users Association.

23   Britain, with France, refers the Suez problem to the UN Security Council.

27-9   The Liberal Party Assembly, Folkestone, opposes both Nasser's nationalisation and the government's handling of the dispute.

29   Clement Davies announces his resignation as Liberal leader.

At the annual meeting of the International Monetary Fund (IMF), Macmillan calls on the Commonwealth finance ministers to associate with the projected European Common Market.

October

1-5   At the Labour Party annual conference, Blackpool, Gaitskell warns the delegates, many of whom sympathise with Nasser, to concentrate their opposition to the government on the use of force; Bevan is finally elected Treasurer by 3 million votes to George Brown's 2.7 million.

3   Macmillan calls for a partial free trade area combining Britain, the Commonwealth and the projected European Common Market.

11-13   The Conservative Party annual conference, Llandudno, fully endorses government policy on the Middle East, while Eden scorns the Opposition's retreat from patriotism.

12   Britain warns Israel that she will assist her ally Jordan, if attacked.

13   The Soviet Union vetoes a UN Security Council resolution opposing Nasser.

16   Eden and Lloyd meet the French Premier and Foreign Minister in Paris, where the Suez expedition is discussed.

18   Walter Monckton, who disagrees with the proposed British military intervention in Suez, resigns as Defence Minister under the cover of ill-health; he is succeeded by Anthony Head.

Eden indicates to the Cabinet that Anglo-French military action would be in concert with Israel.

21   Gomulka is elected the Polish Communist Party leader in a gesture of defiance to the Soviet Union.

23   Demonstrations in Hungary, calling for democratic government and the withdrawal of Soviet troops, turn into insurrection after demonstrators are fired upon.

24   Imre Nagy becomes the Minister-President of Hungary as a State of Emergency is declared; a general strike develops, organised by independent workers' councils.

29   Israel invades the Sinai Peninsula, easily defeating Egyptian troops.

30   Britain and France deliver an ultimatum to Egypt and Israel calling for a withdrawal of both sides to ten miles from Suez; Israel immediately agrees.

Soviet troops move into Hungary.

31   The RAF and the French air force bomb Egyptian airfields when the Egyptians do not withdraw from Suez.

Anthony Nutting, a junior foreign affairs minister, resigns from the government in protest.

In the Commons, Gaitskell attacks the government action as doing 'untold damage to democracy's cause' at a time when Poland and Hungary were striving for their freedom.

November

1   The government survives a Labour vote of censure by 324 to 255 votes amid stormy scenes in the Commons.

Jordan refuses to allow the RAF to use its bases against Egypt.

2   The Liberal Party condemns the government's action in Egypt.

Lord Mountbatten, in disagreement with the Suez intervention, offers his resignation, but this is refused by the government.

The Hungarian government renounces the Warsaw Pact and appeals to the UN and the West against Soviet intervention.

3   There are violent scenes as demonstrations erupt in the Commons over Gaitskell's demands for the government's resignation.

4   In a broadcast, Gaitskell appeals to Conservatives to overthrow Eden.

Bevan addresses a 'Law not War' demonstration in Trafalgar Square which ends in violent clashes with the police.

Soviet forces attack Budapest and take it after a week of ferocious fighting; Nagy takes refuge in the Yugoslav embassy.

5   British and French paratroops land at Port Said, as the Soviet Union threatens to use rockets unless Britain and France accept a ceasefire.

Sir Edward Boyle resigns as Economic Secretary to the Treasury in protest at the government action in Egypt.

Peter Fryer resigns from the *Daily Worker* after his despatches from Budapest are not published, highlighting a mass resignation of intellectuals and workers from the British Communist Party.

Jo Grimond is unanimously elected Liberal leader.

6   British commandos capture Port Said.

The Cabinet, worried over international reaction to the Suez war, is told by Macmillan that unless the war ended, the exchange value of the pound would come under intolerable pressure.

7   Britain and France accept a ceasefire in Egypt, though Britain insists on maintaining a military force until UN troops arrive.

14   Conservative MPs criticise the BBC's anti-government bias during the Suez crisis.

15   A UN Emergency Force lands in Egypt.

The British Communist Party Political Committee denounces 'Fascist and counter-revolutionary elements' in

Hungary, and claims that the party membership is standing firm despite the evidence of mass resignations.

20   Stanley Evans resigns as Labour MP for Wednesbury because of his support for the Suez operation.

22   The government denies any collusion with Israel, to general incredulity.

23-   Eden leaves London for Jamaica, to recover from
Dec 14 exhaustion, leaving Butler as acting-Prime Minister.

27   In the Commons, 112 Conservative MPs sign a motion deploring the refusal of the United States and UN to support Britain over Suez.

December

3   Julian Amery, of the Suez group of Conservative MPs, refers to Britain's 'humiliating withdrawal' under United States and Labour pressure.

4   Macmillan announces a large fall in the gold and dollar reserves and applies to the IMF to draw on the British quota to meet the shortfall.

5   The British and French forces begin their withdrawal from Egypt.

12   The IRA opens a military campaign to end the partition of Ireland with a series of attacks on border posts and military installations throughout Ulster.

17   Petrol rationing is introduced.

18   Eden announces the experimental suspension of the 14-day rule limiting broadcasts of controversial issues.

20   Eden, returned from Jamaica, tells the Commons that he had no foreknowledge of the Israeli attack on Egypt, though he admits that the government knew of the possibility of such an attack.

22   Peter Fryer is expelled from the Communist Party, as the *Daily Worker*'s circulation falls to 63,000.

29   Sinn Fein, the political wing of the IRA, is declared illegal in Northern Ireland.

General

Labour Party membership is 6,537,000.

C.A.R. Crosland's *The Future of Socialism* calls on the Labour Party to reject nationalisation and economic planning in favour of a commitment to equality and welfare.

The *Daily Telegraph* and *Sunday Times* support the government over Suez, while the *Manchester Guardian*, *Economist* and *Observer* are critical; the *Times* is hesitant while the *Daily Mirror*'s hostility is softened as its circulation falls.

John Osborne's *Look Back in Anger* expresses the longing for idealism and hatred of the Establishment by the 'Angry Young Men'.

1957

January

1   Two IRA guerrillas are killed in an attack on Brookeborough, and are given military-style funerals which attract thousands of republicans.

5   The Eisenhower Doctrine is proclaimed in a presidential message to the United States Congress, asking for authority to extend economic and military aid to any Middle Eastern country that desired it.

9   Eden resigns as Prime Minister, with Butler widely seen as his likely successor.

10   Harold Macmillan becomes Prime Minister instead of Butler after the Queen's consultations with Churchill and Lord Salisbury; the choice highlights the informal manner in which Conservative leaders are chosen, and is criticised as an outmoded procedure in a democratic age.

13   Macmillan chooses his Cabinet, with Peter Thorneycroft as Chancellor of the Exchequer and Butler becoming Home Secretary; Selwyn Lloyd remains Foreign Secretary.

21   The Labour 'shadow Cabinet' decides not to pursue the constitutional implications of Macmillan's appointment despite their initial willingness to do so.

22   Israeli forces withdraw from the Sinai peninsula.

24   The Minister of Defence is given greater powers of control over the defence services.

The Gallup poll shows 48 per cent Labour, 43 per cent Conservative and 7 per cent Liberal support.

February

14   Labour wins the Lewisham by-election, turning a Conservative majority of 3,236 into a Labour majority of 1,110.

19   Thorneycroft announces cuts in the social services, raising charges for school meals and milk.

26   The UN General Assembly calls for a peaceful and democratic solution to the Cyprus problem.

March

6	The Gold Coast becomes Ghana, an independent state within the British Commonwealth.
14	EOKA, the Greek Cypriot guerrilla group, offers to suspend its activities if Makarios is released.
16-Apr 2	AEU holds a national shipbuilding strike, the first official national strike since 1926.
21-4	Macmillan meets President Eisenhower in Bermuda, where the strained relationships between Britain and the United States are healed; the United States agrees to supply Britain with guided missiles.
25	The European Economic Community (EEC) is formed by France, West Germany, Italy, Belgium, Luxembourg and the Netherlands; Britain refuses to join.
28	Makarios is released by the British, but is not allowed to return to Cyprus.
29	Lord Salisbury resigns as Lord President of the Council over the decision to release Makarios.

April

4	The Defence White Paper outlines the end of national service in 1960.
9	Thorneycroft's budget provides major tax reliefs, including the abolition of entertainment tax, to create a society where there would be 'room at the top'.
11	Lord Cameron, in a report on the Briggs motor dispute, warns that shop stewards outside trade union control present 'dangerous possibilities and provide an avenue for the introduction of sinister interests'.

May

13	Eight Conservative MPs resign the whip in protest at the government's capitulation to Nasser; an Independent Conservative group is set up.
15	Britain explodes its first thermonuclear bomb.
16	In the censure motion on the government's Suez policy, 14 Conservative MPs abstain.

The first issue of *The New Reasoner*, edited by ex-Communist intellectuals E.P. Thompson and John Saville, begins a 'New Left' which rejects both the Bevanite left and Stalinism.

June

6   The Rent Bill, providing for the progressive abolition of rent controls, is enacted against strong Labour opposition and fears that unscrupulous landlords would benefit.

July

10   Thorneycroft warns against the inflationary dangers in excessive wage rises.

19-26   A national bus strike takes place.

24   The TUC gives the licence for the *Daily Herald* to Odham's Press.

25   Thorneycroft, in a debate on the economy, announces that the government will establish a Council on Prices, Productivity and Incomes despite trade union opposition, but the Council has no enforcement powers and can merely publicise issues.

In a speech at Bedford, Macmillan says that 'most of our people have never had it so good', a phrase seized on by opponents as an indication of complacency and by supporters as an acknowledgement of material success.

30   A Royal Commission on Local Government in the Greater London Area is appointed.

August

7   Reginal Maudling is to supervise government plans for a European free trade area.

31   The Malayan Federation becomes independent.

September

2-6   The TUC Annual Congress, Blackpool, agrees to a motion proposed by Frank Cousins rejecting wage restraint in any form.

4   The Wolfenden Report on homosexuals and prostitutes is published; it recommends the legalisation of homosexual acts between consenting adults.

18   Lord Hailsham becomes Conservative Party Chairman, replacing Oliver Poole.

19   Thorneycroft raises Bank Rate from 5 per cent to 7 per cent, holds down public investment and intensifies the credit squeeze to prevent inflation.

19-21   At the Liberal Party Assembly, Southport, Jo Grimond emphasises the need to attract the new middle-class intelligentsia.

30-
Oct 4   At the Labour Party annual conference, Brighton, Bevan causes consternation among his supporters by successfully opposing a unilateralist motion renouncing nuclear weapons; *Industry and Society*, which sought to replace nationalisation by the state purchase of shares in industry, is adopted as a party programme.

The Gallup poll shows 52 per cent Labour, 33 per cent Conservative and 14 per cent Liberal support.

Unemployment, at 265,000, is 1.2 per cent of the working population.

October

10-12   At the Conservative Party annual conference, Brighton, Lord Hailsham appears on the platform ringing a handbell and calls on delegates to 'beat the daylights' out of the Labour Party; this establishes his popularity with the rank-and-file, though it alienates some of the party establishment.

29   In the parliamentary debate on the economy, Harold Wilson, the Labour Treasury spokesman, establishes his pre-eminence by his humour and grasp of detail.

November

11   Jamaica obtains full internal self-government.

December

5   The Lords debate the House of Lords Reform Bill and accept the principle of women peers by 131 to 30 votes.
12   Macmillan rejects the demand for a separate Welsh Office, similar in status to the Scottish Office, made by the Council of Wales.

General

A symposium of 'Angry Young Men', express in *Declaration* their opposition to consumer values and Establishment complacency and this is mirrored in novels such as John Braine's *Room at the Top*.

The revival of radical thought is having its effect within the Liberal Party as shown in *The Unservile State*, edited by George Watson.

1958

January

6 Thorneycroft resigns from the government, along with his two Financial Secretaries, Nigel Birch and Enoch Powell, when the Cabinet refuses to reduce spending estimates; Heathcote Amory becomes the new Chancellor of the Exchequer.

7 Macmillan leaves on a Commonwealth tour, describing the resignations as 'little local difficulties'.

14 In a speech at Newport, Thorneycroft refuses to organise a rebellion against the party leadership.

February

12 Labour wins the Rochdale by-election, turning a Conservative majority of 1,590 into a Labour majority of 4,530; the Liberals push the Conservatives to the bottom of the poll.

The Victory for Socialism (VFS) group is launched, demanding a unilateralist defence policy and increased nationalisation at home.

17 The Campaign for Nuclear Disarmament (CND) is launched by Bertrand Russell and Canon Collins at a meeting in Westminster's Central Hall.

21 The Council on Prices, Productivity and Incomes issues the Cohen Report condemning wage increases as inflationary; it is welcomed by the FBI but is denounced by the TUC, and Gaitskell calls it 'a political tract, not a scientific report'.

26 Labour opposes the government's policy of nuclear defence in the defence debate in the Commons on the grounds that it relies solely on the nuclear deterrent.

28 Alarmed at the unilateralist stance of the *Daily Herald* and the VFS group, the Labour Party warns the constituency party secretaries that the VFS is setting up a party within a party.

March

6   The Labour leadership agree with the TUC General Council to mount a joint campaign for nuclear disarmament, but rejects the unilateral renunciation of nuclear weapons.

14   Bulganin, the Soviet Premier, criticises Macmillan for allowing the United States to establish US missile bases in Britain.

27   Khruschev becomes the Soviet Premier in succession to Bulganin.

The Liberals win a major victory at the Torrington by-election, turning a Conservative majority of 9,312 into a Liberal majority of 219.

31   In a speech at Halifax, Macmillan makes a personal pledge to prevent unemployment returning to pre-war levels.

April

4   In a CND rally in London 4,000 demonstrate after a march from the nuclear weapons plant at Aldermaston.

15   Amory's budget is uncontroversial, mainly simplifying purchase tax.

25   Ian Macleod, the Minister of Labour announces a small increase in unemployment.

30   The Life Peerages Bill, providing for the creation of non-hereditary and women peers, is enacted.

May

2   The British authorities in Aden declare a state of emergency.

5-   The London busworkers go on strike and, after the TUC
Jun 2   warns Frank Cousins not to spread the strike to other industries, are defeated.

8   The United States Secretary of State, John Foster Dulles, warns the Soviet Union that an attack on Berlin would be regarded as an attack on the Allies.

13   European settlers stage demonstrations in Algiers which become an insurrection against the Fourth French Republic.

21   John Lawrence, the St Pancras Labour group leader, is

suspended from the Labour Party after incidents concerning the raising of a red flag over Camden Town Hall.

29   In an attempt to forestall a military *coup* in Paris, de Gaulle announces his acceptance of the French premiership.

June

13   The Scottish Council of the Labour Party rejects a Scottish Parliament.

15   The Labour Party issues *Learning to Live*, advocating the abolition of the 11-plus examination.

July

3   Amory relaxes the credit squeeze and introduces the option of a 'special deposit' system, whereby the Treasury could compel banks to deposit required amounts in the Bank of England.

11   The Independent Conservatives end their revolt by rejoining the Conservative Party.

17   British troops are sent to Jordan after being requested by a nervous King Hussein following a republican *coup* in Iraq.

24   The Local Government Bill is enacted, substituting a general block-grant system for the Exchequer percentage grants, and giving responsibility for education, health and welfare to the larger borough and urban district councils instead of the county councils.

The Public Records Bill is enacted, providing the Cabinet records to be open to the public after 50 years (unless there are strong objections to individual papers being published).

The first life peerages are announced.

31   Macmillan announces that the state opening of parliament will be televised, a move described by the *Times* as 'a dangerous innovation'.

August

30- Race riots erupt in the Notting Hill area of west London
Sep 7 as a mob of 3,000 whites attack black residents using sticks
and petrol bombs.

September

1-5 The TUC Annual Congress, Bournemouth, condemns
the government's failure to maintain full employment and
demands an expansionist economic policy on the basis of
a planned economy.

3 The government denounces the breakdown of law and
order in Notting Hill, and announces that the principle of
free entry for Commonwealth immigrants will be
re-examined.

18-21 At the Liberal Party Assembly, Torquay, the delegates
call for unilateral abandonment of the hydrogen bomb and
for compulsory secret ballots in the trade unions before strike
action takes place; in a controversial speech, Grimond says
that Liberals want 'to bust open the patronage and privilege
by which both socialists and Tories manipulate our politics',
and describes the Liberals as a 'redbrick party'.

29- The Labour Party annual conference, Scarborough,
Oct 3 promises to introduce legislation to outlaw racial discrimination in public places; it adopts *Plan for Progress*, calling for
a partnership between the state and both sides of industry
to increase investment through a National Investment
Board.

October

8-11 At the Conservative Party annual conference, Blackpool,
Butler resists calls for tighter immigration restrictions and
the deportation of those immigrants who commit criminal
offences by appealing to 'our time-honoured tradition of
hospitality'; Macmillan is interrupted by a far-right group
of Empire Loyalists, who are violently ejected.

21 The first women are admitted to the House of Lords.

22 Ian Macleod, the Minister of Labour, announces the end of compulsory arbitration in industrial disputes.

28   The state opening of parliament is televised for the first time.

The Gallup poll shows 45 per cent Conservative, 41 per cent Labour, and 12 per cent Liberal support.

November

3   Amory announces the abolition of hire-purchase restrictions during the debate on the Address.

28   The Mirror Group of newspapers acquires Amalgamated Press to become the largest periodical and magazine publisher in the world.

December

16   The TUC General Council expresses concern about the possibility of 'ballot-rigging' for elections in the Communist-dominated ETU.

21   In France, de Gaulle is elected the first President of the Fifth Republic.

27   Amory announces the convertibility of sterling for non-resident holders.

General

TUC membership is 8,337,000.

Granada Televison broadcasts candidates and scenes from the Rochdale by-election campaign after preliminary discussions on the legal problem of possible infringement of the election laws, and the BBC takes up such reporting thereafter.

Richard Titmuss, in *Essays on the Welfare State*, points to the pockets of poverty in the midst of the welfare state.

J.K. Galbraith compares private affluence with public squalor in *The Affluent Society*.

1959

January

1   Castro seizes power in Cuba and, after United States opposition to his nationalisation policy, gradually moves closer to the Soviet Union.

25   Britain signs a trade pact with East Germany.

February

19   Macmillan signs an agreement for the independence of Cyprus with the prime ministers of Greece and Turkey.

21   Macmillan and Selwyn Lloyd visit Khruschev in the Soviet Union.

26   In a ballot of local Conservative party members in Bournemouth East and Christchurch, Nigel Nicholson is ousted as the candidate for the next election because of his opposition to the Suez invasion.

28   John Stonehouse, a Labour MP, is expelled from Southern Rhodesia after his calls for majority rule during a visit there.

     Britain agrees with Egypt to settle claims arising from the Suez crisis.

March

1   Makarios returns to Cyprus.

3   In Hola Camp, Kenya, 11 Mau Mau detainees are beaten to death after refusing to work.

     Hastings Banda and other leaders of the Nyasaland African Congress are arrested after riots demanding independence.

4   A Labour censure motion on the government for failing to protest to Southern Rhodesia about the expulsion of John Stonehouse is defeated by 293 to 237 votes.

9-23 Macmillan and Selwyn Lloyd visit de Gaulle in France, Adenauer in West Germany, Diefenbaker in Canada and Eisenhower in the United States.

10   Sir Roy Welensky, the Rhodesian Prime Minister, attacks the British Labour Party's approach to majority rule, and warns that the relationship between a future Labour government and Rhodesia could prove impossible.

30   The CND Aldermaston march attracts 20,000 to Trafalgar Square.

April

7   Amory's budget brings tax reliefs of £350 million, including a reduction in income tax; Labour jeers at its 'electioneering' provisions.

27   In a foreign affairs debate in the Commons, Bevan says that a future Labour Government would stop all nuclear tests.

May

7   The Conservatives make big gains in the municipal elections, returning to their pre-Suez strength.

24   Britain signs a five-year trade pact with the Soviet Union.

28   Amory announces the removal of controls on imports of many consumer goods from the dollar area.

        The Socialist Labour League (SLL), a Trotskyist group led by Gerry Healy, is founded around the *Newsletter* journal, whose editor, Peter Fryer, is forced to resign after a nervous breakdown.

June

3   Singapore becomes a self-governing state.

4   In a surprise vote, the normally conservative Municipal Workers Union (GMWU) votes for a unilateralist defence motion at its conference.

16   The Commons discusses the Hola Camp affair; Alan Lennox-Boyd, the Colonial Secretary, expresses his horror at the deaths, but asks the opposition to place them in the context that 'the authorities had to launch a spiritual and

psychological crusade' against Mau Mau, and that this was bound to provoke resistance.

24   A joint Labour-TUC statement calls for Britain to take a lead in forming a non-nuclear club of countries other than the United States and Soviet Union, though unilateralism is rejected.

July

9   The TGWU rejects the idea of a non-nuclear club at its conference, calling instead for a unilateralist defence policy.

29   The Obscene Publications Bill, sponsored by Roy Jenkins to protect authors and publishers from obscenity charges, is enacted.

August

21   A special conference of the GMWU, called by its President, Jack Cooper, and its General Secretary, Sir Tom Williamson, reverses the unilateralist decision of *4 June*.

September

7-11   The TUC Annual Congress, Blackpool, rejects unilateralism by 5.1 million to 2.8 million votes; it calls for a 40-hour week without loss of pay and opposes any statutory wage regulation.

8   A general election is announced for *8 October*.

11   The Conservatives issue their manifesto, *The Next Five Years*, offering once again to double living standards.

18   Parliament is dissolved.

Labour issues its manifesto, *Britain Belongs To You*, concentrating on improving the social services and expanding the economy.

21   The Liberals issue their manifesto *People Count*, in which Grimond looks forward to a future Liberal government.

28   Gaitskell, in a speech at Newcastle, promises that there will be no rise in income tax and that purchase tax would be abolished.

October

1   Macmillan, in a speech at Nottingham, accuses Labour of turning the election into a mock auction.

8   Polling day in the general election, with a 78.7 per cent turnout (27,862,652 votes); the Conservatives increase their overall majority to 100, the first time in the century a party had increased its representation four times consecutively; 365 Conservative MPs are elected, 258 Labour, six Liberals, and one Independent Conservative; the Conservatives obtain 13,750,875 votes (49.3 per cent), Labour 12,216,172 votes (43.9 per cent), and the Liberals 1,640,760 votes (5.9 per cent).

14   Macmillan reforms his government, with Ian Macleod as Colonial Secretary; Butler succeeds Hailsham as Conservative Party Chairman.

16   Douglas Jay, in an article in *Forward*, argues that Labour should cease to identify itself as a working-class party.

20   Sir Harry Hilton-Foster is unanimously elected Speaker of the Commons.

23   Bevan is unanimously elected Labour's deputy leader.

November

10   The State of Emergency in Kenya is finally lifted.

20   The European Free Trade Association (EFTA) is established, comprising Britain, Denmark, Norway, Sweden, Austria, Switzerland and Portugal; however, it is too loose a federation to be a counterpart to the EEC.

28-9   The Labour Party annual conference, Blackpool, becomes an election post-mortem; Gaitskell argues that Clause IV of the party constitution, committing Labour to 'the common ownership of the means of production, distribution and exchange', should be discarded as an old-fashioned shibboleth; this proposal causes uproar.

December

11   The Crowther Report recommends raising the school leaving age to 16.

16   The Labour NEC approves the establishment of the Young Socialists.

General

Bevan calls for the televising of parliament.

There are now 10 million televison licences in Britain, and the 1959 election is known as the 'television election'.

1960

January

6   Macmillan, confident of his political position at home, begins a month-long tour of Africa.

18   The London Constitutional Conference on Kenya opens, though it is boycotted by the African Nationalists.

The FBI Grand Council rejects statutory limitations on prices, and calls for all sides of industry to maintain the stability of prices and incomes.

25   The African delegates to the Constitutional Conference on Kenya take their place.

The *New Left Review* appears as an independent left-wing socialist journal.

February

3   Macmillan tells the South African Parliament in Cape Town that 'a wind of change is blowing through the continent'.

4   At a meeting of the Warsaw Pact in Moscow, the Chinese observer attacks the notion of 'peaceful co-existence' with the United States propounded by Khruschev, beginning a rift in the Communist world between China and the Soviet Union.

7   Frank Haxell, a Communist, is re-elected ETU President by a small majority, but anti-Communists in the union allege unprecedented ballot-rigging.

8   Butler, as Leader of the Commons, announces changes in Commons procedure aimed at removing as much detail as possible from the floor of the House to make extra time for private Members' bills and backbench questioning of ministers.

13   Gaitskell, speaking in Nottingham, denounces 'the small, professional anti-leadership group' in the party, referring to the VFS group.

17   Britain signs an agreement with the United States to build an early warning station at Fylingdales, Yorkshire, giving

Britain four minutes warning of a nuclear attack.

29- A two-day debate in the Commons ends with 44 Labour
Mar 1 MPs refusing to support a multilateralist Labour
amendment.

March

1 Macmillan, after consultations with MPs of all parties,
announces that parliament will not be televised.

11 Richard Crossman resigns from the 'shadow Cabinet'
after abstaining on the defence vote.

16 The Labour NEC adopts a compromise on the constitutional dispute within the party, retaining Clause IV and also
adopting a declaration of party objectives which stresses the
need for a mixed economy.

17 Labour loses the Brighouse and Spenborough by-election
to the Conservatives, a Labour majority of 47 becoming a
Conservative majority of 666.

21 At an anti-Pass Law meeting in Sharpeville, South Africa,
67 Africans are killed by police; the shootings prompt
demonstrations outside the South African Embassy in
Trafalgar Square and 50 people are arrested; anti-apartheid
sentiment throughout the world is intensified.

31 The Welsh Grand Committee of the Commons is set up
in order to discuss Welsh legislation.

April

4 Amory's budget aims 'to consolidate and fortify our
present prosperity' by increasing the tax on tobacco and
profits in addition to minor tax concessions.

13 Harold Watkinson, Minister of Defence, announces the
abandonment of the Blue Streak missile programme, causing
uproar over the absence of time to debate the issue.

18 Up to 100,000 people demonstrate in Trafalgar Square
after the CND march from Aldermaston.

27 Labour moves a censure vote on the government for its
lack of judgement over the Blue Streak missile.

May

1   A United States spyplane, the U2, is shot down over the Urals and its pilot, Gary Powers, is captured by the Russians.

In a May Day speech in Leeds, Gaitskell attacks the unilateralists, arguing that 'we must stand by our alliance and retain our defences'.

4   The AEU conference votes to adopt a unilateralist policy against Carron's wishes.

10   Writs are issued against 16 ETU officials as the TUC threatens the suspension of the union over the ballot-rigging scandal.

12   The Conservatives make big gains in the municipal elections.

16-19   The Paris Summit conference breaks down as Khruschev denounces President Eisenhower and the United States for the U2 incident.

In an attempt to rethink socialist theory, *International Socialism* is published by a group of neo-Trotskyists.

June

6   The United States agrees to supply Skybolt missiles to Britain.

20   The VFS group, comprising 15 MPs, calls on Gaitskell to resign because of his anti-unilateralist stance.

22   The NEC issues an official Labour Party defence policy statement recommending the abandonment of the independent nuclear deterrent and a concentration on conventional armaments, but reaffirms the need for United States bases in Britain.

23   Amory raises Bank Rate from 5 per cent to 6 per cent and doubles the special deposits banks must hold with the Bank of England in a credit squeeze.

29   Kenneth Robinson, a Labour MP, puts a motion to the Commons asking for homosexuality acts between consenting adults to be legalised as recommended by the Wolfenden Report, but it is defeated by 213 to 99 votes.

July

1   Britain reaches an agreement with Cyprus over the retention of British military bases on the island.

6   Aneurin Bevan, the Labour Party deputy leader, dies.

13   The NEC decides to retain Clause IV after the attempt to drop it from the Labour Party constitution meets strong union opposition.

27   Amory retires to the Lords, to be succeeded as Chancellor of the Exchequer by Selwyn Lloyd; Lord Home becomes Foreign Secretary and Lord Hailsham Lord President of the Council.

         The Labour NEC, in an attempt to defend Gaitskell's position as the threat of a unilateralist victory at the conference grows, adopts a statement affirming the independence of the PLP from all outside bodies.

28   Gaitskell strongly criticises Home's appointment as 'constitutionally objectionable' because the Lords were an appendage rather than a rival to the Commons.

August

16   Cyprus becomes an independent republic.

22   A TUC report on unofficial strikes condemns the attempts by some shop stewards to launch a second shop stewards' movement across industrial boundaries in defiance of union executives, and recommends disciplinary action against unofficial strike leaders.

24   The *Daily Herald* is sold to Odham's Press and freed from the obligation to support Labour and the TUC.

September

5-9   The TUC Annual Congress, the Isle of Man, adopts a unilateralist motion and then, when Carron switches the AEU vote, adopts a multilateralist motion as well; George Woodcock succeeds Vincent Tewson as TUC General Secretary.

22   Rioting erupts between residents and police at Camden Town Hall after leaders of a rent strike are evicted from their homes.

29   Macmillan is interrupted by Khruschev as he addresses the UN General Assembly in New York.

29-   The Liberal Party Assembly, Eastbourne, urges the
Oct 1 government to start entry negotiations into the EEC; support for NATO is reaffirmed while the British manufacture of nuclear weapons is condemned.

The Committee of 100 is formed by Bertrand Russell as a unilateralist group committed to non-violent direct action.

October

1   Nigeria becomes independent within the British Commonwealth.

2   Wedgewood Benn resigns from the Labour NEC after it rejects his attempt to conciliate Cousins and Gaitskell.

3-7   The Labour Party annual conference meets at Scarborough.

5   In the defence debate at Scarborough, the unilateralist motion is passed by 3.3 million to 2.9 million votes; Cousins declares that 'we are the real patriots', but Gaitskell promises to 'fight and fight and fight again' to save the Labour Party.

12-15   The Conservative Party annual conference, Scarborough, backs a policy of firm national defence; Macmillan describes the failure of the summit conference as 'a grievous disappointment for me'.

13   Anthony Greenwood resigns from the shadow Cabinet to stand against Gaitskell for the Labour leadership.

18   The *Victory For Sanity* manifesto, written by William Rodgers, calls for a campaign to be organised to support Gaitskell.

20   Harold Wilson stands against Gaitskell on the grounds of the need to preserve party unity, forcing Greenwood to withdraw.

November

1   Macmillan announces that a Polaris missile base will be set up in Scotland, at Holy Loch.

3   Gaitskell is re-elected Labour leader against Wilson by 166 to 81 votes.

10   George Brown is elected Labour deputy leader against the unilateralist Fred Lee.

17   Michael Foot returns to the Commons on being elected Labour MP for Ebbw Vale in a by-election caused by the death of his hero, Bevan.

     Wedgewood Benn becomes Lord Stansgate on his father's death.

23   Benn rejects the peerage in order to remain in the Commons.

25   The Campaign for Democratic Socialism (CDS) is adopted as the title of the pro-Gaitskell campaign launched in an attempt to reverse the unilateralist victory.

December

13   In the defence debate 50 Labour backbenchers refuse to follow Gaitskell.

     The Gallup poll shows 47 per cent Conservative, 37 per cent Labour and 14 per cent Liberal support.

1961

January

19   Selwyn Lloyd announces a partial relaxation of hire-purchase restrictions.

20   John Kennedy is inaugurated as United States President.

February

1   Enoch Powell, the Minister of Health, announces an 11 per cent increase in NHS expenses, and doubles prescription and other charges to meet the increase.

9   Macmillan announces a Royal Commission on the Press to investigate the increasing monopoly in the industry.

22   A Labour-TUC joint statement on defence seeks to blur the differences within the party, but a compromise put forward by Richard Crossman and Walter Padley is rejected as conceding too much to the unilateralists.

March

1   Cecil King, editor of the *Daily Mirror*, assures Labour MPs that the *Daily Herald* would remain a distinct paper in its politics.

7   In a debate in the Lords, Lord Salisbury strongly criticises the government's policy of giving independence to African countries and makes a personal attack on Macleod.

8   At the Commonwealth Prime Ministers meeting in London, Hendrik Verwoerd announces that South Africa will leave the Commonwealth.

15   Foot and four other Labour MPs vote against the Army and Air estimates.

16   The Labour Whip is withdrawn from Foot and his dissenting colleagues; Foot, in *Tribune*, accuses the party leadership of conducting a witch-hunt.

21   The House Committee on Privileges rejects Benn's claim that he is not a peer.

April

11   Conservative backbench MPs unsuccessfully attempt to amend the Criminal Justice Bill in order to bring back birching as a punishment.

12   The FBI, at its Brighton conference, calls for a tripartite body of government, employers' and union representatives to oversee developments in the economy.

13   The Commons votes by 221 to 152 that Benn should not be admitted on the grounds that he is no longer a member of the Commons.

The Conservatives make gains in the borough and county council elections, and in the LCC elections.

17   Lloyd's budget delights Conservatives by raising the starting point of surtax.

26   Butler announces the intention to appoint a joint select committee of both Houses to consider reforming the composition of the Lords.

May

4   Benn is triumphant in the Bristol South-East by-election caused by his own elevation to the peerage, increasing the Labour majority from 5,827 to 13,044.

8   The House votes 250 to 177 not to allow Benn to take his seat because he belongs properly to the Lords.

11   Macmillan announces an independent inquiry into the security services under Lord Radcliffe after the spy George Blake is sentenced to 42 years' imprisonment.

17   Edward Heath, Lord Privy Seal and minister with special responsibility for European affairs, argues in the Commons that Britain would find it advantageous to join the Common Market.

31   South Africa becomes an independent republic outside the Commonwealth.

Far-reaching changes for Welsh local government are proposed by the Local Government Commission for Wales, which recommends that the present 13 administrative counties should be reduced to five.

June

3-4	Kennedy and Khruschev meet in Vienna in their only face-to-face encounter; Khruschev forms a poor opinion of his opponent.
28	Mr Justice Winn, after a 38-day trial, declares J. Byrne to be the winner of the ETU Presidential election after Frank Haxell and four other Communists had been found guilty of conspiring by fraudulent means to falsify the result.

July

20	The Plowden Report points to the technical difficulties of controlling government expenditure and calls for general surveys of spending over a period of years, together with a constructive parliamentary control.
25	Lloyd introduces special deflationary measures to stem the growing imbalance in the balance of payments; he raises Bank Rate from 5 per cent to 7 per cent and announces a 'pay pause' for government employees, causing outrage among teachers and nurses in particular.
26	In the Commons debate on Lloyd's measures, Harold Wilson, for Labour, attacks the spirit of national complacency encouraged by the government.
28	The Election Court rules Benn to be disqualified from the Commons, and declares Malcolm St Clair, the defeated Conservative, to be MP for Bristol South-East; Benn declares this to show 'the fundamentally undemocratic character of the law', and refuses to compromise.
31	Macmillan announces that formal negotiations will begin for Britain to enter the European Common Market.

August

2-3	In the Commons debate on the decision to enter the EEC, Conservative ex-Ministers Sir Derek Walker-Smith and Robin Turton join left-wingers like Michael Foot in attacking the government; Gaitskell is equivocal in his approach.
10	Britain formally applies for EEC membership.

13   East Germany seals off the border between East and West
Berlin.

14   Jomo Kenyatta, the Kenyan Nationalist leader, is
released from British detention.

17   The Berlin Wall is constructed, alarming Western leaders
that a war is about to begin.

22-3   Lloyd sees the TUC and employers' leaders to discuss
the establishment of a tripartite body to oversee economic
planning.

September

4-8   The TUC Annual Congress, Portsmouth, attacks the
'pay pause', rejects a unilateralist defence policy and
supports the entry negotiations into the EEC; it also decides
to expel the ETU from its membership after the ballot-
rigging scandal.

17   The Public Order Act is invoked after a mass sit-down
in Trafalgar Square, organised by the Committee of 100,
ends with the arrest of 1,314 people.

21-3   At the Liberal Party Assembly in Edinburgh, Grimond
calls for workers to be represented on company boards.

October

2-6   At the Labour Party annual conference, Blackpool,
Gaitskell succeeds in reversing the unilateralist victory of the
previous year by 4.5 million to 1.7 million votes; in addition
Cousins's demand for sharper public ownership proposals is
defeated by 3.7 million to 2.4 million votes; *Signposts For The
Sixties* is adopted, stressing the need of 'planning for expansion' as the means to overcome faltering industrial growth.

5   In his Mansion House speech, Lloyd appeals for the
co-operation of both sides of industry to maintain the value
of sterling, and talks of the need to set up machinery to
co-ordinate the national effort and create a sense of national
purpose.

9   Ian Macleod becomes Leader of the Commons and
Conservative Party Chairman, succeeding Butler, who
remains as Home Secretary and deputy Prime Minister.

11-14   At the Conservative Party annual conference, Brighton, Butler promises legislation to curb Commonwealth immigration.

November

1   The Commonwealth Immigrants Bill, ending the principle of free entry for Commonwealth citizens, is introduced.

12   In executive elections to the ETU anti-Communists win a total victory.

13   In his Guildhall speech, Macmillan stresses the need for increasing interdependence between the three groups of the free world — the United States, the European Community and the Commonwealth — and sees Britain as excellently placed to facilitate this process.

16   Gaitskell, in what he regards as his most important speech, attacks the Commonwealth Immigration Bill as a 'plain anti-colour measure in practice', but the Bill is given a second reading by 284 to 200 votes.

Wilson becomes Labour Foreign Affairs spokesman.

The Electricity Council grants a wage award to power supply workers in defiance of the government, breaching the 'pay pause' ordered by Lloyd.

December

28   Lord Home, the Foreign Secretary, says at Berwick-on-Tweed that a crisis of confidence had arisen in the UN because of double standards; the founder members, whose aim was peace, were being judged more harshly than the newer members, who were pro-Communist and wanted colonial independence,

General

Ralph Miliband's *Parliamentary Socialism* calls upon socialists to reject the Labour Party's stress on purely parliamentary action.

Raymond Williams, in *The Long Revolution*, continues the New Left's interest in cultural analysis.

1962

January

1   Postal workers begin a work to rule, precipitating a series of union protests against the 'pay pause'.

17   The TUC Economic Committee agrees to join the proposed tripartite body, the National Economic Development Council (NEDC), on condition that they do not need to preach pay restraint.

24   The TUC General Council overcomes opposition led by Cousins and agrees by 21 to eight votes to be represented on the NEDC; the ETU is readmitted to the TUC, having been purged of its Communist leadership.

February

5   Gaitskell and Wilson denounce Lord Home's speech of *28 December* as totally insensitive to the existence of imperialism.

8   The NEDC is established as a tripartite body to run the economy on the French model of indicative planning.

12   Six members of the Committee of 100 are sentenced to imprisonment for conspiring to enter an RAF base.

26   The IRA calls off its Border Campaign in the face of the apathy of the Irish public, 'whose minds have been deliberately distracted from the supreme issue' of Irish unity; thereafter the IRA becomes a peaceful pressure group with a socialist programme.

28   Len Williams becomes Labour Party General Secretary after Morgan Phillips suffers a stroke.

March

5-6   In the Commons defence debate, Harold Watkinson, Minister of Defence, maintains the V-bomber force as a nuclear deterrent.

7   The NEDC holds its inaugural meeting, chaired by

Lloyd, and commissions a series of reports on the general economy and on specific industries.

14   The Liberals win a spectacular by-election victory at Orpington, turning a Conservative majority of 14,760 into a Liberal majority of 7,855.

31   The 'pay pause' ends, to be succeeded by the observation of a 2½ per cent 'guiding light' for pay rises.

April

5   The Radcliffe Committee reports on security, pointing to the danger of Communist activity in the Civil Service unions, but recommending no major changes in the security services.

9   Lloyd's budget is a neutral one, which imposes a levy on speculative gains in an attempt to curry trade union co-operation.

10   Heath stresses the need for political as well as economic unity at the West European Union meeting.

18   The Commonwealth Immigrants Bill is enacted.

May

6   Gaitskell's speech in Glasgow is disrupted by Young Socialist supporters of unilateralism, leading to allegations of Trotskyist infiltration of Labour's youth section.

10   The Conservatives lose heavily to the Liberals in the local government elections.

12   The dock employers breach the 'guiding light' principle by granting a 9 per cent pay rise to prevent a dock strike.

21   John Hare, Minister of Labour, announces that 77 industries had already had wage rises in excess of 2½ per cent.

June

2   Macmillan spends a cordial weekend with de Gaulle discussing Britain's entry into the EEC.

7   Duncan Sandys, the Commonwealth Secretary, says that

disruption of the Commonwealth is too high a price to pay for EEC entry.

14   Derek Walker-Smith and Peter Walker, two Conservative MPs, issue an anti-EEC pamphlet, *A Call to the Commonwealth*.

The Conservative candidate loses his deposit in the West Lothian by-election.

16-17   On Foot's urging, the CND Conference agrees not to run parliamentary candidates.

20   Reginald Maudling, in a letter to his Barnet constituents, calls for Conservatives to adapt to the new conditions of the 1960s by emphasising the need for national purpose.

27   The Pilkington Committee on Broadcasting reports, advocating a second BBC channel and calling on the television companies to give minor parties a fair chance of broadcasting time; no definite rules on what is a political broadcast are drawn up, however.

The Gallup poll shows 39 per cent Labour, 35 per cent Conservative and 25 per cent Liberal support.

July

1   Fighting breaks out in a Trafalgar Square rally of the new National Socialist Movement as its leader, Colin Jordan, declares that 'Hitler was right'.

12   At the Leicester North by-election, held by Labour, the intervention of a Liberal pushes the Conservative candidate into a poor third place.

13   In a major Cabinet reshuffle, dubbed 'the night of the long knives', Macmillan dismisses seven Cabinet Ministers, including Selwyn Lloyd and Lord Kilmuir, the Lord Chancellor; Butler remains deputy Prime Minister though he loses the Home Office to Henry Brooke; a more dynamic team is appointed, including Reginald Maudling as Chancellor of the Exchequer.

17   The LCC refuses to co-operate with the government's plans for a Greater London Council.

19   Henry Brooke, the Home Secretary, makes an abortive attempt to deport a Jamaican woman who had shoplifted £2 worth of goods.

21   Anthony Eden, Lord Avon, at a Young Conservative

rally at Leamington Spa, says that 'Lloyd has been harshly treated', an implied criticism of Macmillan.

26   During a censure debate, Macmillan announces that a National Incomes Commission is to be established to draw attention to important wage claims.

30   Reminding the government of Britain's Commonwealth commitments, 40 Conservative MPs table an anti-EEC motion.

August

6   Jamaica becomes independent within the Commonwealth.

31   Trinidad and Tobago become independent within the Commonwealth.

September

3-7   At the TUC Annual Congress, Brighton, George Woodcock defends union participation in the NEDC, while rejecting the hostile atmosphere created by the government in which a prices and incomes policy is impossible; the Congress is equivocal on the question of EEC entry.

6   An important reorganisation of the Liberal Party takes place, with Donald Wade appointed deputy leader in charge of policy in order to relieve Grimond's workload.

9   Gaitskell joins the Commonwealth Labour leaders in denouncing entry into the EEC.

19   The communiqué after the Commonwealth Prime Ministers meeting is a victory for Macmillan in that it does not condemn EEC entry.

The Royal Commission on the Press, chaired by Lord Shawcross, can find 'no acceptable legislative or fiscal way' to remove the danger of monopoly control of communications.

19-22   A successful Liberal Party Assembly at Llandudno, held in the wake of the Liberal by-election victories, blurs its politically risky commitment to a Federal Europe by stressing that this does not mean the end of all national sovereignty.

October

2-5   At the Labour Party annual conference, Brighton, Gaitskell rallies the left's support by attacking the EEC as meaning 'the end of a thousand years of history', but he alienates his traditional revisionist supporters like Roy Jenkins.

3   In the Mansion House speech, Maudling announces that he is injecting £42 million spending power into the economy by releasing post-war credits, and he promises an increase of £70 million in public investment and loans to local authorities.

9   Uganda becomes independent within the Commonwealth.

10-13   The Conservative Party annual conference, Llandudno, supports the government in its EEC negotiations.

11   Hugh Foot resigns as Britain's UN representative in protest at the British government's defence of the Southern Rhodesian government.

22   President Kennedy announces a total naval blockade of Cuba after the discovery of secret Soviet missile bases there.

William Vassall, an Admiralty clerk, is sentenced to 18 years' imprisonment for espionage after he is blackmailed by the Russians over his homosexual activities.

23   In a letter to Khruschev, Bertrand Russell blames the West for precipitating the Cuban crisis by its 'unjustifiable action'.

24   The Labour NEC condemns President Kennedy's action in imposing a blockade around Cuba as of doubtful legality, while 'Hands Off Cuba' demonstrations take place outside the US Embassy in Grosvenor Square.

25   Macmillan gives his full support to Kennedy, saying that 'there is no wavering or break among the Allies'.

28   Khruschev ends the Cuban missile crisis by agreeing to halt the building of missile bases and to dismantle existing bases; in return, Kennedy lifts the blockade.

November

5   Maudling announces new tax allowances for industrial investment and a reduction of purchase tax on cars.

8 George Brown beats off Harold Wilson's attempt at the Labour deputy leadership by 133 to 103 votes.

Thomas Galbraith, the Under-Secretary for Scotland, resigns over his associations with Vassall.

Brooke says that the government will increase the penalties against incitement to racial hatred.

14 Macmillan sets up a new Radcliffe judicial tribunal to investigate press reports of the Vassall affair.

22 Labour wins the South Dorset by-election as a result of the intervention of an anti-Common Market candidate, turning a Conservative majority of 6,693 to a Labour majority of 704.

December

5 Dean Acheson, a former United States Secretary of State, causes British outrage by saying that Britain was 'about played out' as an independent power.

9 Tanganyika becomes an independent republic within the Commonwealth.

11 United States Defence Secretary MacNamara visits London and is warned by Peter Thorneycroft, Minister of Defence, that the cancellation of the Skybolt missile might lead to the rise of anti-American feeling in Britain.

15-16 Macmillan visits de Gaulle at Rambouillet to discuss EEC entry.

18 Britain agrees that Nyasaland has the right to secede from the Central African Federation.

19 Macmillan visits President Kennedy at Nassau, as 120 Conservative MPs call on Britain to retain the independent deterrent.

21 Kennedy offers the Polaris missile as a compromise after the cancellation of Skybolt.

General

Labour Party membership is 6,296,000.

1963

January

9   Lord Hailsham is given special responsibility for the north-east, where unemployment at 7 per cent is far above the national average.

14   Convinced after the Polaris deal that Britain is subordinate to the United States, de Gaulle effectively vetoes Britain's application to the EEC, saying that Britain 'is insular . . . and linked by her trade, her markets and her suppliers to a great variety of countries, many of which are distant'.

18   Hugh Gaitskell, the Labour leader, dies suddenly at the age of 56.

21   Macmillan, speaking in Liverpool, says that unemployment is caused by uncertainty about world trade, the EEC situation, and the timing of an election.

22   A Franco-German treaty of co-operation is signed by de Gaulle and Adenauer, creating a powerful axis within the EEC.

24   The NEDC adopts a target of 4 per cent annual growth.

29   Heath criticises de Gaulle bitterly after Britain's application to join the EEC is formally rejected.

February

7   In the contest for the Labour leadership, Harold Wilson leads on the first ballot with 115 votes, helped by the split in the Labour right between George Brown with 88 votes and James Callaghan with 41 votes.

14   In the second ballot, Wilson is elected Labour leader with 144 votes to Brown's 103.

Unemployment reaches 878,000, or 3.9 per cent, in the coldest winter since 1947.

March

4   Thorneycroft, as Minister of Defence, announces an overhaul of the entire defence structure, integrating the three service ministries with his own.

In the Commons defence debate, Denis Healey for Labour promises that a future Labour government would discontinue Polaris.

7   Two reporters are imprisoned following their refusal to divulge the sources of their information on the Vassall affair.

8   Discontent with Macmillan's leadership is expressed at the Conservative Central Council, where Heath is mentioned as a successor.

22   John Profumo, the War Secretary, denies to the Commons that there was truth in the rumours that there had been any impropriety in his relationship with Christine Keeler, a model who had been having an affair with a Soviet attaché.

25   Captain Terence O'Neill becomes Ulster's Prime Minister, succeeding Lord Brookeborough (premier since 1943) and promises a modernisation of Northern Ireland's sectarian image.

26   In the debate on the rejection of Chief Enahoro's appeal for political asylum from Nigeria, the government's majority falls to 56 and two Conservatives vote against the government.

An unemployment demonstration takes place outside parliament.

27   The Beeching report on *The Reshaping of British Railways* calls for the closure of many lines.

April

3   Maudling's budget, based on a policy of 'expansion without inflation', reduces taxes by £269 million, mostly as income tax reliefs, and provides tax concessions to firms setting up in areas of high unemployment.

6   Britain signs a Polaris missile agreement with the United States.

10   Macmillan tells the 1922 Committee of Conservative backbenchers that he will lead the party at the next election.

12   The annual Aldermaston march attracts 100,000 to Trafalgar Square, the last highpoint of CND activity.

13   Powell announces a ten-year plan of community care under an expanding NHS.

Lord Poole becomes joint Conservative Chairman with Macleod.

20   The first report of the National Incomes Commission rejects the 40-hour agreement in the Scottish building industry.

22   A general strike in British Guiana leads to rioting.

25   The Radcliffe Tribunal clears Sir Thomas Galbraith and Lord Carrington, the First Lord of the Admiralty, of all suspicion in the Vassall case, and censors the press for its reporting of the affair.

May

9   The local elections are a disaster for the Conservatives; Labour is the main beneficiary, as the Liberals lose their previous electoral momentum.

30   The government decides to bring the Peerage Bill into force after the next election.

June

5   Profumo resigns as War Secretary after admitting to the House that he had lied about his relationship with Christine Keeler, providing a salacious story for the press and public to enjoy.

17   In the Commons debate on the Profumo affair, Wilson condemns the government over its security aspects, while Nigel Birch calls for Macmillan himself to resign; 27 Conservatives abstain in the division.

21   Macmillan appoints Lord Denning to head a judicial inquiry into the security aspects of the Profumo case.

Unemployment declines to 480,000, or 2.1 per cent.

July

5-20 A Sino-Soviet summit conference in Moscow fails to resolve the differences between the two sides; as a result the split between China and the Soviet Union widens to divide the whole Communist movement.

8 At the TGWU conference, Scarborough, Wilson hails the idea of an incomes policy as 'a great adventure' for Labour.

16 A Labour amendment to the Peerage Bill that it come into immediate effect passes the Lords by 105 to 25 votes, forcing the government to give way on the issue.

18 Labour moves a censure motion on the government for encouraging slum landlordism by its 1957 Rent Act, after the activities of Rachman, a brutal landlord, are revealed.

25 Lord Home for Britain signs the Nuclear Test Ban Treaty with the United States and Soviet Union to ban all overground nuclear tests.

31 The Peerage Bill is enacted and Wedgewood Benn immediately disclaims his peerage.

The London Government Bill is enacted against strong Labour opposition, setting up a 32-borough Greater London Council (GLC) by amalgamating the LCC and Middlesex County Council; the Inner London Education Authority (ILEA) is retained as a permanent institution after a Labour campaign.

August

5 A nuclear test ban treaty is signed by Britain, the United States and the Soviet Union, after revelations that strontium-90 released by nuclear tests is poisoning the atmosphere; France and China refuse to sign.

15 The Stratford by-election demonstrates the unpopularity of the government, as the Conservative majority of 14,129 is reduced to only 3,470.

20 Benn is elected Labour MP in the Bristol South-East by-election with no official Conservative or Liberal opposition.

September

2-6   At the TUC Annual Congress, Brighton, the AEU delegation refuses to follow Carron's wishes and votes with the TGWU delegation 'in complete opposition to any form of wages restraint' and to call for more public ownership.

10-14   The Liberal Party Assembly at Brighton calls for a Ministry of Expansion to overcome economic stagnation, while Grimond calls for passion in politics as part of the fight against the enemy of complacency.

11   Les Cannon, one of the leaders of the anti-Communist faction, is elected ETU President.

26   Lord Denning's report on the Profumo affair is published.

30-Oct 4   At the Labour Party annual conference, Scarborough, Wilson calls for the identification of socialism with the new age of scientific planning and technology.

October

1   Britain agrees to join discussions about a mixed-manned nuclear fleet under NATO auspices.

8   Macmillan goes into hospital for an operation on his prostate gland.

8-12   The Conservative Party annual conference meets at Blackpool.

10   Lord Home announces Macmillan's resignation to the delegates; Lord Hailsham renounces his peerage to become Quintin Hogg and announces his candidacy for the leadership; Butler and Maudling are also candidates, though less publicised.

12   Butler presents his reformist view of modern Conservatism and British society, but fails to arouse enthusiasm among the delegates.

15   The main Conservative contenders for the leadership visit Macmillan at the King Edward VII hospital.

17   After the consultation process is completed, Lord Home emerges as the new Conservative leader, to strong dissatisfaction in some sections of the party; the process acutely highlights the outmoded manner in which Conservative leaders are chosen.

19   Home becomes Prime Minister and renounces the

peerage to become Sir Alec Douglas-Home; Wilson describes him as an 'an elegant anachronism' and a symbol of the Conservative failure to adapt to a competitive and technological age.

20   Macleod and Powell refuse to join the government, but Butler agrees to serve as Foreign Secretary and Lloyd becomes Leader of the Commons; John Hare succeeds Macleod as Conservative Party Chairman.

23   The Robbins Committee calls for the expansion of higher education to cover all those who are qualified for it; the government accepts the report and Quintin Hogg is appointed Education Secretary.

November

7   Home is elected a Conservative MP in the Kinross and West Perthshire by-election.

22   President Kennedy is assassinated in Dallas, Texas; Lyndon Johnson takes over as President.

The Gallup poll shows 49 per cent Labour, 37 per cent Conservative, and 12 per cent Liberal support.

December

12   Kenya becomes an independent republic within the Commonwealth.

19   The British Monopolies Commission recommends the abolition of price maintenance on car electrical equipment, presaging the general abolition of resale price maintenance.

31   The Central African Federation is dissolved.

General

Hugh Carleton-Greene, the BBC Director General, announces that the satirical show, *That Was The Week That Was*, will end because 'the political content of the programme will be difficult to maintain'.

1964

January

13   In his *Spectator* review of Randolph Churchill's book, *The Fight for the Tory Leadership*, Ian Macleod professes his belief that Macmillan was determined to have any candidate who was not Butler.

21   The *Rookes v Barnard* judicial decision threatens the right of the trade unions to strike, by returning to the pre-1906 period when unions were liable to damages for strike action.

26   Wilson, in a speech at Swansea, proposes the increased intervention of the state in the economy in order to direct investment along productive channels.

28   Powell denounces the NEDC and the whole idea of regulation of prices and incomes as nonsensical in a non-Communist economy.

February

10   The TUC sells its share of the *Daily Herald*, to be renamed the *Sun*, to International Publishing Corporation (IPC).

17   Home, in the BBC *Panorama* programme, affirms that the economy has never been stronger.

18   The trade deficit of £120 million is the largest ever recorded.

25   The Resale Prices Bill is published, abolishing resale price maintenance by which manufacturers can enforce prices on retailers.

26   Denis Healey says that Labour has no interest in Polaris as a deterrent, but indicates a flexible position with regard to its value as part of the NATO fleet.

March

10   On the second reading of Heath's Resale Prices Bill, 21 Conservatives vote against and over 20 abstain; the Bill passes as Labour abstains.

11   The FBI Grand Council rejects the NEDC plans for prices and profit controls.

April

9   Home announces that there will be no election until the autumn.

      In the first elections to the GLC Labour wins control with 64 Labour and 36 Conservative councillors elected.

14   Maudling's budget takes £100 million in increased indirect taxes, but is widely seen as dull.

16   The Committee of Public Accounts criticises the Ferranti company's profit on the Bloodhound missile as excessive (Ferranti later offers to repay £4 million).

22   Greville Wynne, a British spy sentenced in Moscow is exchanged for Gordon Lonsdale, a Soviet spy sentenced in England three years earlier.

May

9   The Conservatives are able to check Labour gains in the Midlands in the local elections.

June

30   Spain breaks off negotiations with Britain for the construction of warships in protest at the continuing British rule in Gibraltar.

      Ray Gunter, in *Socialist Commentary*, warns the unions that the state will intervene in their affairs unless they reform themselves; the article causes intense anger among union leaders.

July

6   Nyasaland becomes independent as Malawi.

15   The Councils of the FBI, British Employers' Confederation and the National Association of British Manufacturers agree in principle to merge into one single body.

16   The Resale Prices Bill is enacted.

27   Winston Churchill retires from the Commons after 64 years.

August

2   United States aircraft attack North Vietnam after claiming that a United States ship had been attacked by North Vietnamese torpedo boats.

September

4-5   At the Liberal Party Assembly, Grimond looks to the floating voter to strengthen the Liberals, though the heady days of Orpington are gone.

7-11   The TUC Annual Congress, Blackpool, demands legislation to give unions the protection of the 1906 Trade Disputes Act once again.

8   The ETU conference at Blackpool votes to exclude Communists from holding office in the union.

11   Labour issues its manifesto, *The New Britain*, demanding a national plan for expansion and opposition to national nuclear deterrents.

15   A general election is announced for *15 October*.

The Liberals issue their manifesto, *Think For Yourself — Vote Liberal*, putting forward a radical but non-socialist programme.

17   The Conservatives issue their manifesto, *Prosperity With A Purpose*, pledging to maintain the nuclear deterrent and calling for economic growth.

Wilson challenges Home to a televised debate in an obvious attempt to imitate the 1960 Kennedy-Nixon televised debates in the United States.

21   Malta becomes independent within the Commonwealth.

Grimond demands the right to participate in any televised debate, thereby ending any possibility of a debate taking place.

25   Parliament is dissolved.

October

15   Polling day, with a turnout of 77.1 per cent (27,657,148 votes cast); Labour wins with a tiny overall majority of four, ending 13 years of Conservative government; 317 Labour MPs, 304 Conservatives and nine Liberals are elected; Labour obtains 12,205,808 votes (44.1 per cent), the Conservatives 12,002,642 votes (43.4 per cent), and the Liberals 3,099,283 votes (11.2 per cent); in a surprise result, Patrick Gordon Walker, Labour's Foreign Affairs spokesman, is defeated at Smethwick after a racist campaign against him.

Khruschev is replaced as Soviet leader by Alexei Kosygin as Premier and Leonid Brezhnev as Communist Party Secretary.

16   Wilson becomes Prime Minister and forms a Labour government, with James Callaghan as Chancellor of the Exchequer, George Brown as Economic Affairs Secretary, and Sir Frank Soskice as Home Secretary; in surprise moves, Wilson appoints Patrick Gordon Walker as Foreign Secretary and Frank Cousins Minister of Technology, though neither have seats in the Commons; James Griffiths becomes the first Secretary for Wales.

China explodes its first atomic bomb.

22   The Conservative Central Office is reorganised, with Butler losing his key position as Chairman of the Research Department (held since 1945), though John Hare (now Lord Blakenham) remains as Chairman.

24   Northern Rhodesia becomes the independent republic of Zambia.

26   Callaghan imposes a 15 per cent surcharge on imports, in order to deal with a balance of payments deficit of £800 million, causing an international outcry.

27   Wilson states that a Rhodesian declaration of independence would be 'an open act of defiance'.

November

3   Wilson says that Peter Griffiths, the new Conservative MP for Smethwick elected after a racist campaign, should be treated as 'a parliamentary leper'.

4   A Joint Statement of Intent is signed by Brown for the government with the TUC and the main employers' organisations to plan economic growth, restrain wages within any rises in productivity and to stabilise prices.

11   Callaghan's budget raises pensions and abolishes prescription charges, but increases taxes on petrol and 1965 income tax rates.

16   Wilson, in his Guildhall speech, stresses the need to 'keep sterling strong and see it riding high'.

17   The government states its intention of banning the export of arms to South Africa.

23   Callaghan raises Bank Rate to 7 per cent as sterling weakens.

25   Devaluation is avoided as the government arranges a major loan of US$3,000 million from foreign banks.

Wilson agrees to the sale of 16 Buccaneer aircraft to South Africa, despite his election pledges.

December

1   Wilson states in the Commons that the Polaris missile base at Holy Loch is to be retained.

4   Sidney Silverman introduces his Murder (Abolition of the Death Penalty) Bill, suspending capital punishment for five years.

12-13   At the Labour Party annual conference in Brighton, Wilson attacks 'trade union luddites and board room luddites' who wish to turn back to the old days of class conflict.

16   After consultations with President Johnson in Washington, Wilson outlines an agreement for an Atlantic Nuclear Force, retaining Polaris missiles under NATO control; the Conservatives accuse him of surrendering British control of nuclear weapons.

17   The government announces that prescription charges will be free from *February 1965*.

21   Silverman's Bill suspending capital punishment obtains a second reading by 355 to 170 votes.

General

The Institute for Workers Control (IWC) is established

by a group of socialists, and soon attracts support from the left-wing of the trade union movement.

Herbert Marcuse, in his book *One Dimensional Man*, argues that with the absorption of the working class into capitalist society, the prospect of social transformation has ended, and only rebellion by the most oppressed is left as an alternative; the analysis soon becomes popular with a new student left.

1965

January

14   The Premiers of Northern Ireland and the Irish Republic meet for the first time.

Aircraft workers demonstrate in London against the government's policy on contracting the industry.

21   Patrick Gordon Walker loses the Leyton by-election, as a Labour majority of 7,926 becomes a Conservative majority of 205, and he immediately resigns as Foreign Secretary.

Frank Cousins retains Nuneaton for Labour with a majority reduced from 11,702 to 5,241.

Edward du Cann succeeds Blakenham as Conservative Party Chairman.

22   Michael Stewart is appointed Foreign Secretary.

24   Winston Churchill dies at the age of 90.

31   Butler retires from politics to become Master of Trinity College, Cambridge.

February

2   A Royal Commission on the role of trade unions in modern society, to be chaired by Lord Donovan, is announced by Wilson.

4   The Confederation of British Industry (CBI) is established, merging the main employers' federations; John Davies is its first Director General.

Soskice warns that considerable evasion of immigration controls is taking place.

11   Brown announces the establishment of a Prices and Incomes Board as new machinery for reviewing prices and incomes.

Wilson promises President Johnson British support for a 'measured response' by the United States against the Vietcong.

16   Home appoints Maudling as his Foreign Affairs spokesman and Heath as his Treasury spokesman.

The Trade Disputes Bill, giving legal protection to unions

on strike by reversing *Rookes v Barnard*, is given a second reading.

21- Arthur Bottomley, the Commnonwealth Relations
Mar 3 Secretary, and Lord Gardiner, the Lord Chancellor, visit Rhodesia on a fact-finding mission.

25 The Conservative Central Office publishes the new procedure for the election of a Conservative leader; a candidate must obtain an overall majority of votes cast, plus 15 per cent more votes than the runner-up, to win on the first ballot of MPs, with a simple overall majority on a second ballot.

March

4 Silverman leads a group of 50 Labour MPs who call for the government to dissociate itself from United States actions in Vietnam.

9 Wilson, in a Commons speech, urges an attack on the immigration problem by the integration of existing immigrants, a ban on racial discrimination and the despatch of missions overseas in order to overcome evasions of immigration controls.

17 Aubrey Jones, a Conservative MP under pressure from his Birmingham constituency party over his liberal views on immigration, accepts the chairmanship of the Prices and Incomes Board.

24 David Steel wins the by-election at Roxburghshire, Selkirkshire and Peebleshire, turning a Conservative majority of 1,739 into a Liberal majority of 4,607.

April

1 Stewart defends the United States actions in Vietnam in a Commons debate, to the support of the Conservatives and the criticism of his own backbenchers.

The GLC is inaugurated.

6 Callaghan's budget increases both direct and indirect taxes, and introduces capital gains tax and a corporation tax; the TSR-2 aircraft is cancelled on the grounds of cost.

8 Brown's White Paper on prices and incomes policy

intends to set a norm of 3 to 3½ per cent rises in annual incomes.

9   Soskice introduces a Race Relations Bill to prohibit racial discrimination in places of public resort.

14   Wilson, in a speech to the Economic Club in New York, declares his 'unalterable determination' not to devalue sterling, and threatens the Americans 'we shall knock hell out of you' in economic competition.

19   The CND demonstration in Trafalgar Square, attracting 150,000, demonstrates a growing opposition to the Vietnam War.

27   Callaghan cuts the import surcharge to 10 per cent.

29   Wilson, backed by Home and Grimond, warns the Rhodesian government against a unilateral declaration of independence.

30   At a special TUC conference, the prices and incomes policy is approved by 6.6 million to 1.8 million votes; the TGWU whose General Secretary is a member of the government, opposes the policy.

A White Paper on steel nationalisation is issued.

May

6   In the debate on the steel nationalisation White Paper, the government wins by 310 to 306 votes after Brown heads off a threat to vote against the Paper by two Labour back-benchers, Woodrow Wyatt and Desmond Donnelly, by hinting that less than full public ownership may be involved.

7   Ian Smith's Rhodesia Front wins a landslide victory in Rhodesian elections.

13   The Conservatives make big gains at Labour and Liberal expense in the local elections.

24   A Bill to legalise private homosexual actions passes the Lords by 94 to 49, despite Lord Montgomery's opposition.

26   The government refuses to allow Leo Abse leave to introduce a bill which would legalise homosexual acts between consenting adults.

June

2	The government survives an Opposition amendment to defer corporation tax by the Speaker's casting vote.
3	Bank Rate is reduced to 6 per cent in an effort to create confidence in the economy.
15	As the balance of payments situation worsens, a Bank of England report states that Britain is living on borrowed time unless incomes are brought under control.
23	In the *Guardian*, Grimond calls for a Liberal-Labour coalition.
27	The *Sunday Express* claims that 100 Conservative MPs want Heath as their leader; a claim that indicates Conservative unrest with Home.

July

7	The government is defeated in the Commons on the Finance Bill.
8	Harold Davies, the British government representative, arrives in Hanoi in an abortive attempt to arrange peace talks between North Vietnam and the United States.
12	Tony Crosland, the Education Secretary, issues a circular requesting local education authorities to submit plans within a year for reorganising secondary education on comprehensive lines.
20	The Lords gives Silverman's Bill suspending capital punishment a second reading by 204 to 104 votes.
22	Home resigns as Conservative leader.
27	Callaghan deflates the economy further, holding back £350 million of public investment and restricting spending on housing, schools, hospitals and local authority projects; defence spending is cut by £100 million.
	In the first ballot for the Conservative leadership, Edward Heath leads with 150 votes, against 133 votes for Reginald Maudling and 15 votes for Enoch Powell; Heath does not have a big enough majority and a second ballot is called.
28	Heath is unanimously elected Conservative leader after Maudling withdraws; Maudling becomes his deputy, Home his Foreign Affairs spokesman and Macleod his Treasury spokesman.

President Johnson announces that United States military strength in South Vietnam will rise to 125,000, and that further forces would be committed as needed; the United States is thereby committed to the Vietnam War.

August

2   A White Paper on immigration policy is issued, restricting entry to 7,500 permits per year for professional and skilled workers.

3   As reserves fall by £140 million (after a fall of £91 million in July), panic grips the City as rumours of devaluation abound.

5   The Trade Disputes Bill is enacted.

September

2   Sir Harry Hilton-Foster, the Speaker of the Commons, dies suddenly.

6-10   The TUC Annual Congress, Brighton, agrees to a compulsory early warning scheme for potential wage rises by 5.2 million to 3.3 million votes.

16   Brown's National Plan is published, envisaging a 25 per cent increase in national output by 1970; Heath describes it as 'the biggest publicity gimmick the government has so far produced'.

22-5   At the Liberal Party Assembly, Scarborough, Grimond calls on Labour to break with its left and align with the Liberals.

27-   At the Labour Party annual conference, Blackpool, the
Oct 10 government's support for United States policy in Vietnam is upheld by 3.6 million to 2.5 million votes.

October

4-8   Inconclusive talks between Wilson and Ian Smith, the Rhodesian Premier, fail to avert a crisis as Smith threatens independence to preserve white rule.

7   Heath presents *Putting Britain Right Ahead*.

12   A White Paper is issued proposing a Parliamentary Commissioner, or Ombudsman, to act as an appeal against unjust administrative decisions.

12-15   The Conservative Party annual conference, Brighton, witnesses a bitter debate on Rhodesia, as Lord Salisbury attacks the Conservative Executive for refusing to support the Rhodesian government or to oppose sanctions on 'our friends and kinfolk'; Heath calls for a middle way to be found, and warns the British government that 'a blank cheque from us is not there'.

21   In his Mansion House speech, Callaghan expects the payments deficit to be eliminated within a year, while Lord Cromer warns against a premature relaxation of economic restraint.

25-30   Wilson visits Rhodesia, where he warns against a unilateral declaration of independence but tells Joshua Nkomo and Ndabaninge Sithole, the two African nationalist leaders who had been excluded from the London talks, that Britain will not use force against Rhodesia.

26   Dr Horace King, a Labour MP, is elected Speaker of the Commons.

27   Herbert Bowden, the Leader of the Commons, announces reforms in parliamentary procedure to speed up the work of the House; ten-minute bills are to be taken after government business rather than before, and a second reading committee would handle the second reading of non-controversial bills.

November

8   The Murder (Abolition of the Death Penalty) Bill is enacted.

The Race Relations Bill is enacted.

11   The Rhodesian government declares independence; all purchases of Rhodesian sugar and tobacco (70 per cent of her exports to Britain) are banned.

15-16   The Southern Rhodesia Bill, authorising economic sanctions, is enacted within ten hours of publication; in the Lords, Salisbury opposes the declaration of independence, but describes Ian Smith as 'a man of outstanding rectitude and honesty'.

December

1	More major sanctions are imposed on Rhodesia.
8	The Rent Bill is enacted, giving greater security to tenants.
16	Oil sanctions are imposed on Rhodesia.
20-1	In the Commons debate on a Rhodesian oil embargo, the Conservatives abstain, but their internal divisions become clear as 31 Conservatives vote for the government and 50 vote against.
22	Roy Jenkins is appointed Home Secretary and proceeds to encourage legislation relaxing the over-strict morality suffered by many in Britain.

1966

January

11 At the Lagos Commonwealth Prime Ministers' conference, Wilson is attacked for not using force against Rhodesia, but reassures the premiers that sanctions will bring Smith down in 'a matter of weeks rather than months'.

25 Wilson offers to talk to Smith about peaceful ways of ending the rebellion.

27 Labour retains the Hull North by-election with a majority increased from 1,181 to 5,351; Richard Gott, standing in opposition to the government's Vietnam policy, obtains only 253 votes.

31 96 Labour and Liberal MPs cable Senator Fulbright, the United States Senate Foreign Affairs Committee Chairman, asking him to continue to oppose the extension of 'this cruel and dangerous war'.

The Vietnam Solidarity Committee (VSC) is formed by Bertrand Russell.

February

22 The Defence White Paper cuts defence spending by 16 per cent over the next four years, but retains the 'East of Suez' role.

Christopher Mayhew resigns as a junior defence minister over the abandonment of aircraft carriers in favour of the shore-based F111-A aircraft, but his resignation speech attacks the East of Suez policy.

28 A general election is announced for *31 March*.

March

2 Britain protests to Portugal about the building of oil storage tanks at Beira, but is told that they are for Mozambique, not Rhodesia.

6 The Conservatives issue their manifesto *Action, Not Words*, calling for an end to state interference in the market and for ruthless competition to be the mainspring of the economy, with the state giving welfare only to the poorest.

7   Labour's manifesto, *Time For Decision*, stresses the role of economic planning and the achievements of the government.

10   Parliament is dissolved.

The Liberal manifesto, *For All The People*, calls for entry into the EEC and a withdrawal of British forces from east of Suez.

31   Polling day, with a turnout of 75.8 per cent (27,264,747 votes); Labour wins by a large overall majority of 97; 363 Labour MPs, 253 Conservatives, twelve Liberals, one Irish Republican and Labour, and the Speaker are elected; Labour obtains 13,096,629 votes (48.1 per cent), the Conservatives 11,418,455 votes (41.9 per cent), and the Liberals 2,327,457 votes (8.5 per cent).

April

19   In a reshuffle of his 'shadow Cabinet', Heath retires Lloyd and Sandys to the back benches.

21   The Queen's Speech announces the government's readiness to join the EEC if British and Commonwealth interests are safeguarded.

27   Wilson announces informal talks between Britain and Rhodesia to explore the possibility of negotiations.

May

3   Callaghan's budget imposes a selective employment tax on employers to shift employment away from the expanding service sector to the declining manufacturing sector, and also announces that the import surcharge is to end in November.

16-
Jul 1   The National Union of Seamen strike over demands for higher wages and a 40-hour week.

23   The government declares a State of Emergency as the strike begins to affect trade.

24   Wilson announces a Royal Commission under Sir John

Maud to undertake a review — 'the biggest this century' — of local government in England and Wales.

26   British Guiana achieves its independence as Guyana.

June

15   At a PLP meeting, Wilson stresses the unique role Britain enjoys in the area east of Suez because of its military commitments there, and a motion calling for military withdrawal from the region is defeated by 225 to 54 votes.

The Abortion Bill, introduced as a private Member's Bill by David Steel in order to make abortion legal, is given its second reading by 233 to 29 votes.

20   Wilson alleges that the seamen's strike is a result of agitation by 'a tightly-knit group of politically motivated men'.

29   As the United States bombing of North Vietnam is extended to non-military areas in Hanoi and Haiphong, Wilson dissociates himself from the new actions.

July

1   Bank Rate is raised to 7 per cent and special deposits are doubled in an attempt to avert a sterling crisis.

3   Cousins resigns from the government over plans to regulate wages, which he describes as 'a contradiction of the philosophy upon which our party is based'; Benn takes his place as Minister of Technology.

4   Legislation to give statutory powers to the Prices and Incomes Board is published, requiring prior notification of increases in prices and incomes.

5   Leo Abse uses the ten-minute rule to introduce his Sexual Offences Bill making homosexual acts between consenting adults over 21 legal, and it passes on a free vote by 244 to 100 votes.

7   In a Commons debate on Vietnam, Wilson is attacked by Heath for his dissociation from the latest United States bombing and by the left for his general support for the Americans in the war; 32 Labour MPs abstain on the division.

14   Gwynfor Evans wins the Carmarthen by-election for the

Welsh Nationalists, turning a Labour majority of 9,233 into a Plaid Cymru majority of 2,436.

16-18   Wilson, during his visit to Moscow, fails to persuade the Soviet leaders to put pressure on North Vietnam to compromise with the United States.

20   The government imposes a 'wage freeze' — a statutory halt to any rises in incomes, profits or dividends for six months in order to reduce demand; Brown offers his resignation after the failure of his prices and incomes policy, but it is refused.

25   The Iron and Steel Bill, providing for the nationalisation of the steel industry, is given a second reading against vigorous Conservative and Liberal opposition by 328 to 247 votes.

27   The TUC General Council approves the wage freeze by 20 to 12 votes, against Woodcock's advice that it would be unworkable.

31   The Colonial Office is wound up and merged into the Commonwealth Relations Office.

August

3   In the additions to the Prices and Incomes Bill incorporating the wage freeze 26 Labour MPs abstain, bringing the government majority down to 52.

10   George Brown is appointed Foreign Secretary and Michael Stewart becomes Economic Affairs Secretary.

The time limit for publication of Cabinet papers is reduced to 30 years.

12   The Prices and Incomes Bill is enacted.

18   Mao Tse-tung and Lin Piao appear together at a mass rally in Peking which launches the Chinese Cultural Revolution which soon becomes the inspiration for a student revolt in the Western world.

September

5-9   The TUC Annual Congress, Blackpool, defeats the opposition of the TGWU to the wage freeze by 5 million to 3.9 million votes.

6-15 At the Commonwealth Prime Ministers' conference, Wilson overcomes the critics of his Rhodesian policy by winning three months 'breathing space' to end the crisis.

21-4 The Liberal Party Assembly, Brighton, denounces the wage freeze as 'an unprecedented government intervention in the process of collective bargaining'; the Young Liberals emerge as a political force, shocking the older delegates by their demands for workers' control of industry and embarrassing the leadership when they succeed in referring back a resolution on NATO, leaving the party without a clear policy on the Atlantic Alliance.

October

3-7 At the Labour Party annual conference, Brighton, Cousins attacks the government's incomes policy, warning that 'if the law is unfair, trade unionists since time immemorial have opposed the law', but the government policy is supported by 3.8 million to 2.5 million votes; the government suffers a defeat over its support for United States policy in Vietnam by 3.8 million to 2.6 million votes; Wilson makes it clear that the government would act independently of conference decisions.

An Order in Council prevents newspaper owners from granting a wage bonus to their employees.

6 Brown puts forward new proposals for ending the Vietnam War on the basis of reconvening the Geneva Conference, of which Britain was a co-chairman, but this is rejected by both North and South Vietnam.

13-16 At the Conservative Party annual conference, Blackpool, Heath stresses the need for more free enterprise, tax incentives and reform of the trade unions; he avoids conflict over Rhodesia by opposng UN intervention and calling for more talks with the Smith regime.

November

10 The government announces that it will seek to join the EEC.

14 Wilson, in his Guildhall speech, calls upon the 'Merchant

Venturers of the City of London' to be ready for the tough competition within the EEC.

16-17 In the Commons debate, the two front benches support EEC entry, while the back benches of both sides are divided.

23 Duncan Sandy's motion to restore capital punishment for the murder of policemen and prison warders is defeated in a Commons free vote by 292 to 170 votes.

Unemployment in November is 541,083, but sterling is healthy and the balance of payments is in surplus.

December

1-3 Wilson meets Ian Smith on HMS *Tiger*, where he proposes a new constitution for Rhodesia and a return to legality.

4 Smith rejects the *Tiger* terms.

7-8 In the Commons debate on the Rhodesian talks, Wilson attacks the Conservatives for supporting racialism after they oppose both the *Tiger* terms and UN sanctions.

12 The Industrial Reorganisation Bill is enacted, setting up the Industrial Reorganisation Corporation (IRC) to assist the private sector through state direction of investment.

16 The UN adopts selective mandatory sanctions on Rhodesia.

General

TUC membership is 8,868,000.

In 'The Longest Revolution', an article in *New Left Review*, Juliet Mitchell calls for an independent women's movement.

1967

January

15-17   Wilson and Brown visit Rome, beginning their tour of European capitals to argue for British membership of the Common Market.

17   Jo Grimond resigns as Liberal leader.

18   In the Liberal leadership ballot, Jeremy Thorpe obtains six votes against three for Eric Lubbock and three for Emlyn Hooson; Thorpe is unanimously elected Liberal leader after Lubbock and Hooson withdraw.

20   The wage freeze is succeeded by a period of 'severe restraint' with wage rises dependent on increases in productivity and efficiency.

25   After an address by Douglas Jay, President of the Board of Trade, to the finance and economic affairs group of the PLP, attacking the EEC, Wilson warns all ministers of their collective responsibility to support Cabinet decisions.

27   Wilson becomes the first British Prime Minister to speak to the Consultative Assembly of the Council of Europe, and commits Britain to the spirit of European unity.

February

7   The National Front is founded as a merger of several Fascist and racist groups.

10   Large scale rioting occurs in Aden against the British authorities.

21   In a Commons motion, 108 MPs warn the government of their opposition to EEC entry.

March

2   Wilson warns his backbenchers against constant rebellions, saying that 'every dog is allowed one bite, but a different view is taken of a dog that goes on biting'.

13-21   Students at the London School of Economics stage a sit-in over disciplinary action made against two left-wing lecturers.

15 Shinwell resigns as PLP Chairman after a dispute over discipline with Richard Crossman, the Leader of the Commons.

21 Herbert Bowden, the Commonwealth Relations Secretary, tells the Commons that sanctions against Rhodesia are 'biting very deeply'.

22 The Iron and Steel Bill is enacted.

The Parliamentary Commissioner Bill is enacted, setting up an Ombudsman on the Scandinavian model to investigate administrative abuses by government; the Ombudsman has no real powers, though.

April

7 The UN mission leaves Aden, complaining bitterly of the lack of British co-operation.

10-15 The Conservatives make big gains in local elections, and Labour loses control of London for the first time since 1934 when 82 Conservative councillors are elected against 18 Labour in the GLC elections.

11 Callaghan's budget is neutral, giving no tax concessions and imposing no large increases in taxation.

May

2 Wilson announces that the Cabinet has decided that Britain should apply for EEC entry.

In the Scottish burgh elections, the SNP do well, gaining 60,000 votes in Glasgow, though no seats.

British service families are withdrawn from Aden after reprisals are threatened over the killing of six Arab children in a landmine explosion.

10 After a three-day debate, the Commons agrees to apply for EEC entry by 488 to 62 votes, with 34 Labour and 26 Conservative MPs voting against; 51 Labour MPs abstain, including seven Parliamentary Private Secretaries who are forced to resign.

16 de Gaulle warns of the 'formidable obstacles' to British membership of the Common Market.

23   Lord Chalfont is appointed the chief British negotiator for EEC entry.

June

5-10   In a six-day war, Israel emerges as the dominant power in the Middle East after defeating Egypt, Syria and Jordan.

Brown announces British neutrality in the Arab-Israeli war.

13   Despite bad trade figures, Callaghan predicts a balance of payments surplus for the year.

19   Brown announces independence for Aden.

The period of severe restraint in wage rises is succeeded by a 'period of moderation' in which all rises are to be held below the 1966 norm of 3 to 3½ per cent.

July

7   Civil war in Nigeria begins in earnest as Nigerian forces attack the seceded eastern state of Biafra.

10   At the EEC Ministerial Council, Brussells, Couve de Murville, French Foreign Minister, warns that British entry could 'affect the very existence of the Common Market'.

13   The Lords give the Sexual Offences Bill, introduced by Leo Abse (on *5 July 1966*) a second reading by 111 to 48 votes.

15-19   The Dialectics of Liberation conference at the Round House in London is addressed by radicals like Herbert Marcuse, Stokely Carmichael and R.D. Laing; it testifies to an increasing radicalism on the left.

17   The government's majority falls to 56 on the measure delaying wage rises for a further year, as 22 Labour MPs abstain.

20   A committee under Mr Justice Latey advocates a reduction in the voting age from 21 to 18.

24   Callaghan tells the Commons that 'devaluation is not the way out of Britain's difficulties'.

Patrick Gordon Walker, the Education Secretary, announces dearer school meals and welfare milk, combined with an increase in family allowances.

25   Margaret Herbison, the Minister for Social Security, resigns in protest at the move away from the principle of universality in the NHS.

27   The Defence Policy Statement, which drastically reduces British military forces east of Suez, causes 19 Labour MPs to abstain.

August

28   In a Cabinet reshuffle, Wilson takes personal charge of the Department of Economic Affairs, with Peter Shore acting as his deputy; Tony Crosland becomes President of the Board of Trade.

September

4-8   The TUC Annual Congress, Brighton, votes against the government's wage restraint policies.

5   Sir Humphrey Trevelyan, the British High Commissioner in Aden, recognises the Nationalist forces there, to Conservative consternation.

10   In a referendum, Gibralter votes by 12,138 to 44 to remain under British rule.

11   Anthony Barber becomes Conservative Party Chairman, after Edward du Cann has thoroughly overhauled Conservative organisation and finances.

18-   A dock strike in London and Liverpool adds to growing
Nov 28 balance of payments problems.

20-3   At the Liberal Party Assembly in Blackpool, the Young Liberals are defeated when delegates support NATO and reject a radical motion calling for the unification of all Europe, Eastern as well as Western.

21   Labour loses the safe seat of Walthamstow West at a by-election, as a Labour majority of 8,725 is turned into a Conservative majority of 62.

25   A ceasefire is agreed in Aden as negotiations for independence begin.

October

2-6   The Labour Party annual conference, Scarborough, supports government policy on wage restraint and on EEC entry, but calls for a dissociation from United States policy in Vietnam.

8   Clement Attlee dies at the age of 84.

18-21   At the Conservative Party annual conference, Brighton, Heath successfully resists the pro-Smith section of the party led by Lord Salisbury.

26   Callaghan, in his Mansion House speech, argues that sterling 'could begin a new stage in the world monetary system' if it was put at the service of the EEC.

27   An anti-Vietnam War demonstration outside the United States embassy in London turns into violence.

    The Abortion Bill is enacted.

31   The Queen's Speech proposes to reform the House of Lords in order 'to eliminate its present hereditary basis'.

    The Gallup poll shows 45 per cent Conservative, 38 per cent Labour, and 14 per cent Liberal support.

November

2   Winifred Ewing wins the Hamilton by-election for the SNP, turning a safe Labour majority of 16,576 into a SNP majority of 1,799.

7   Hugh Scanlon, a prominent supporter of the left-wing Intstitute for Workers Control (IWC), is elected President of the powerful Amalgamated Engineering Federation (AEF) union.

    The government's economic policies are criticised in a letter signed by 46 Labour MPs, who call for 'a decisive break with the traditional remedy of deflation'.

8-10   George Thomson, the Commonwealth Relations Secretary, holds unsuccessful talks with Ian Smith in Salisbury, Rhodesia.

17   Heavy pressure is placed on sterling as rumours of devaluation abound.

18   Callaghan announces that the pound has been devalued from US$2.80 to US$2.40.

19   Wilson, in a television broadcast on the devaluation, says that 'this does not mean that the pound in your pocket . . . has been devalued', provoking protests at his mendacity.

27   de Gaulle effectively vetoes British entry into the Common Market, arguing that it 'would destroy the partnership of which France is a member'.

29   Callaghan becomes Home Secretary after the failure of his economic policies highlighted by devaluation, while Roy Jenkins becomes Chancellor of the Exchequer.

British troops withdraw from Aden.

December

5   In the Commons debate on devaluation, Jenkins says that the measure has given the British economy the chance of export-led growth, but sharp criticism of a Letter of Intent to the IMF promising deflationary policies leads 16 Labour MPs to abstain and 18 Labour MPs to vote against the government.

14   Wilson affirms the arms embargo on South Africa, provoking sharp criticism from both the Conservatives and the CBI, and opposition within the Cabinet led by Brown.

20   The decision to maintain an arms embargo on South Africa ends a post-devaluation struggle for power within the Cabinet with a victory for Wilson.

1968

January

16   In a major deflationary package, government spending is cut by £716 million, including a withdrawal of British military forces from east of Suez by 1971 and the cancellation of the F-111 aircraft; the housing programme is cut, while charges for NHS prescriptions and dental treatment — the issue on which Wilson resigned with Bevan in 1951 — are imposed; Lord Longford resigns over the deferment of the raising of the school leaving age to 16.

The left-wing *Tribune* group of MPs led by Michael Foot propose an alternative programme of expansion combined with tougher controls on capital.

18   On the motion approving the government policy on the cuts 25 Labour MPs abstain, while Desmond Donnelly resigns the Labour Whip in protest at the withdrawal east of Suez.

February

6   Home in South Africa pledges that the embargo on arms would be reversed by a future Conservative government.

8-9   During Wilson's visit to Washington, President Johnson expresses concern on British withdrawal east of Suez.

21   Heath and the 'shadow Cabinet' demand immediate controls on the influx of Asians expelled from Kenya and a tougher immigration policy.

22   Callaghan announces the introduction of emergency legislation to prevent the entry of many of the Kenyan Asians.

25   Home returns to England from South Africa convinced that there could be a satisfactory formula for a Rhodesian settlement.

27   The Commonwealth Immigration Bill, creating a voucher system for Kenyan Asians, is given a second reading by 372 to 62 votes, with 35 Labour and 15 Conservative

MPs voting against it.

March

1   The Commonwealth Immigration Bill is enacted after an all-night sitting of the Lords.

4   The Rhodesian government executes three Africans in defiance of a Royal Prerogative of Mercy, provoking a bitter reaction in the Labour government which prevents consideration of Home's peace proposals.

15   George Brown resigns from the government over his exclusion from Cabinet decision-making; he remains as Labour's deputy leader and is succeeded as Foreign Secretary by Michael Stewart.

17   Central bank governors meeting in Washington agree to a two-tier system for gold in order to end the growing world financial crisis.

         An anti-Vietnam War demonstration in front of the United States embassy in Grosvenor Square erupts into violence.

19   Jenkins's budget, designed to secure structural changes in the economy, imposes a major increase of £923 million in indirect taxation; Jenkins tells the Commons that 'we must have a stiff budget followed by two years of hard slog'.

27   A Conservative attempt to get the Rhodesian negotiations restarted is defeated in the Commons by 331 to 237 votes.

         Desmond Donnelly is expelled from the Labour Party.

28   Three serious by-election defeats highlight Labour's loss of a significant proportion of working-class voters; in Dudley, a Labour majority of 10,022 is turned into a Conservative majority of 11,656.

April

4   Martin Luther King, the black United States civil rights leader, is assassinated in Memphis, Tennessee; race riots erupt in Washington and 40 other cities.

5   In a major reorganisation of his government, Wilson appoints Barbara Castle as the Secretary for the new

Department of Employment and Productivity (taking over and enlarging the Ministry of Labour), while Richard Crossman is appointed to co-ordinate the social services.

9   The Race Relations Bill is published, making racial discrimination illegal and setting up a Race Relations Board as an enforcement agency.

12   Wilson formally relinquishes his overall supremacy of the Department of Economic Affairs, thereby acknowledging Jenkins's supremacy in economic policy-making.

20   Enoch Powell makes an inflammatory speech in Birmingham in which he forecasts 'a river of blood' unless the problems of black and Asian minorities in the inner cities are resolved by encouraging voluntary repatriation.

21   Heath dismisses Powell from the 'shadow Cabinet'.

23   The Commons gives the Race Relations Bill a second reading by 313 to 209 votes; the Conservative opposition to the Bill leads Humphrey Berkeley to resign the Conservative Whip.

Several hundred London dockers stop work and demonstrate in support of Powell.

May

3   Clashes between students and police in Paris begin the 'students revolt' in France, setting off a wave of strikes and occupations by workers and serving as a model for the European far left.

5   Spain closes the border with Gibralter.

9   The Conservatives and, in Scotland, the SNP make big gains at Labour's expense.

10   Cecil King, the Chairman of International Publishing Corporation (IPC), launches a violent attack on Wilson in the *Daily Mirror*, and calls for a fresh leader for the Labour Party; Labour rallies around Wilson in reaction.

15   The AEF holds a one-day strike against the government's incomes policy.

21   The new Prices and Incomes Bill extending government powers over wages receives a second reading by 290 to 255 votes, with 34 Labour MPs abstaining.

30   Cecil King is dismissed as IPC Chairman after his attack on Wilson.

The Gallup poll shows 56 per cent Conservative, 28 per cent Labour and 11 per cent Liberal support.

June

6   Senator Robert Kennedy is assassinated after his victory in the California primary.

12   Michael Stewart, with Conservative support, resists the demand for an arms embargo to Nigeria, then involved in civil war.

13   The Donovan Commission on the trade unions reports, pointing to the growth of unofficial strikes and calling for a move away from centralised wage bargaining, and a Commission on Industrial Relations to investigate labour difficulties; it does not recommend legal sanctions against unofficial strikers, however, to the chagrin of the Conservatives and the CBI.

18   The Lords oppose government sanctions against Rhodesia by 193 to 184 votes, in a symbolic protest.

20   In retaliation for the Lords vote on Rhodesia, Wilson announces the end of all-party talks on the reform of the House of Lords, and the intention to introduce 'comprehensive and radical' reforms instead.

26   The Fulton Report on the future of the Civil Service is published.

July

10   The Prices and Incomes Bill is enacted.

In the interests of party unity the PLP decides not to discipline 23 Labour MPs who voted with the Opposition in the committee stage of the Prices and Incomes Bill.

24   Harry Nicholas is elected Labour Party General Secretary by the NEC after Sir Len Williams is appointed Governor-General of Mauritius.

August

14   Heath, speaking in Canberra, Australia, promises to

reverse the government's decision to withdraw east of Suez.

20-1   Soviet troops, supported by Warsaw Pact states, occupy Czechoslovakia to end the reform movement there.

September

2-6   The 100th TUC Annual Congress, Blackpool, rejects a statutory incomes policy by 7.7 million to 1 million votes and by an overwhelming majority endorses the demand for equal pay for women.

16   The Marylebone Cricket Club (MCC) announces that Basil D'Oliveira, a Cape Coloured, is to tour South Africa after all, having initially dropped him from the team.

17   John Vorster, the South African Prime Minister, cancels the MCC cricket tour.

18-21   The Liberal Party Assembly, Edinburgh, rejects Grimond's call for a completely independent and self-governing Scotland in favour of a major devolution of power through four separate parliaments within the United Kingdom.

20   Heath, in a speech at York, calls for a register of immigrants and their dependants, and the restriction of work permits to 12 months at a time.

30-   The Labour Party annual conference, Blackpool, passes
Oct 4 by five to one a motion calling for the repeal of the statutory wages policy; Castle and Jenkins make clear that the government would ignore the conference.

October

5   A demonstration calling for civil rights for Catholics in Derry turns into violence as police attack peaceful demonstrators.

9-12   At the Conservative Party annual conference, Blackpool, Powell warns that unless something is done about immigration, 'the character of England itself will be changed . . . in a way its people neither chose nor desired'.

9-13   Wilson renews his talks with Ian Smith on board HMS *Fearless*, and new peace proposals are elaborated which involve a concession by Wilson on Smith remaining in power.

16   The Commonwealth Relations Office is wound up and merged into the Foreign Office.

21   Richard Crossman, in the Granada Lecture, condemns the trivialisation of serious political issues into superficial personality clashes by television.

22   The *Fearless* proposals are endorsed by the Commons by 177 to 56 votes, but 49 Labour MPs vote against them and over 100 abstain.

23   In a joint statement, the CBI and TUC accept the need for a Commission on Industrial Relations proposed by the Donovan Commission report, but insist that it should not have power to investigate industrial relations.

25   The Race Relations Bill is enacted.

27   A massive anti-Vietnam War demonstration of 100,000 testifies to a renewed far left in Britain.

November

1   The Department of Health and Social Security (DHSS) is established, merging the Ministries of Health and Social Security, with Richard Crossman as its head; the Civil Service Department is to take responsibility for the Civil Service from the Treasury, with the Prime Minister as its head.

2-7   George Thomson, Minister without Portfolio, visits Rhodesia to push the *Fearless* talks further, but his discussions are inconclusive.

4   Wilson reaffirms the Attlee pledge (of *28 October 1948*) guaranteeing the constitutional status of Northern Ireland in a meeting with Captain O'Neill, but demands immediate reform to give Catholics equal rights.

7   The Representation of the People Bill, reducing the voting age to 18 is published.

21   A White Paper on House of Lords reform is approved by the Lords by 251 to 56 votes, and by the Commons by 270 to 111, the opposition comprising MPs of all parties.

22   Captain O'Neill announces a limited reform package which fails to satisfy the civil rights movement.

December

9   O'Neill says in a televised broadcast that 'Ulster stands at the crossroads'.

11   William Craig, the hardline Unionist Minister of Home Affairs in Northern Ireland, is dismissed.

General

Labour Party membership is 6,087,000.

Cathy Come Home, a BBC Television play, begins an important drama series dealing with major social problems, usually from a left-wing viewpoint.

1969

January

1-4   A civil rights march from Belfast to Derry is ambushed by Protestants at Burntollet.

2   Rupert Murdoch becomes the proprietor of the popular *News of the World*.

3   The Cabinet approves legislation to regulate trade unions.

7-15   At the Commonwealth Prime Ministers' conference, Wilson rejects demands by Kenneth Kaunda of Zambia to withdraw the *Fearless* terms and overthrow the Smith regime by force.

17   *In Place of Strife*, the White Paper on trade union legislation, is introduced in the Commons by Barbara Castle; it introduces penal sanctions to enforce the provisions of a law which would impose compulsory strike ballots in some disputes and a 'cooling off' period for unofficial strikes; it is criticised by the CBI and the Conservatives as inadequate, while the Labour Party and the trade unions are alarmed.

A Commission on Industrial Relations is established, with Woodcock as chairman.

20   Richard Nixon is inaugurated as United States President.

24   Students at the London School of Economics (LSE) break down control gates and the governors close the School for a month.

25   Heath, in a speech at Walsall, makes concessions to Powell by calling for even tighter immigration controls and generous financial assistance to immigrants who wish to leave Britain.

February

3   The Parliament Bill to reform the Lords wins its second reading by 285 to 135 votes, with opposition from 105 Conservatives and 27 Labour MPs (the Conservatives and Liberals enjoyed a free vote).

20   Denis Healey, the Defence Secretary, introduces the Defence White Paper by telling the Commons that it would 'set the seal on Britain's transformation from a world power to a European power' by its concentration on NATO.

21   Vic Feather becomes acting TUC General Secretary.

March

3   The Commons endorses *In Place of Strife* by 224 to 62 votes, with the Conservatives and 39 Labour MPs abstaining and 53 Labour MPs voting against.

18   A bitter strike at the Ford car factories, involving 42,000 workers and losing £1,000,000 a day, ends after 3 ½ weeks.

26   The Labour NEC votes against *In Place of Strife* by 16 to five votes, with Callaghan defying Cabinet responsibility to vote against in his position as party Treasurer.

27-31   Wilson visits Lagos in an unsuccessful attempt to end the Nigerian Civil War.

April

3   The Cabinet unanimously reaffirms its support for *In Place of Strife*, thereby ending Callaghan's revolt.

15   Jenkins's budget restrains demand again, this time by £340 million in tax increases; he says 'the improvement has been a good deal slower than we hoped' because Britain's competitive position had been destroyed by irresponsible industrial action, and announces that the government has decided to proceed with trade union legislation.

16   Castle tells the Commons that penal sanctions would not involve workers being sent to prison, and says that the collection of any debt from fines would come from the wage packet.

17   Wilson announces that the Parliament Bill is to be abandoned after it had been effectively held up in its committee stage by the combined opposition of Foot (who wanted the Lords abolished) and Powell (who did not want any change).

Wilson stresses to the PLP that the passage of the trade union legislation is 'essential to the government's continuance in office'.

Bernadette Devlin, a socialist republican, is elected as

Unity MP for Mid-Ulster at the age of 21.

19   Violent rioting erupts in Derry and Belfast as Ulster police columns attempt to break through nationalist barricades.

28   O'Neill resigns as Northern Ireland's Prime Minister under pressure from Unionist hardliners, and Major James Chichester-Clark succeeds him.

de Gaulle resigns as French President after being defeated in a referendum on regional reform; the chances of British entry into the EEC are enhanced as a result.

29   Wilson constructs an 'inner Cabinet' of seven (unnamed) ministers to plan and co-ordinate long-term policies.

May

1   100,000 workers strike against the government's trade union proposals in response to a call from the Liaison Committee for the Defence of Trade Unions (LCDTU).

6   In local government elections in Scotland, the SNP makes only small gains.

7   Douglas Houghton, the PLP chairman, warns the Cabinet that backbench support for a trade union bill would not be forthcoming.

Smith's proposals for a Rhodesian republic mark the effective end of the *Fearless* negotiations.

12   After discussions with trade union leaders on a possible alternative to regulatory legislation, the government agrees not to publish a bill until after the Whitsun recess.

13   Callaghan is excluded from the inner Cabinet discussing trade union reform.

19   The TUC issues *Programme for Action*, giving the General Council limited powers to intervene in strikes; these proposals are described as ineffective by John Davies, the CBI Director General.

21   Wilson tells the TUC leaders that their proposals, though an advance on the previous situation, are not yet strong enough.

June

5   The TUC special conference, Croydon, rejects the

government's *In Place of Strife* proposals by 8.2 million to 0.3 million votes, and Hugh Scanlon warns of industrial action if the government continues on its course.

9   Powell attacks Heath for 'sheer incomprehension of the very magnitude of the danger' caused by immigration.

11   The report of the Redcliffe-Maud Commisson on Local Government proposes far-reaching changes for the complete redrawing of the local government map in England; outside Greater London, 61 new local government areas are proposed, with three — Birmingham, Liverpool and Manchester — having similar structures to the GLC.

18   Wilson, in a major defeat for his government, announces that the *In Place of Strife* proposals were being abandoned in favour of the TUC's voluntary approach.

19   The report of the four Boundary Commissioners recommends major alterations to 322 constituencies to increase the total to 635, though the changes benefit the Conservatives.

20   Callaghan introduces the House of Commons (Redistribution of Seats) (No 2) Bill, relieving the Home Secretary of the statutory need to lay the Boundary Commission reports before Parliament.

24   Rhodesia is declared a republic.

26-   A Port Talbot steel strike of 130 blastfurnacemen provides
Aug 4 the first test for the TUC's voluntary approach, but the strike is settled after TUC approaches have been rebuffed.

July

2   The government's bill to defer the Boundary Commission report obtains its second reading by 298 to 246 amidst Conservative charges of gerry-mandering the next election.

3   The government's agreement with the TUC is condemned by the opposition in the Commons as a shameful retreat, and Heath affirms that new legislation would be introduced by a future Conservative government.

21   In the committee stage of the government's bill to defer the Boundary Commission report, the Lords, by 270 to 96 votes, demand that any changes be implemented by March 1970.

August

12-14   Riots break out in Derry after a provocative Protestant parade there, and Ulster police are unable to break the nationalist resistance; 'no go' areas are set up by the people in the city.

14   British troops move into Derry, though they respect the 'no-go' areas.

15   British troops are moved into Belfast after overnight rioting in which ten people are killed and 100 wounded in the Catholic slum area of the city; the troops are greeted by the Catholics as saviours.

19   The Downing Street Declaration is issued by Wilson and Chichester-Clark promising reform in Ulster, though the border is to be maintained.

The balance of payments goes into surplus, but unemployment reaches 568,079 or 2.5 per cent.

September

1   Campbell Adamson is appointed Director General of the CBI.

1-5   The TUC Annual Congress, Portsmouth, demands the repeal of the Prices and Incomes Act by 4.6 million to 4.2 million votes; Vic Feather becomes General Secretary.

8   Jack Jones succeeds Cousins as TGWU General Secretary, forming a powerful left-wing alliance with Scanlon.

17-20   The Liberal Party Assembly in Brighton adopts a new constitution which tightens up party administration and establishes a disciplinary board with the power to expel individuals who are not genuine Liberals; there are rumbles of discontent at the failure of Thorpe to maintain the Liberal momentum.

25   The Royal Commission on the Reform of Local Government in Scotland proposes a two-tier system of seven regional and 37 district authorities, a major reduction in the number of local authorities from the 430 of the existing system.

26   Rupert Murdoch buys the *Sun* from IPC and proceeds to make it highly popular by mixing salacious stories and pictures with right-wing politics.

29- At the Labour Party annual conference, Brighton, the
Oct 3 government programme, *Agenda for a Generation*, proposing
a wealth tax, is agreed by 3.5 million to 2.2 million votes,
with the TGWU and AEF voting against.

October

5 The Department of Economic Affairs (DEA) is abolished.
8 Reg Prentice resigns from the government over its failure
to give adequate resources to the Ministry of Overseas Aid
from which he had been moved.
8-11 The Conservative Party annual conference, Brighton,
votes (against the leadership's wishes) to restore capital
punishment; a demand for the compulsory repatriation of
immigrants is defeated by 1,349 to 954 votes.
10 Lord Hunt's report into the Ulster disturbances recommends the abolition of the 'B-Specials', a militia hated by
the Catholics, and the establishment of a new militia, the
Ulster Defence Regiment (UDR); the recommendations are
accepted by the government.
13-27 An unofficial coalminers' strike in Yorkshire spreads to
involve 121,000 miners; 979,000 working days are lost in
the largest miners' strike since 1944.
14 The government defeats the Lords amendment to its bill
deferring the Boundary Commission report by 272 to 229
votes.
16 The Lords reject the Bill by 299 to 78 votes in what is
becoming a bitter political and constitutional clash.
22 The Divorce Reform Bill is enacted, bringing to an end
a period of libertarian social legislation.

The Gallup poll shows 46 per cent Conservative, 44 per
cent Labour and 7 per cent Liberal support.

November

5 The South African rugby tour is disrupted by anti-
apartheid demonstrators led by Young Liberal activist, Peter
Hain.
6 The statutory 3.5 per cent limit on dividend increases is
to be abolished by the end of the year.

13   Callaghan moves the rejection of the draft orders relating to the Boundary Commission reports on the grounds that local government organisation had to be considered first, and the Commons supports him by 303 to 250 votes, against bitter Conservative opposition.

16-17   The British Communist Party Congress defeats, by 295 to 118 votes, a motion by pro-Soviet elements led by Palme Dutt, and condemns the Soviet invasion of Czechoslovakia.

December

8   In a foreign affairs debate on Vietnam, dominated by the news of a massacre at My Lai, carried out by American soldiers, 44 Labour MPs abstain and 49 vote against the government's support of the United States.

16   The Commons votes to make the abolition of capital punishment permanent by 343 to 185 votes.

18   The Lords vote, by 220 to 174 votes, to abolish the death penalty permanently.

1970

January

11   The Provisional IRA and Provisional Sinn Fein are set up by delegates at a Sinn Fein conference in Dublin disgusted by the Official IRA's military quietism.

17   Powell criticises government aid to improve housing and social services in immigrant areas as merely encouraging immigrants to stay.

18   Heath repudiates Powell's views on race as 'an example of man's inhumanity to man, which is absolutely intolerable in a Christian civilised society'.

19   Anti-apartheid protesters daub a dozen cricket grounds with slogans protesting at the forthcoming MCC tour of South Africa.

26-9   Wilson visits the United States, where he becomes the first foreign statesman to attend the National Security Council.

28   Castle presents a bill providing equal pay for women doing equal work to be introduced in 1975.

30   The Conservative leadership meets at the Selsdon Park Hotel, Croydon, and formulates an election strategy stressing law and order, free market policies, the reduction of taxes, stricter immigration controls, and legal regulation of trade unions.

Gold and dollar reserves rise by £21 million to £1,074 million, the highest for two years, while the balance of payments is in surplus for the sixth successive month.

February

4   A bill is published to compel local authorities to end the 11-plus examination and develop comprehensive schools.

A White Paper on local government reform in England on the lines of the Redcliffe-Maud report is published.

13   After the MCC reduces the number of matches in its South African tour under pressure from anti-apartheid protestors and the government, Sir Peter Rawlinson, in an attempt to highlight the need for more law and order, stresses that 'the government is acknowledging the licence to riot'.

27   The Committee of Vice-Chancellors agrees to allow students to see their academic records, to check that they contain no political comments, after the occupation of Warwick University sets off a series of occupations by students.

A conference on women's history at Ruskin College, Oxford, spontaneously becomes the first national conference of the women's liberation movement, elaborating demands for equal pay, equal education and opportunity, 24-hour nurseries and free contraception and abortion on demand.

March

5   The government Defence White Paper is approved by 251 to 230 votes after 36 Labour left-wing MPs abstain in defiance of a three-line whip; Bob Mellish, the Labour Chief Whip, bitterly attacks them as damaging the party in a pre-election period.

19   Labour has a good result in the South Ayrshire by-election, its majority falling from 12,053 to only 10,886; as opinion polls are favourable, the government sees good portents in holding an early election.

April

9   The Conservatives retain control of the GLC in elections which see a moderate swing to Labour.

14   Jenkins's budget gives only minor tax concessions despite an all-time revenue surplus of £2,444 million, as he wishes to concentrate on guiding the economy into steadily increasing growth and to avoid charges of electioneering.

21   The Alliance Party is formed in Northern Ireland as an attempt to unite Protestants and Catholics into a non-sectarian party which accepts the union with Britain.

May

7   Labour makes large gains in the municipal elections.

14   Zambia and Uganda threaten to withdraw from the Commonwealth Games unless the MCC drops its tour of South Africa.

18   A general election is announced for *18 June*.

22   The MCC calls off its South African tour after strong government pressure is placed upon it.

26   The Conservative election manifesto, *A Better Tomorrow*, pledges to cut government spending, introduce a legal framework for trade unions and to maintain a military presence east of Suez.

27   The Labour manifesto, *Now Britain's Strong, Let's Make It Great To Live In*, is imprecise about the future, relying mainly on the government's record.

28   The Liberal manifesto, *What A Life!* is little noticed, its commitment to self-government within Britain undercut by the nationalist challenge.

29   Parliament is dissolved.

The Equal Pay Bill is enacted after unopposed readings in Parliament.

June

3   Tony Benn, in a speech at Westminster Central Hall, says that the flag of racialism hoisted by Powell is beginning to look like the same flag which flew over Dachau and Belsen.

11   Enoch Powell attacks the distortion of statistics on Commonwealth immigration and speculates on the enemies of Britain in the Civil Service.

15   The balance of payments figures for May show a deficit of £31 million.

18   Polling day, with a turnout of 72.0 per cent (28,344,798 votes); the Conservatives win a surprise victory, upsetting the opinion pollsters, with 330 Conservative MPs, 287 Labour, six Liberals, one Independent Labour, one SNP, two Irish Republicans, one Irish Republican Labour, one Ulster Protestant Unionist, and the Speaker, a Conservative overall majority of 31; the Conservatives obtain 13,145,123 votes (46.4 per cent), Labour 12,208,758 votes (43.1 per

cent) and the Liberals 2,117,035 votes (7.5 per cent); George Brown is among the defeated MPs and resigns as Labour's deputy leader.

19   Heath becomes Prime Minister, and forms a Conservative government with Ian Macleod as Chancellor of the Exchequer, Reginald Maudling as Home Secretary and Sir Alec Douglas-Home as Foreign Secretary.

24   Home expresses his readiness to discuss the sale of arms to South Africa.

30   Home and Anthony Barber, the minister responsible for restarting negotiations with the EEC, begin a new round of talks aimed at British entry into the Common Market.

Margaret Thatcher, the Education Secretary, withdraws the Crosland circular (of *12 July 1965*) on comprehensive education, and stresses that local education authorities have the freedom to retain the old structure of education if they so wish.

July

3   Clashes between the army and Catholics as troops search for arms in the Falls Road area of Belfast leads to a Provisional IRA bombing campaign.

7   Macleod rules out tax cuts in the autumn.

8   Roy Jenkins is elected Labour's deputy leader with 133 votes; Michael Foot polls 67 and Fred Peart 48.

16   A State of Emergency is declared as a dockers' strike begins to affect trade.

Foot is elected to the shadow Cabinet.

20   Ian Macleod dies suddenly of a heart attack.

23   Two CS gas bombs are thrown into the Commons chamber intending to remind MPs of life in Northern Ireland; a drastic review of security in the Commons is ordered.

25   Barber is appointed Chancellor of the Exchequer, with Geoffrey Rippon taking over the EEC negotiations.

29   A settlement of the dockers' strike is reached with the offer of higher pay.

31   Peter Thomas succeeds Barber as Conservative Party Chairman.

August

6   Robert Carr, the Employment Secretary, stresses that there is no incomes policy but advises the chairmen of the nationalised industries to take the national interest into account when negotiating pay rises.

21   The Social Democratic and Labour Party (SDLP), a moderate nationalist party, is founded in Northern Ireland.

September

6   An attempt to hijack an Israeli El Al Boeing aircraft fails, and Leila Khaled, a Palestinian guerrilla, is arrested after a forced landing at Heathrow.

7-11   The TUC Annual Congress, Brighton, unanimously approves a resolution opposing any legislation that would 'restrict the freedom of the trade union movement', and delegates warn of a prolonged and bitter dispute with the government if the anti-union legislation proceeds.

7   Heath calls an emergency Cabinet meeting after a Palestinian threat to blow up two other aircraft and their passengers on a Jordanian airfield, unless Khaled is released.

9   A third aircraft is hijacked and landed at the Jordanian airfield.

12   The three aircraft are blown up, though the passengers are safely held.

16   Fierce fighting erupts in Jordan after King Hussein acts against the Palestine Liberation Organisation (PLO), the main Palestinian guerrilla group, in response to the hijackings.

23-6   The Liberal Party Assembly meets at Eastbourne in a dispirited mood after the poor election result.

27   The war in Jordan is ended by an agreement in Cairo.

28-
Oct 2   At the Labour Party annual conference, Blackpool, the policy of controlling incomes is rejected by 3.1 million to 2.8 million votes; Jenkins stresses the need for Labour to be free of trade union domination.

30   Leila Khaled is released; the government is criticised by Powell and Sandys for surrendering to terrorism.

October

7-10   The Conservative Party annual conference, Blackpool, demands an end to state interference in the market to support 'lame duck' industries; Heath promises 'a change so radical, a revolution so quiet and yet so total' that it will take more than one parliament to implement.

15   A new Department of Trade and Industry is set up under John Davies, merging the old Board of Trade and Ministry of Technology.

A new Department of the Environment under Peter Walker unites the old Ministries of Housing, Local Government, Transport, and Public Works.

Barber, in his Mansion House speech, reaffirms the government's determination to reduce state spending.

25   The Archbishop of Canterbury and 100 African bishops express their deep disquiet over arms sales to South Africa in a letter to the Prime Minister.

27   Barber presents an autumn budget of reductions in income and corporation tax, the ending of free school milk, and increases in charges for the social services; the IRC is to be wound up.

28   The Defence White Paper reaffirms the government decision to retain a military presence east of Suez, but on a limited scale.

29   Lord Rothschild becomes head of a new section of the Cabinet Office, the Central Policy Review Staff, 'the Think Tank', which is to advise the Cabinet on policy.

November

2   The Prices and Incomes Board is wound up.

5   The 'dirty jobs' strike of public service workers ends after two months when the employers, fearful of the threat to public health, give in to the union demand for higher wages; the government is infuriated.

Dr Arikpo, the Nigerian Foreign Minister, warns of the adverse effect on British economic interests in Nigeria if the arms sales to South Africa go ahead.

9   On the government motion to renew sanctions against Rhodesia 23 Conservative MPs vote against.

11 Rolls Royce, on the verge of bankruptcy, is given government aid of £42 million.

25 Lord Hall is dismissed as Chairman of the Post Office, leading postal workers to hold one-day strikes and demonstrations against the possible privatisation of the service.

December

3 The Industrial Relations Bill is published, providing for unions to be registered to enjoy legal status, pre-strike ballots and 'cooling-off' periods to be compulsory, and fines to be imposed on unions and individuals who disobey.

7 The ETU work-to-rule causes widespread cuts in electricity supplies to industry, hospitals and homes.

8 In response to a call from the Liaison Committee for the Defence of Trade Unions (LCDTU), 350,000 workers strike, the main effects being felt in London and Liverpool.

14 The electricians' dispute is called off by the ETU after manifestations of extreme public hostility.

15 The Industrial Relations Bill is given a second reading by 324 to 280 votes, against vociferous Labour opposition.

16 Campbell Adamson, Director General of the CBI, describes the Industrial Relations Bill as 'a considerable landmark in our industrial history'.

General

Conservative Party membership is estimated at 1.5 to 1.7 million; TUC membership is 9,402,000.

Lord Coleraine, in *For Conservatives Only*, calls for the rejection of the concept of the 'middle ground' in politics, which is a concession to socialism.

1971

January

4   President Pompidou makes favourable comments regarding British entry into the Common Market.

12   Selwyn Lloyd is elected Speaker of the Commons.

        Robert Carr is nearly killed by a bomb planted at his home by the Angry Brigade, an anarchist group.

14-22 At the Commonwealth Prime Ministers' conference, Singapore, Heath stresses the need for arms sales to South Africa to counter the growing Soviet presence in the Indian Ocean, but meets with bitter opposition.

20-1   In the Commons debate on EEC entry, Rippon says that the main problems for the government are the level of the British financial contribution to the Community and the treatment of Commonwealth products, particularly dairy products from New Zealand and sugar from the West Indies.

20-   A national postal workers' strike is defeated by the
Mar 8 government's intransigence.

February

4   Frederick Corfield, the Minister of Aviation Supply, announces to general astonishment that Rolls Royce is to be nationalised to avoid bankruptcy.

        A White Paper states that Britain is under a legal obligation to supply anti-submarine helicopters to South Africa under the 1955 Simonstown Agreement.

5   The first British soldier is killed in Belfast.

8   Powell attacks the decision to nationalise Rolls Royce as casting discredit on the principles of capitalism and free enterprise.

15   The new decimal currency comes into circulation within Britain.

16   A White Paper makes new proposals for local government reform to take effect from April 1974; the number of local authorities is to be reduced from 1,800 to 500, to be organised in a two-tier system of 51 county and 455 district councils; six metropolitan counties are to be organised along the lines of the GLC.

21   The TUC holds a mass demonstration of 140,000 trade unionists in a seven-mile march ending at Trafalgar Square in protest at the Industrial Relations Bill.

24   An Immigration Bill is published, establishing a single system of control for Commonwealth and 'alien' immigrants, while giving freedom of entry to 'patrials' — those whose parents or grandparents were born in the United Kingdom.

March

1   A major one-day strike by 1,750,000 workers, with the AUEW officially supporting its own strikers, takes place against the Industrial Relations Bill.

8   The Immigration Bill obtains a second reading by 295 to 265 votes, against Labour accusations that it is blatantly racist.

18   A special TUC Congress at Croydon advises unions not to register as unions under the Industrial Relations Bill and not to recognise its provisions.

The AUEW holds another one-day strike against the Industrial Relations legislation.

23   Chichester-Clark resigns as Ulster Prime Minister after pressure from Unionist hardliners and Brian Faulkner succeeds him.

24   The Industrial Relations Bill is given a third reading by 307 to 269 votes after the opposition challenge to 57 amendments (breaking the previous record of 43 divisions in 1907) leads to voting lasting 11 hours 38 minutes.

30   Barber's budget cuts taxes by £546 million and replaces selective employment tax and purchase tax with value-added tax (VAT).

April

6   In a meeting with leaders of the CBI Carr expresses concern about the private sector's inability to match the state sector's toughness on wages.

26   Wilson, in a speech in Birmingham, warns of the danger of accepting the wrong terms for EEC entry too quickly.

27   In yet another victory for the government's pay policy, the Amalgamated Society of Locomotive Engineers and Firemen (ASLEF) accepts a limited pay rise after the failure of its rail go-slow.

May

11   As 120 Labour MPs introduce a backbench motion opposing EEC entry, 100 Labour MPs sign an advertisement in the *Guardian* supporting the Common Market.

11-12   At the EEC ministerial meeting in Brussels, Rippon demands that 'the dialogue of the deaf must end' if the obstacles to Britain's entry are to be overcome.

13   Labour makes big gains in the local government elections.

15   Heath, in a speech at Aberdeen during the critical phase of EEC negotiations, says that 'it is not only Britain's destiny but all Europe's that is now being determined'.

21   In a joint press conference in Paris, Heath and Pompidou seal their *entente*.

27   The Conservatives lose the Bromsgrove by-election, their majority of 10,874 being turned into a Labour majority of 1,868.

June

7   Agreement is reached at the EEC ministerial meeting at Luxembourg over the import of Commonwealth sugar and the problem of the sterling balances.

23   Sir Keith Holyoake, the New Zealand Prime Minister, approves the EEC agreement as a substantial concession to his country.

      In protest at the threat to close Upper Clyde Shipbuilders (UCS) 100,000 workers strike in western Scotland.

25   Thatcher announces an extra £132 million spending on primary school buildings.

July

7   A White Paper on British entry into the EEC is published.

9   In a television broadcast, Wilson is equivocal on Labour's attitude to the terms of Common Market entry.

14   Heath opposes a referendum on EEC entry at a special meeting of the Conservative Party Central Council, on the grounds that legislation is the duty of elected MPs.

Parliament agrees to end free school milk by 211 to 188 votes.

17   At a special Labour party conference on the EEC in London, Wilson makes a ferocious attack on the British terms of entry, dismaying pro-Market MPs like Roy Jenkins, the deputy leader; no vote is taken. At a private PLP meeting, Jenkins rejects Wilson's stand on the EEC and calls upon Labour MPs to see 'beyond the narrow, short-term political considerations of the moment' to recognise the wider national interest. Barber, fearful of rising unemployment, announces further cuts of £425 million in tax, together with the abolition of all statutory restrictions on hire purchase.

21-6   A debate on the EEC White Paper in the Commons reveals widespread opposition to the British terms of entry, though no vote is taken.

29   The government announces the closure of the UCS yards at Clydebank and Scotstoun.

30   An occupation and 'work-in' of the UCS yards begins, led by Communist shop stewards Jimmy Reid and Jim Airlie.

August

6   The Industrial Relations Bill is enacted.

9   Internment without trial is introduced in Northern Ireland as troops arrest republican sympathisers; a major intensification of violence is the result with a total of 35 people killed and 200 houses burned down in August alone.

15   In the United States President Nixon virtually ends the post-war Bretton Woods financial settlement by suspending the conversion of dollars into gold; he imposes a 90-day freeze on prices and incomes.

September

3   Workers at the Plessey plant at Alexandria, near Glasgow, follow the UCS example by occupying the plant to prevent the removal of equipment.

6-10   The TUC Congress, Blackpool, rejects the EEC terms of entry with virtual unanimity; delegates pass a motion by 5.6 million to 4.5 million votes instructing, rather than advising, member unions not to register or obey the provisions of the Industrial Relations Act.

15-18   The Liberal Party Assembly, Scarborough, supports the EEC entry terms and demands a common European foreign policy and monetary union.

24   Home announces the expulsion of 105 Soviet diplomats, trade and business officials on charges of espionage.

27-8   Talks at Chequers on the Ulster situation between Heath, Faulkner and Lynch prove to be inconclusive.

29   The Democratic Unionist Party (DUP) is formed in Ulster by supporters of Ian Paisley, dissatisfied with the compromising attitude shown towards Catholics by the Unionist party.

October

4-8   The Labour Party annual conference, Brighton, calls for a sweeping nationalisation programme, including the public ownership of the banks and insurance companies; delegates oppose the EEC entry terms by a majority of five to one.

13-16   The Conservative Party annual conference, Brighton, supports the EEC entry terms by 2,474 to 324 votes; delegates carry a motion demanding the restoration of the death penalty for the murderers of policemen and prison warders.

18   Heath announces that Conservative MPs will have a free vote in the EEC debate.

20   Robert Mellish, the Labour Chief Whip, announces a three-line whip, ordering Labour MPs to vote against the EEC entry terms.

21   The Commons debate on British entry terms to the EEC begins.

26   Urging him to abstain rather than vote for a Conservative government, 101 Labour MPs send a letter to Roy Jenkins.

28   After a six-day debate, Parliament approves British terms of entry into the EEC by 356 to 244 votes; 69 Labour MPs, led by the deputy leader, Roy Jenkins, vote for entry in defiance of their party, while 39 Conservative MPs vote against.

The Immigration Bill is enacted.

November

10   Roy Jenkins, challenged for the Labour deputy leadership, obtains 140 votes, against 96 for Foot and 46 for Benn, and he is forced into a second ballot.

15   Heath, in his Guildhall speech, points to the possibility of a reunified Ireland as 'a solution to the Ulster crisis.

Sir Keith Joseph, the Health and Social Services Secretary, abandons a proposal for a sliding scale of charges on NHS prescriptions because of administrative difficulties and the opposition of chemists and the medical profession.

Communist China takes its seat at the UN.

Wilson visits Northern Ireland and Dublin in an unsuccessful attempt to find a solution to the Ulster crisis.

15-24   Home visits Salisbury, Rhodesia, for talks with Smith.

16   The Compton Committee, investigating allegations of brutality against detainees in Northern Ireland, finds that physical ill-treatment had taken place, but not brutality as defined by the Committee (i.e. cruelty or a pleasurable infliction of suffering).

17   Jenkins is re-elected Labour deputy leader on the second ballot with 140 votes; Foot polls 126 votes.

23   Barber announces an increase in public spending of £160 million.

24   Home reaches an agreement with Ian Smith on a constitutional settlement for Rhodesia with separate racial rolls of voters but more African seats; a Commission under Lord Pearce is to test African opinion before the agreement can be fully ratified.

25   Wilson proposes a settlement of the Ulster crisis by the Irish Republic declaring its loyalty to the Queen and ending its theocratic nature, paving the way for a United Ireland, though internment is to be retained; this solution is rejected by all.

December

2   In a pithead ballot, miners vote by 58.8 per cent to 41.2 per cent for industrial action in pursuit of higher pay.

7   Libya nationalises British Petroleum's £80 million investment in oil and withdraws Libyan government deposits in British banks.

16   Michael Foot and Peter Shore, two ardent anti-Common Marketeers, are given responsibility in Labour's 'shadow Cabinet' for EEC legislation.

18   The United States devalues the dollar by 7.9 per cent, beginning a period of floating exchange rates in the world economy.

20-1   Heath meets President Nixon in Bermuda to discuss the change in Britain's relationship with the United States, which was in danger of becoming more distant with Britain's entry into the EEC.

General

TUC membership is 10,002,000.

Ralph Harris, a leading figure in the Institute of Economic Affairs, argues in *Down with the Poor* that poverty can only be reduced through the free operation of the market.

1972

January

9 A national coalminers' strike begins.

11 The Pearce Commission begins to test African opinion about the Home-Smith agreement.

20 As unemployment reaches 1,023,583, or 4.3 per cent, Heath is shouted down in the Commons by the opposition as the announcement is made.

22 Heath signs the Treaty of Accession to the EEC, together with the Prime Ministers of Ireland, Denmark and Norway.

30 British troops kill 13 demonstrators in Derry on 'Bloody Sunday'.

February

1 After the 'Bloody Sunday' killings, Maudling is assaulted in the Commons by Bernadette Devlin, who later expresses sorrow that she had not strangled him.

  Lord Justice Widgery is appointed to carry out an inquiry into the events surrounding 'Bloody Sunday'.

2 The British Embassy in Dublin is burned down by a mass demonstration in protest at 'Bloody Sunday'.

3 On hearing of the death of a picketing miner at Scunthorpe, Tom Swain, a Labour MP, warns of 'another Ulster' in Yorkshire.

9 A State of Emergency is declared as the miners' strike begins to erode fuel supplies.

10 Violent clashes at Saltley Coke Depot lead to its closure after a mass demonstration of trade unionists threatens to swamp the police.

11 There are complete power cuts throughout the country as a result of the miners' strike.

  A committee of inquiry into the coal dispute is set up under Lord Wilberforce.

17 The government obtains a second reading for the EEC enabling legislation by 309 to 301 votes, and Jeremy Thorpe is physically attacked by Labour MPs for supporting the government.

18   After the report of the Wilberforce Commission is rapidly drawn up, the Cabinet accepts its finding that the miners have a just case, but the NUM rejects the Cabinet's surrender, desiring better terms.

19   Heath concedes the NUM demands for better wages and working conditions in a major defeat of the government's pay policy.

22   The Official IRA set off a bomb at Aldershot army barracks which kills seven cleaning women.

28   The miners return to work following their acceptance of the government's offer in a ballot.

John Davies, the Trade and Industry Secretary, announces £35 million financial assistance to enable the UCS yards to continue in business, thereby ending the successful work-in.

March

18   William Craig addresses 70,000 demonstrators of the new Ulster Vanguard movement in Belfast and calls on them to 'liquidate the enemy'.

21   Barber's budget reduces taxation by £1,200 million in order to expand domestic demand in the face of rising unemployment.

22   The Industrial Development Executive, similar to the IRC, is set up to direct state investment into helping the private sector; it is another indication of the government's U-turn on the economy.

24   Heath announces that the Stormont Parliament is to be suspended and that the province is to be placed under direct rule; William Whitelaw is to head the new Northern Ireland Office.

27-8   A two-day general strike called by Ulster Vanguard in protest at the suspension of Stormont paralyses Northern Ireland.

29   The 'shadow Cabinet' decides to support a Conservative backbench amendment to hold a referendum before Britain enters the EEC.

April

7   Carr becomes Lord President of the Council and is succeeded as Employment Secretary by Maurice Macmillan; Lord Carrington becomes Conservative Party Chairman.

10   Jenkins resigns as Labour's deputy leader in protest at the 'shadow Cabinet' decision to support a referendum on EEC entry.

18   The Conservative backbench amendment to the EEC enabling legislation, to hold a referendum before Britain enters the EEC, is defeated by 284 to 235 votes.

19   Macmillan orders a 'cooling off' period to prevent a rail work-to-rule.

The Widgery report exonerates British actions on 'Bloody Sunday', but casts doubt on the wisdom of killing 13 civilians.

25   Edward Short is elected Labour deputy leader by 146 votes to 116 for Foot.

May

4   Labour wins control of over 50 cities and boroughs in local elections in England and Wales.

13   After the resumption of a rail work-to-rule, the Industrial Relations Court orders a ballot of railworkers.

23   The Pearce Commission in Rhodesia reports that African opinion is overwhelmingly against the Home-Smith agreement, and Home announces the continuation of sanctions as a result.

26   The first Strategic Arms Limitation Agreement (SALT) between the United States and the Soviet Union, restricting the building of anti-ballistic missile systems, is signed in Moscow.

31   The rail ballot shows an overwhelming vote for industrial action.

June

12   The government settles the rail dispute on the union's terms.

16   Five dockers are threatened with arrest for refusing to appear before the Industrial Relations Court over the 'blacking' of a London firm, but the Official Solicitor quashes the order when 30,000 dockers strike in protest.

23   Barber announces that sterling is to 'float' as a currency on the foreign exchange markets.

26   An IRA ceasefire is arranged in Northern Ireland.

July

3   The ceasefire in Ulster is nearly broken when British troops prevent the Ulster Defence Association (UDA), a Protestant paramilitary force, from setting up their own no-go areas.

9   The Provisional IRA ends the ceasefire.

18   Maudling resigns as Home Secretary over allegations that he had received substantial sums of money from John Poulson, a businessman accused of corruption.

21   Five dockers are finally jailed for contempt of the Industrial Relations Court, and the main docks immediately strike in protest.

24   The Aldington-Jones report on containerisation of the docks appears, recommending high severance pay for dockers made redundant by the new technology.

26   The TUC General Council calls a one-day General Strike at the end of the month in protest at the imprisonment of the five dockers, but the dockers are then released as the Official Solicitor intervenes.

28   A national dock strike begins as the Aldington-Jones report is rejected by the dockers.

31   In Operation Motorman British troops end the no-go areas in Belfast and Derry.

August

8   General Amin, the Ugandan dictator, says that Asians living in Uganda are the responsibility of Britain and must leave the country within 90 days.

16   The national dock strike is called off by a TGWU delegate conference, though Jack Jones and the delegates are

subjected to violent abuse by picketing dockers.

September

4-8   The TUC Annual Congress, Brighton, expels 32 small unions for registering with the Industrial Relations Court in defiance of TUC rules.

19-23   At the Liberal Party Assembly, Margate, Thorpe points to the growing polarisation of British politics and says that Liberals are ready for their greatest assault on the two-party system.

24-5   In a two-day referendum, Norway votes by 53.5 per cent to 46.5 per cent to leave the EEC, leading Labour leaders to intensify the pressure for a referendum in Britain.

26   Heath's counter-inflationary proposals are issued, limiting pay increases to £2 per week for a year and limiting prices to 5 per cent.

29   The Franks Committee recommends the repeal of Section 2 of the 1911 Official Secrets Act, which orders imprisonment for the disclosure of information by Crown servants; the Committee recommends that the Section should be restricted to matters of national interest.

October

2-6   The Labour Party annual conference, Blackpool, takes a further swing to the left by adopting a sweeping nationalisation programme involving major industries like shipbuilding, insurance and the banks.

9   Barber announces that Minimum Lending Rate (MLR) is to replace the old Bank Rate as it provides greater flexibility.

11-14   The Conservative Party annual conference, Blackpool, defeats a Powellite motion condemning the government for accepting the expelled Ugandan Asians by 1,721 to 736 votes.

16   The government begins talks with the CBI and TUC over a voluntary prices and incomes policy.

17   The European Communities Bill, providing for British entry into the EEC, is enacted.

26   The Local Government Bill, providing for a two-tier structure of 44 county and 300 district councils, is enacted.

Cyril Smith wins the Rochdale by-election, turning a Labour majority of 5,171 into a Liberal majority of 5,093.

November

2   The negotiations for a voluntary prices and incomes policy collapse over the government's refusal to control all prices, including food and rents.

5   Peter Walker becomes the new Trade and Industry Secretary as Davies becomes Lord President of the Council with special responsibility for EEC relations.

6   Heath announces statutory controls of all pay, prices, rents and dividends for 90 days, angering Powell and the Conservative right as the adoption of an incomes policy is another reversal of his government's original free enterprise principles.

The Gallup poll shows 45 per cent Labour, 37 per cent Conservative and 15 per cent Liberal support.

December

1   Two bombs in Dublin kill two people and injure 127, leading to the immediate passage of the Offences Against the State Bill by the Irish Parliament; the devices are later suspected of being set off by British agents.

6   Two men and two women, alleged to be members of the anarchist group the Angry Brigade, are sentenced to ten years' imprisonment for conspiring to cause explosions.

7   The Liberals win a spectacular victory in the Sutton and Cheam by-election turning a Conservative majority of 12,696 into a Liberal majority of 7,417.

13   The PLP refuses to nominate representatives to the European Parliament.

18   Uganda nationalises 41 foreign-owned farms and tea estates, 34 of them British.

20   The report of the Diplock Commission is issued as a
White Paper advocating the suspension of trial by jury in
Northern Ireland.

General

Inflation reaches an annual 7.1 per cent.

1973

January

1 Britain formally joins the EEC; Heath forecasts 'a future of better jobs and a higher standard of living'.

16 The British delegations take their place in the European Parliament, with Labour boycotting the assembly.

27 A ceasefire is negotiated in Vietnam.

February

14-23 A national gasworkers' strike wins an improved wages offer after causing over 600 industrial plants to close for lack of gas.

27 Civil servants hold a strike for the first time in their history.

28 A joint Labour-TUC policy document on the economy — *Economic Policy and the Cost of Living* — is issued, launching the Social Contract; it promises price controls, industrial democracy and economic growth to influence a new climate of collective bargaining.

March

1 Dick Taverne retains his seat fighting as a Democratic Labour candidate in the Lincoln by-election, and increases his majority from 4,750 to 13,191.

6 Barber's budget is neutral, with marginal fiscal changes, as he seeks economic growth without inflation.

8 A referendum in Northern Ireland is boycotted by the Catholic minority, and consequently returns a massive majority for retaining partition.

The Provisional IRA open a bombing campaign in England; two bombs in central London kill one person and injure 200.

20 A government White Paper on Northern Ireland is issued, proposing an elected assembly which would choose an executive which must statutorily include members of the Catholic minority.

April

1   'Phase Two' of the incomes policy, whereby a compulsory standstill is replaced by pay increases limited to £1 plus 4 per cent, begins; it is administered by a Pay Board and a Prices Commission.

10   Heath, in his Guildhall speech, declares that the militants are losing support as people become increasingly impatient with 'pointless, ritualistic strikes'.

12   In the first elections to the new local authorities in England and Wales, Labour takes control of all six new metropolitan authorities and recaptures the GLC, where 58 Labour councillors, 32 Conservatives and two Liberals (the first Liberals to be represented in County Hall for 30 years) are elected.

30   President Nixon announces the resignation of two of his top aides over the Watergate scandal, when spies burst in to Democratic headquarters; the resulting affair paralyses the United States government.

May

1   The TUC organises a one-day strike against the government's incomes policy, in which 1.6 million workers take part.

10   In the first elections for the new district councils, Labour emerges as the victor, but the Liberals capture Liverpool on the basis of their community politics.

19   The Royal Navy is ordered to provide protection for British trawlers within the 50-mile limit of Icelandic waters after they come under harassment from Iceland, which is concerned about its fishing rights.

21   Anthony Lambton, the Defence Under-Secretary for the RAF, resigns over the 'unhappy justification' of links with call-girls.

24   Lord Jellicoe, the Lord Privy Seal, also resigns over the call-girl incident.

June

7   The Labour NEC issues *Programme For Britain*, including a call to nationalise the top 25 companies; Wilson personally repudiates this pledge, which disappears from the final programme.

28   The Unionists win a big majority in elections to the new Northern Ireland Assembly, but they are badly splintered into moderate and hardline parties.

The Campaign for Labour Party Democracy is established in an attempt to change the Labour Party constitution by making the leadership more accountable to the membership.

July

5   The National Health Service (Reorganisation) Bill is enacted, the most far-reaching reorganisation of the NHS since its foundation, structuring the administration in three tiers — area health authorities, regional health authorities, and a central department.

10   The *Times* carries reports of massacres by Portuguese troops of 400 people in Mozambique in 1971 and 1972.

18   The Social Security Bill is enacted, restructuring state retirement pensions into a single basic flat-rate pension.

19   The government announces tax changes to help poorer families.

August

3   Two brothers, Kenneth and Keith Littlejohn, convicted in Dublin of bank raids, claim that they are British intelligence agents.

The Gallup poll shows 38 per cent Labour, 31 per cent Conservative and 28 per cent Liberal support.

September

1   The Iceland government unilaterally extends its territorial waters to 50 miles, declaring that no other country can fish there.

3-7   The TUC Annual Congress, Blackpool, rejects calls to boycott talks due to be held in Downing Street on 'Phase Three' of the Prices and Incomes policy; 20 unions are expelled for registering with the Industrial Relations Court; Len Murray is elected TUC General Secretary.

10   The Liberals propose a tripartite federal system for Britain.

13   In a special report, the Pay Board calls for rigorous restrictions on the restoration of pay rises lost by workers in the 'Phase One' freeze.

18   The CBI leaders demand for the relaxation of price controls is rejected by Heath in the Downing Street talks.

18-22   The Liberal Party Assembly, Southport, senses electoral triumph as Thorpe warns trade unionists that the price of full employment must be the limitation of collective bargaining; a group around Trevor Evans, the Liberal leader of Liverpool council, wishes to build on the party's endorsement of community politics to replace Labour as the main party of the left.

October

1-5   The Labour Party annual conference, Blackpool, reaffirms non-cooperation with the EEC until the issues are submitted to the people at either a referendum or election; *Labour's Programme, 1973* is adopted, a radical programme which seeks 'a fundamental and irreversible shift in the balance of power and wealth in favour of working people'.

6-24   The Arab-Israeli war, in which Egypt wins initial victories, leads to a quadrupling of oil price rises by the Organisation of Petroleum Exporting Countries (OPEC), many of whom are angry at the tacit support given to Israel by the West.

6   Britain imposes an immediate arms embargo on the Middle East belligerents.

10   Spiro Agnew resigns as United States Vice-President after being accused of bribery while Governor of Maryland.

10-13   At the Conservative Party annual conference, Blackpool, Powell attacks the interventionist economic policy of the government, after which Barber calls him a 'frustrated fanatic'.

The Industrial Relations Court seizes £100,000 from the AUEW for contempt of court.

13   At the conference, Heath proposes annual summits of European leaders to maintain the initial momentum of British entry and to move towards a closer political and monetary union in the EEC.

18   In the Commons debate on the Middle East arms embargo, Wilson argues that Israel was discriminated against in much the same way that the Spanish Republic was discriminated against in 1936; in the vote, the embargo is upheld by 251 to 175 votes, with 17 Conservatives and all the Liberals against the embargo, and 15 Labour MPs supporting it.

Joseph Godber, the Minister of Agriculture, warns the Commons of significant rises in food prices in the coming months as Britain adapted to EEC conditions.

21   President Nixon dismisses the Attorney General and the Special Investigator in order to protect himself from the scandal concerning a break-in at the Democratic Party head-quarters at the Watergate Hotel.

22   The Industrial Relations Court takes £75,000 of its fine imposed on the AUEW on *10 October* from its political fund, a move which provokes accusations of political prejudice.

25   The Local Government (Scotland) Bill is enacted, instituting a two-tier system of nine regional councils and 53 district councils.

31   The Kilbrandon Commission reports, recommending the devolution of power to Scotland and Wales, but rejecting independence.

November

1   'Phase Three' of the prices and incomes policy comes into operation, with pay increases limited to 7 per cent or £2.25 per week.

Roy Jenkins is elected to the 'shadow Cabinet' with a large vote.

8   Margo Macdonald wins the Glasgow Govan by-election for the SNP turning a Labour majority of 7,142 into a SNP majority of 571 in a sign that the SNP is breaking into industrial Scotland.

12   An overtime ban by miners is imposed and production falls by 22 per cent within a week.

13   The government announces an assumption of emergency powers to deal with the miners' overtime ban, a go-slow by power workers and a work-to-rule by railworkers; Minimum Lending Rate (MLR) is increased to an unprecedented 13 per cent.

19   In a censure debate in the Commons, Heath says that the government had deliberately embarked on an expansionary economic policy, and points to 1973 as the highest investment growth year for ten years; some Conservatives call for substantial cuts in government spending and higher taxes in order to control a 10 per cent rate of inflation.

Peter Walker, the Trade and Industry Secretary, announces a 10 per cent reduction in all fuel and petrol supplies.

20   Walker introduces the Fuel and Electricity (Control) Bill, giving the government powers to ration and control the supply and distribution of all petrol.

21   The NUM rejects an increased pay offer from the Coal Board; Joe Gormley, the NUM President, declares that 'the fight is no longer with the Board . . . but with the government and Phase Three'.

22   Heath warns the miners of the constitutional implications of their action, but Gormley challenges him to call an election on the issue of the unions.

26   Wilson demands that his 'shadow ministers' should stop publicly bickering after fierce exchanges between Tony Benn and Reg Prentice, and he insists that front bench speeches must be cleared by party headquarters before being made.

27   Wilson proposes a peace offer of higher pay for the miners within Phase Three, and condemns the use of industrial action to bring down a government.

29   Powell makes a personal attack on Heath for his economic policies, declaring his fears for 'the mental and emotional stability' of the Prime Minister.

December

2   William Whitelaw becomes Employment Secretary as the industrial situation deteriorates, and is succeeded as Northern Ireland Secretary by Francis Pym.

5-9   Whitelaw holds a conference at Sunningdale, attended by the power-sharing parties but boycotted by hardline Unionists; an agreement to set up a Council of Ireland is reached.

6   New government restrictions on the use of fuel by cars and offices comes into force.

In a mood of panic, the London Stock Exchange falls 19.7 points in the morning.

11   Sir Michael Clapham, the CBI President, warns in a speech at Newcastle that Britain 'is walking on the edge of a precipice', and calls on the government to abandon its growth target and concentrate on economic survival.

12   ASLEF, one of the rail unions, begins an overtime ban.

13   Heath announces in the Commons that many areas of commerce and industry are to begin a three-day week, that continuous process users are to be limited to 65 per cent of normal electricity consumption, and that other severe cutbacks in power are to come into effect.

14-15   A summit conference of EEC heads of government at Copenhagen makes no progress on the Community's political, monetary or economic problems.

17   Barber's mini-budget reduces government spending by £1,200 million, especially in defence, education, health and social services.

28   The power engineers call off their proposed overtime ban.

1974

January

1   The power-sharing Executive in Northern Ireland is established under Brian Faulkner,

8   The Department of Energy is established under Lord Carrington.

9-10   Parliament meets to discuss the industrial and economic crisis, with Heath resisting pressure for a *7 February* election.

14   The talks between the government and TUC on the coal dispute collapse.

21   The government rejects as inadequate the TUC peace offer not to use a miners' settlement as a precedent for higher wage claims.

24   The NUM calls a strike ballot.

28   ASLEF announces a series of one-day stoppages over pay restructuring.

29   The Labour Party and NUM leaders publicly dissociate themselves from the threat of Mick McGahey, the Communist Vice-President of the NUM, to appeal to troops for support if the army is called in.

February

4   An IRA bomb kills 12 people on a Manchester to Catterick bus.

5   The NUM calls an all-out strike after it receives an 81 per cent majority for industrial action in a ballot.

7   A general election is announced for *28 February*.

Powell announces that he is not standing in the election.

8   Parliament is dissolved.

The Labour manifesto, *Get Britain Back To Work*, rejects a statutory incomes policy but calls for greater state intervention in the economy.

10   The miners' strike begins.

The Conservative manifesto, *Firm Action For A Fair Britain*, attacks Labour's extreme socialist policies and claims the election is about whether the government or the unions will run Britain.

11   ASLEF calls off its industrial action.

13   The Liberal manifesto, *You Can Change the Face of Britain*, proposes a penal tax on wage settlements as a means of controlling inflation.

17   Wilson announces 'a great, new Social Contract' with the unions.

23   Powell, in a Birmingham speech, disclaims the Conservatives and says that he will vote Labour in order to get Britain out of the EEC.

26   Campbell Adamson, the Director General of the CBI, dismays Conservatives by calling for the repeal of the keystone of the government's trade union policy, the Industrial Relations Act.

28   Polling Day, with a turnout of 78.8 per cent (31,340,162 votes); the election on 'who runs the country' is indecisive, with Labour having slightly more seats and fewer votes than the Conservatives, while the Liberals are grossly under-represented; 301 Labour, 296 Conservatives, 14 Liberals, eleven various Unionists, seven Scottish Nationalists, two Plaid Cymru, two Independent Labour, one Irish SDLP and the Speaker are elected; the Conservatives have 11,872,180 votes (37.9 per cent), Labour 11,645,616 votes (37.2 per cent), and the Liberals 6,059,519 votes (19.3 per cent).

March

2   Heath offers Thorpe a Cabinet post in a coalition government.

3   As Thorpe comes under Liberal pressure to refuse a coalition, Heath indicates that a new inquiry into reforming the electoral system could be set up.

4   The Parliamentary Liberal Party rejects a coalition with the Conservatives despite the offer of a Speakers Conference on all-party lines to consider the introduction of proportional representation.

Wilson becomes Labour Prime Minister again and forms a government with Denis Healey as Chancellor of the Exchequer, Roy Jenkins as Home Secretary and James Callaghan as Foreign Secretary; the left is well represented by Foot as

Employment Secretary and Benn as Industry Secretary.

6   The NUM Executive recommends an acceptance of a £103 million pay settlement.

7   Eric Varley, the Energy Secretary, announces a return to the five-day week and an end to the emergency controls on power supplies.

8   Tony Crosland, the Environment Secretary, announces an immediate freeze on rents to the end of the year.

11   The miners' strike ends as the men accept the pay offer.

Barber announces that he is retiring from the Commons; Heath reshapes his 'shadow Cabinet', with Robert Carr as Treasury spokesman.

12   In the Queen's Speech debate, Wilson announces that he will not resign as a result of 'a snap division, or even perhaps . . . a more substantial one'.

26   Healey's budget provides for a major increase in taxes and prices, and a promise of a wealth tax; he warns that unless inflation is halted, 'the resulting political and social strains may be too violent for the fabric of our democratic institutions to withstand'.

31   The Greater London Young Conservatives demand a complete overhaul of the party's organisation and leadership.

April

1   Callaghan, at the EEC foreign ministers' conference, calls for 'a root and branch review' of EEC policies and a fundamental renegotiation of British terms of entry.

The reorganisation of local government outside Greater London comes into effect.

3   Shirley Williams, the Prices and Consumer Affairs Secretary, introduces the Prices Bill, giving the government increased powers to regulate retail prices through a Prices Commission.

11   Jenkins announces an amnesty for illegal immigrants in Britain.

30   The Trade Union and Labour Relations Bill, repealing the Industrial Relations Act in favour of a pro-union law protecting the closed shop, is introduced by Foot.

May

3   The Industrial Relations Court orders the seizure of all AUEW assets because of the union's continuing contempt of court.

5   Wilson attacks the Industrial Relations Court as 'the putrefying corpse of Tory legislation'.

8   The industrial crisis ends when the AUEWs debt is paid anonymously.

15   A Loyalist general strike against the power-sharing Executive in Ulster cripples the province.

19   Merlyn Rees, the Northern Ireland Secretary, declares a State of Emergency as the strike continues.

21   Len Murray of the British TUC leads an abortive 'back to work' march in Ulster.

22   Wilson accuses Loyalists in Ulster of 'sponging on Westminster', as the Executive leaders ask that the army be used to break the strike.

23   The National Front candidate, with 11.5 per cent, is just behind the Liberal in the Newham South by-election, and pushes the Conservative into fourth place.

28   Faulkner resigns from the Executive with Ulster on the verge of collapse, and the Executive is dissolved in admission of defeat; the triumphant Loyalists end the strike.

June

11   William Whitelaw becomes Conservative Party Chairman.

15   A student, Kevin Gately, is killed after clashes between anti-Fascist demonstrators and police protecting a National Front meeting in Red Lion Square, London.

17   An IRA bomb damages Westminster Hall, injuring 11 people.

19   The government is defeated by 306 to 299 votes over a clause in the Finance Bill enabling trade unions to reclaim tax relief for any funds lost to the Industrial Relations Court.

20   The government is defeated by 311 to 290 votes over plans for more state control over private industries and firms.

26   In a further elaboration of the Social Contract, the TUC General Council approves wage restraint coupled with social and economic reform in *Collective Bargaining and the Social Contract*.

28   The Liberal National Executive votes by 22 to twelve to reject any parliamentary alliance that does not include both Labour and Conservative.

July

2   Nurses and paramedical staff threaten to refuse to serve 40 penthouse suites in Charing Cross hospital.

5   Barbara Castle, the Health and Social Services Secretary, resolves the Charing Cross hospital dispute by calling for the eventual withdrawal of all private medical services.

8   Angered by Castle's threat to withdraw private services, hospital consultants decide to campaign for the retention of pay-beds.

11   In a White Paper, Varley proposes the public ownership of the offshore oil and gas industries.

The Speaker casts his vote for the government after a tied vote on the closed shop in the Trade Union and Labour Relations Bill committee stage.

14   Foot announces the establishment of a Royal Commission on the Distribution of Income and Wealth under Lord Diamond.

16   The Lords return the Trade Union and Labour Relations Bill to the Commons because the third Commons reading is declared null and void after the finding of a technical fault with the closed shop vote on *11 July*; the Speaker then deleted the closed shop from the Bill.

22   Healey's mini-budget reduces VAT to 8 per cent, eases dividend controls and spends an extra £50 million in food subsidies.

25   Benn offers a £1.75 million loan to the action committee of Glasgow employees of the Beaverbrook newspapers to set up a workers' co-operative publishing the *Scottish Daily News*.

26   Benn offers loans and grants to the Meriden co-operative to produce motorcycles.

31   The Trade Union and Labour Relations Bill is enacted, abolishing the Industrial Relations Court.

Benn makes a commitment to nationalise the shipbuilding and associated industries.

August

9   Richard Nixon resigns as United States President over the Watergate affair; Gerald Ford succeeds him.

15   Benn issues a White Paper, *The Regeneration of British Industry*, proposing a National Enterprise Board (NEB), to take over selected private companies and to draw up planning agreements with the largest companies.

September

2-6   The TUC Annual Congress, Brighton, endorses the Social Contract by a large majority, the AUEW delegation abstaining after coming under pressure not to vote against.

3   Powell is adopted as a Unionist candidate for South Down.

5   Sir Keith Joseph, in a speech at Preston, implicitly criticises Heath by blaming inflation on the policy of giving full employment top priority.

7   A White Paper on devolution proposes directly elected assemblies for Scotland and Wales.

10   The Conservative election manifesto, *Putting Britain First*, pledges to work out a voluntary incomes policy, with the law to be used only in the last resort.

17-21   At the Liberal Party Assembly, Brighton, Thorpe keeps his coalition options open in his bid to bring about 'a complete realignment of the political forces in Britain'.

16   The Labour manifesto, *Britain Will Win With Labour*, bases economic and social policy on the Social Contract and pledges that the people will be able to have a binding vote on Britain's EEC membership.

17   The Liberal manifesto, *Why Britain Needs a Liberal Government*, calls for the break-up of the old two-party dominated system.

18   A general election is announced for *10 October*.

20   Parliament is dissolved.

October

5   The IRA bombs pubs in Guildford, killing five people.

10   Polling Day, with a turnout of 72.8 per cent (29,189,104 votes); Labour wins by an overall majority of only three; 319 Labour MPs, 276 Conservatives, thirteen Liberals, eleven SNP, ten various Unionists, three Plaid Cymru, one Irish SDLP, one Irish Republican and the Speaker; Labour obtains 11,457,079 votes (39.2 per cent), the Conservatives 10,462,565 votes (35.8 per cent), and the Liberals 5,346,704 votes (18.3 per cent).

14   The 1922 Committee of Conservative backbenchers discusses the party leadership question and agrees to ask Heath not to make a snap decision on his future.

17   Jack Jones calls for unions to show moderation in their approach to the growing economic crisis.

19   Joseph, in a speech at Birmingham, calls for birth control in the poorest sections of society, provoking widespread dissension within the Conservative Party.

23   The South African government treats the visit of eleven British ships as a diplomatic victory.

27   Callaghan accuses South Africa of political manipulation of the visit and calls for a review of the Simonstown Agreement.

November

3   Edward du Cann is elected chairman of the 1922 Committee in a clear criticism of Heath.

5   The AUEW Executive, by 27 to 25 votes, rejects a left-wing demand for a wage rise of £50 per week.

6   Wilson demands that Benn and two junior ministers, Judith Hart and Joan Lestor, conform to collective responsibility after the three vote for a NEC resolution condemning the naval visit to South Africa.

12   Healey presents an emergency budget providing £1,500 million relief for industry while promising to hold public spending down.

14   Heath indicates in a letter to the 1922 Committee that he will stand for election as soon as new rules are devised to elect a leader.

Ian Mikardo is defeated as PLP chairman by Cledwyn Hughes in a setback for the Labour left.

20   Heath announces the appointment of a special committee

under Lord Home to review the procedure for electing a leader.

21   A bomb explosion in a Birmingham pub, blamed on the IRA, kills 21 and injures 182 people.

27-30   The Labour Party annual conference, London, passes a sharply critical motion against the EEC by 3 million to 2.8 million votes.

29   The Prevention of Terrorism Bill, giving wide powers to the police to hold suspects for five days and to deport them to Ireland, is enacted two days after its introduction.

December

3   Roy Mason, the Defence Secretary, announces a £4,700 million reduction in spending spread over ten years, including substantial cuts in British forces east of Suez.

7   Wilson, in a speech in London, announces that he will personally recommend Britain remaining within the EEC in a referendum if he agreed with the re-negotiated terms.

9-10   A compromise agreement on the British financial contribution to the Community budget is agreed at the EEC summit in Paris.

11   The Commons defeats a motion to restore the death penalty for terrorists by 369 to 217 votes.

12   The left-wing in the NUM is defeated when the supporters of the Social Contract in the Executive water down pay demands by 14 to 12 votes.

50 Labour MPs vote against the Defence White Paper as making 'fake' cuts in defence spending.

17   New rules for electing a Conservative leader are published, stipulating that the winner must obtain a simple majority plus 15 per cent of the votes eligible (rather than cast) on the first ballot, and that other candidates may enter a second ballot.

19   Edward Short, the leader of the Commons, announces details of financial assistance to the opposition parties in parliament, dependent on the seats won at the preceding election.

29   Benn, in a letter to his British constituents, calls for a

fundamental condemnation of EEC membership as destroying British sovereignty and the supremacy of Parliament.

General

Inflation reaches an annual 16 per cent.

1975

January

12   Reg Prentice, the Education Secretary, announces the phasing out of direct grant grammar schools from September 1976.

23   Wilson announces that a referendum on British membership of the EEC will take place by the end of June if negotiations are completed in time.

27   Heath accepts the new rules for electing a Conservative leader, and announces that the first ballot will be held on *4 February*.

31   The Industry Bill is published, establishing the National Enterprise Board, seen by Benn as a major instrument of state direction of the economy

February

4   Margaret Thatcher defeats Heath in the first ballot for the Conservative leadership; she obtains 130 votes, to 119 for Heath and 16 for Hugh Fraser; Heath withdraws, and Whitelaw stands in his place.

6   The NUM rejects a NCB pay offer, which has to be improved twice before being accepted; Arthur Scargill, the union's Yorkshire Area President, says triumphantly that 'the Social Contract has been breached'.

10   Thatcher is elected the first woman leader of a major British political party, with 146 votes to 79 for Whitelaw, 18 for Sir Geoffrey Howe, 18 for James Prior, and eleven for John Peyton.

18   Thatcher retains Whitelaw as her deputy, while Reginald Maudling becomes Foreign Affairs spokesman and Sir Geoffrey Howe Treasury spokesman; Joseph becomes head of Policy and Research, and Lord Thorneycroft Conservative Party Chairman; Heath is left out of the 'shadow Cabinet'.

24   The Commons votes by 354 to 182 to allow its proceedings to be broadcast by radio, but rejects television coverage by 275 to 263 votes.

26   The Commons approves the White Paper providing for a referendum on EEC membership by 312 to 262 votes.

28   Reg Prentice bitterly attacks the left and demands that 'the unions must not welsh' on their bargain with the government; he is publicly repudiated by Wilson for his use of language.

March

10-11   The EEC summit in Dublin agrees to a budget-correcting mechanism to help Britain, a move which satisfies the British government that it has successfully renegotiated the terms of entry into the Common Market.

10   John Gollan retires, and is succeeded as General Secretary of the British Communist Party by Gordon McLennan.

18   The Cabinet decides by 16 to seven votes to recommend that Britain stay within the Common Market.

20   The Commons decides on, by a free vote of 142 to 47, the scheme to help opposition parties fulfil their parliamentary functions more effectively by providing them with finance.

Tony Crosland, the Environment Secretary, introduces the Community Land Bill, taking into local authority ownership land subject to development.

21   The Labour Party's Scottish conference at Aberdeen defeats a resolution calling for wide-ranging powers for a Scottish Assembly, and instead seeks an Executive with powers similar to those of the Secretary for Scotland.

24   Foot introduces the Employment Protection Bill, providing for the establishment of an Advisory Conciliation and Arbitration Service (ACAS) to settle industrial disputes, protection of the closed shop and rights against unfair dismissal; it is denounced by the CBI as 'biased to the trade unions and one-sided'.

26   The Referendum Bill is published, providing for a national count with a simple majority of votes cast deciding the outcome.

27   Wilson, in his reply to a parliamentary question, says that dissident ministers are free to express their views on the EEC, but not from the despatch box.

April

9   ·The Commons approves the White Paper on the EEC renegotiation terms by 396 to 170 votes, with 145 Labour MPs voting against, 138 voting for and 32 abstaining.

Eric Heffer, the Minister of State for Industry, is dismissed after speaking against the government from the back benches.

15   Healey's budget reduces public spending by £900 million, reduces food and housing subsidies, and increases direct and indirect taxes to meet the growing crisis; he blames excessive wage rises for inflation.

24   After the Ryder report, Wilson announces that the governnment is taking a majority shareholding in British Leyland (BL).

26   A special Labour Party Conference votes for withdrawal from the EEC by a two-to-one majority.

28   The Employment Protection Bill is given a second reading by 270 to 244 votes.

30   Saigon finally falls to Communist forces, bringing the long Vietnam War to an end.

May

5   Castle says that private beds in the NHS are to be ended as soon as the necessary Bill is passed.

7   When 56 Labour MPs vote on a left-wing amendment to the Defence White Paper, the government survives due to Conservative support.

8   The Referendum Bill is enacted.
       The Prices Bill is enacted.

17   Jack Jones tells a TGWU rally that they must be prepared to accept wage rises as a flat amount across the board.

18   Benn claims that entry into the Common Market had cost Britain 1,137,000 jobs.

28   Wilson warns of the damage to employment if Britain withdraws from the EEC.

June
4   The Commons is broadcast over radio for the first time.

5   In the referendum, Britain votes (on a turnout of 64 per cent) to remain within the EEC by 17,378, 581 votes (67.2 per cent) against 8,470,073 (32.8 per cent); only Shetland and the Western Isles vote against.

10   In an assertion of his victory over the anti-EEC left, Wilson shifts Benn from the Industry Department to become Energy Secretary; Varley exchanges posts to become Industry Secretary.

16   The 1955 Simonstown Agreement with South Africa is ended.

18   The PLP decides to end its boycott of the European Parliament.

20   After threatening a strike, the National Union of Railwaymen (NUR) accepts a 30 per cent pay rise from a reluctant British Railways.

22   Jack Jones says that collective bargaining could be voluntarily suspended for one year if the government takes action on prices.

25   Mozambique attains its independence from Portugal, threatening Smith's government in Rhodesia.

26   Labour loses the Woolwich West by-election, where a Labour majority of 3,541 is turned into a Conservative majority of 2,382.

     US$934 million are lost from Britain's reserves in May and June.

July

9   The TUC General Council vote by 19 to 13 for a policy of wage restraint with a £6 per week rise for workers earning less than £7,000 per year.

11   The White Paper on counter-inflationary policy calls for pay rises of £6 per week for those earning less than £8,500 per year.

22   The Conservatives abstain on the counter-inflationary White Paper, while 54 *Tribune* Group MPs vote against; Heath, in a television interview, expresses his regret at the Conservative abstention.

     Sam Silkin, the Attorney General, seeks to restrain publication of the Crossman Diaries.

30   The Royal Commission on the Distribution of Wealth reports, noting the continuing trend to the equalisation of wealth in Britain.

August

5   Peter Shore, the Trade Secretary, announces an independent inquiry into industrial democracy (with Sir Alan Bullock appointed as its chairman on *3 December*).

11   A DHSS consultative document calls for new licensing laws for private nursing homes, arousing strong protests by the medical profession and the Conservatives.

September

1-5   The TUC Annual Congress, Blackpool, votes to accept the General Council document, *The Development of the Social Contract*, by 6.9 million to 3.4 million votes.

9   William Craig resigns as Ulster Vanguard leader after his policies of power-sharing with the Catholics are defeated; Ian Paisley emerges as the undisputed leader of hardline Loyalism.

15   Thatcher, in a speech in the United States, attacks the 'persistent expansion of the state, and the relentless pursuit of equality'.

16-20   At the Liberal Party Assembly, Scarborough, Thorpe calls for a permanent prices and incomes policy, and for a national investment fund.

29-   At the Labour Party annual conference, Blackpool, Foot
Oct 3   and Jones successfully attack left-wing opposition to an incomes policy; Wilson warns of extremists who are trying to infiltrate the constituency parties.

October

1   Lord Justice Widgery refuses to grant an injunction to prevent publication of the Crossman Diaries.

7-10   At the Conservative Party annual conference, Blackpool, Joseph attacks the idea of the mythical 'middle ground' and calls for a genuine consensus in politics based on the market economy.

9   Official figures show a 2½ per cent fall in real personal income in the second quarter of 1975, the biggest fall in 20 years.

November

5   After a meeting with TUC and CBI leaders at Chequers, Healey announces that it had been agreed that there should be indicative planning to concentrate public aid on viable and profitable sectors of the economy, rather than an immediate deflation or general import controls.

8   The *Scottish Daily News* co-operative ceases after only six months.

10   Angola attains its independence from Portugal in another portent of doom for the Smith regime in Rhodesia.

12   The Employment Protection Bill, described by Foot as the greatest advance by the trade union movement since the 1825 repeal of the Combination Laws, is enacted.

    The Petroleum and Submarine Pipelines Bill, providing for the establishment of the British National Oil Corporation (BNOC), is enacted.

    The Sex Discrimination Bill, providing for women to be given the same treatment as men when they apply for jobs, is enacted.

    The Industry Bill and the Community Land Bill are enacted.

15-17   The Rambouillet Summit of the six major powers — the United States, Japan, Britain, France, Italy and West Germany — issues a declaration reaffirming their commitment to world economic recovery.

16   The British Communist Party Congress passes a resolution calling for political liberalisation in the Soviet Union and Eastern Europe by an overwhelming majority.

22   A White Paper, *Our Changing Democracy*, calls for a legislative assembly with a cabinet and chief executive in Scotland, but only an executive assembly for Wales, run on the committee system.

December

5   Merlyn Rees, the Northern Ireland Secretary, ends

detention without trial after 52 months.

17   Healey imposes selective import controls on textiles, clothing and footwear in order to ease unemployment in those industries.

19   Healey announces an indefinite delay in introducing a wealth tax.

General

Inflation reaches an annual 25 per cent.

Conservative Party membership is estimated at 1.5 million.

Stuart Holland, in *The Socialist Challenge*, calls on the Labour Party to adopt indicative planning in order to defend the British economy from the multinational companies.

1976

January

5   The Provisional IRA kills ten Protestants at Whitecross in South Armagh in a massacre which appalls both Catholics and Protestants; the Special Air Service (SAS) is sent to Ulster by the Wilson government in response.

13   Britain applies for credit of £1,000 million from the International Monetary Fund (IMF).

18   The Scottish Labour Party is formally established, with two MPs, Jim Sillars and John Robertson.

27   John Methven succeeds Campbell Adamson as Director General of the CBI.

29   Norman Scott, a male model, makes public allegations of having had an affair with Jeremy Thorpe.

February

3   George Thomas is unanimously elected Speaker, reducing Labour's majority to vanishing point.

4   The Parliamentary Liberal Party reaffirms its faith in Thorpe.

19   A White Paper on Public Expenditure anticipates a decline in total government expenditure from 1975/6 to 1978/9; it is denounced by the *Tribune* Group as a 'mockery of Labour's whole industrial strategy'.

     Iceland breaks diplomatic relations with Britain over the fisheries dispute.

21   Joan Lestor resigns as a junior minister in protest at the public expenditure White Paper.

March

4   The Ulster Convention is dissolved in disorder.

10   The government is defeated on the public expenditure White Paper by 284 to 256 votes after 37 Labour MPs abstain, forcing a motion of confidence.

11   The government survives the confidence motion by 297 to 280 votes.

16   Wilson announces his surprise resignation because he had reached the age of 60.

25   In the first ballot for the Labour leadership, Foot with 90 votes and Callaghan with 84 emerge as the front runners; Jenkins, with a disappointing 56 votes, and Benn, with a surprisingly high 37 votes, withdraw; Healey, with only 30 votes, continues while Crosland, with 17 votes, is defeated.

        A New Trade Union and Labour Relations Bill is enacted.

30   In the second ballot for the Labour leadership, Callaghan leads with 141 votes to Foot's 133, but Healey's 38 votes force a third ballot.

April

5   In the third ballot for the Labour leadership, Callaghan wins with 176 votes to Foot's 137.

        Callaghan becomes Labour Prime Minister, with Crosland as Foreign Secretary and Foot as Lord President of the Council and Leader of the Commons; Castle is excluded from the government.

6   Healey's budget provides, in return for the TUCs acceptance of a voluntary pay policy, tax reliefs with the highest VAT rate cut from 25 per cent to 12 ½ per cent; however, duties on petrol, alcohol and tobacco are raised.

7   John Stonehouse, caught up in criminal proceedings, resigns the Labour Whip and the government loses its overall majority; this leads to a dispute over the composition of the select committees.

May

3   The Commons agrees by 288 to 280 votes that the select committees should maintain a government majority despite its lack of an overall majority in the Commons.

5   The TUC General Council agrees to limit wage rises to 4 per cent from *1 August*, with a maximum of £4 and a minimum of £2.50 per week.

6	The Conservatives make big gains at both Labour and Liberal expense in the local elections.
8	After further allegations by Norman Scott against Jeremy Thorpe, a fellow Liberal, Richard Wainwright, publicly speculates why Thorpe had not sued Scott for libel.
10	Thorpe resigns as Liberal leader over the Scott affair.
12	Jo Grimond becomes interim Liberal leader until the new method of electing a leader by the whole membership can take effect.
27	Michael Heseltine seizes the mace after a government Whip breaks an agreed pair to vote for a government motion; the motion, suspending Standing Orders in the Commons so that legislation to nationalise the shipbuilding and aircraft manufacturing industries can be expedited, passes by 304 to 303 votes.
28	In protest at the breaking of the government Whip's pair, Thatcher calls off all pairing arrangements and co-operation with the Leader of the Commons.

June

1	Crosland signs a six-month agreement with Iceland for 24 British trawlers to fish up to 20 miles off the Icelandic coast.
7	In a pithead ballot, the NUM members vote by 53.4 per cent to support pay restraint in their wage demands.
9	The Hansard Society Commission under Lord Blake recommends a system of proportional representation on the West German model as preferable to the existing electoral system of 'first past the post'.
16	A special TUC conference votes by 9.2 million to 0.5 million for the new pay policy.
22	Thatcher resumes pairing arrangements after Callaghan agrees to a further vote on the motion to suspend Standing Orders (which the government wins).
27	An Air France aircraft is hijacked by Palestinian guerrillas and flown to Entebbe airport in Uganda.
	The Gallup poll shows 44 per cent Conservative, 40 per cent Labour and 11 per cent Liberal support.

July

3   Israeli commandos free the hostages at Entebbe, but a British citizen, Mrs Dora Bloch, who had been transferred to a hospital, is murdered.

7   In the ballot for the Liberal leadership, David Steel is elected by 12,541 to 7,032 votes for the more radical John Pardoe.

10   Four British mercenaries are executed in Angola, despite personal appeals for clemency from the Queen and Callaghan.

12   At the EEC summit in Brussels, the United Kingdom is allocated 81 seats in the 410-strong European Parliament, with 63 seats for England, ten for Scotland, five for Wales, and three for Northern Ireland.

21   Christopher Ewart-Biggs, the British Ambassador to the Irish Republic, is killed by an IRA car bomb outside Dublin.

22   To arrest the decline in the value of the pound, Healey announces a reduction of £1,012 million in public expenditure, mainly in local authority loans, defence, education, health and social services; he also declares a limit on the growth in money supply of 12 per cent.

25   Heath displays a public aloofness towards Thatcher in a television appearance.

28   Britain breaks diplomatic relations with Uganda over the murder of Mrs Dora Bloch.

       The Labour NEC and the TUC General Council agree to extend the Social Contract for three years in affirming the priorities of industrial democracy and indicative planning.

August

2   The Lords uphold a court ruling that Fred Mulley, the Education Secretary, was unreasonable in directing Tameside Council in Lancashire to abolish its grammar schools.

19   A Lords select committee recommends the 'first past the post' system, for the first direct elections to the European

Parliament, despite the systems of proportional representation used in other countries.

27   John Stonehouse finally resigns from the Commons to face criminal proceedings.

30   The traditional Notting Hill carnival turns into a riot against the police, 325 of whom are hurt by stone-throwing crowds.

September

4   25,000 Protestants and Catholics take part in a peace march in Derry, but the 'peace people' soon disintegrate over internal divisions on partition.

6-10   The TUC Annual Congress at Brighton carries by an overwhelming majority a motion calling for a return to free collective bargaining in the next year, amid warnings of a rank and file revolt if the informal pay restraint continues.

7   The NECs home policy committee calls for the nationalisation of the four main clearing banks, a policy derided openly by Callaghan as 'an electoral albatross'.

9   Mao Tse-tung, the Chinese Communist leader, dies.

10   In the Cabinet reshuffle which follows the acceptance by Roy Jenkins of the EEC Commission Presidency, Merlyn Rees becomes Home Secretary.

14-18   At the Liberal Party Assembly, Llandudno, David Steel tells delegates that the party would join any coalition which would further the Liberal cause, particularly with regard to proportional representation; delegates vote by a large majority to reject a prices and incomes policy, despite the leadership's contrary wishes.

17   Whitelaw calls for a virtual end to immigration if racial tolerance is to prevail.

24   Ian Smith, under growing pressure from African nationalist guerrillas, agrees to accept majority rule within two years.

27-   The Labour Party annual conference, Blackpool, rejects
Oct 1   the government White Paper on reducing public expenditure and also supports those councils which refuse to implement cuts; delegates also vote for the nationalisation of the banks; however, Callaghan condemns the idea that 'you could just spend your way out of a recession'.

28   Healey cancels a flight to Hong Kong as the pound falls to US$1.637 (from US$2.024 in January).

29   To meet the sterling crisis, the government announces that it will borrow £2,300 million from the IMF; Healey declares that the alternative is 'economic policies so savage that they would lead to rioting in the streets'.

October

4   The Conservatives issue *The Right Approach*, a programme which expresses hostility to state intervention and defence cuts, but reserves the right to help industries in economic trouble and calls for co-operation with the trade unions.

5-8   At the Conservative annual conference, Brighton, Howe tells delegates that Conservatives must represent the real interests of ordinary trade unionists.

12   Castle tells the NEC that the government should confront the IMF rather than accept the political defeat which would flow from capitulating to its demands.

21   Michael Foot is elected Labour deputy leader with 166 votes to 128 for Shirley Williams.

November

4   Labour loses two by-elections at Walsall North and Workington, losing its majority irrevocably.

8   The government adopts a guillotine motion on six major Bills to deal with the savage Lords amendments to them.

19   John Davies becomes Conservative Foreign Affairs spokesman when Maudling returns to the back benches.

22   The Race Relations Bill, strengthening the laws against racial discrimination, is enacted.

34   Foot introduces the Devolution Bill providing for separate assemblies in Scotland and Wales, and he indicates that the government is willing to consider a referendum on the proposals.

December

1   The 'shadow Cabinet' agrees to oppose the Devolution
         Bill; Alick Buchanan-Smith, the Scottish Affairs spokesman,
         and Malcolm Rifkind, his deputy, resign in protest.
6   In opposition to the Conservative leadership, Heath sup-
         ports the case for full and effective devolution in Scotland.
15   Healey presents a mini-budget reducing public spending
         by £2,500 million over two years; these reductions include
         £300 million on defence and £570 million on road and school
         construction; indirect taxes are increased and some of the
         government's shares in British Petroleum (BP) are sold.
16   The Devolution Bill is given a second reading by 292 to
         247 votes, with 60 MPs (including Heath) abstaining and
         ten Labour MPs voting against.
21   In the Commons vote on Healey's economic measures,
         26 Labour MPs vote against the government, which wins
         by 219 to 51 votes as a result of Conservative abstentions.

General

Inflation falls to an annual 15 per cent.

Labour Party membership is 6,499,000.

TUC membership is 11,036,000.

Robert Bacon and Walter Eltis, in *Britain's Economic Problem: Too Few Producers*, argues that inflation and unemployment are caused by an increasing reliance on service industries.

The Glasgow Media Group, in *Bad News*, argues that the media are biased against the left and working-class struggles.

1977

January

3   The IMF grants a standby credit of 3,360 million Special Drawing Rights (£2,300 million) to the British government, the largest credit ever granted.

6   Roy Jenkins becomes President of the European Commission.

10   The Bank for International Settlements opens a US$3,000 million credit facility to the Bank of England, and a US$1,500 million loan from West German banks is negotiated.

14   Anthony Eden dies, at the age of 79.

20   Jimmy Carter is inaugurated as United States President.

26   The Bullock Report on Industrial Democracy recommends that companies employing over 2,000 workers be compelled to accept on their Boards of Directors equal numbers of workers' representatives, elected by trade unions, and ownership representatives elected by shareholders.

28   Callaghan promises the introduction of legislation on industrial democracy by the summer.

31   Healey, at a dinner for overseas bankers, says that inflation is as great an evil as unemployment.

February

10   Callaghan describes a third year of pay restraint as an 'inevitable policy'.

15   Callaghan retreats from his commitment to legislate on the Bullock Report after encountering intense resistance to the proposals from the CBI, and offers a compromise whereby the Bullock proposals would be replaced by lower levels of participation.

17   The Lords declare the Bill to nationalise shipbuilding to be a 'hybrid', thereby forcing its procedure through the House to be slowed down.

19   Tony Crosland, the Foreign Secretary, dies suddenly.

21   Dr David Owen is appointed Foreign Secretary at the age of 38, the youngest Foreign Secretary since Eden took the post in 1935.

22   To speed up the passage of the Devolution Bill, the government attempts to introduce a guillotine, but is defeated by 312 to 283 votes when 22 Labour MPs vote against and 15 abstain; this defeat effectively ensures that the legislation will not have the time to become law.

March

2   Eric Varley, the Industry Secretary, announces that ship repairing is to be dropped from the Bill nationalising shipbuilding in order to facilitate its passage.

Jack Jones calls for an immediate and statutory price freeze in order to avoid a wage explosion.

10   In a visit to Washington, Callaghan enthuses over the co-ordination of British policies with the United States and emphasises the strength of the 'special relationship'.

11   The Labour Party in Scotland calls for an immediate referendum to break the deadlock on devolution.

17   In order to avoid the defection of the Labour left after a debate on the reductions in public expenditure, the government refuses to contend an Opposition motion to adjourn the Commons; Thatcher calls the refusal 'defeat with dishonour' and calls a motion of no-confidence which seems likely to be passed.

The Aircraft and Shipbuilding Industries Bill, providing for public ownership, is enacted.

23   The government survives the no-confidence vote by 322 to 298 after Callaghan and Steel announce the 'Lib-Lab pact' whereby the Liberals support the government in return for regular consultations over policy and the holding of free votes on proportional representation for the elections to the European Parliament.

29   Healey's budget gives tax concessions equivalent to a 4½ per cent pay increase, though some of these are made conditional on the union acceptance of renewed wage restraint after August.

April

4   An increased tax on petrol proposed in Healey's budget is withdrawn as a result of Liberal opposition.

5   Deng Xiao-Peng becomes First Vice-Chairman of the Chinese Communist Party and soon establishes himself as the new Chinese leader, committed to economic and political reform.

15   David Owen meets Smith in Rhodesia to press a new constitution.

Heath, in a speech in Glasgow, calls for the proposed Scottish Assembly to have revenue-raising powers, a greater concession to Scottish nationalism than the government is prepared to give.

17   Jack Jones calls for an early return to free collective bargaining in a sign of growing discontent with the Social Contract.

27   Labour loses the Ashfield by-election in a mining consti-tuency, where a Labour majority of 22,915 is turned into a Conservative majority of 264.

May

2-14   An abortive General Strike is held in Northern Ireland, with limited success, by hardline Loyalists under Ian Paisley.

5   The Conservatives make sweeping gains in local elections in England and Wales; they recapture the GLC, where 64 Conservative and 28 Labour councillors are elected; the Na-tional Front obtains 119,000 votes (5.3 per cent) in the GLC elections and push the Liberals into fourth place in 32 of the 92 seats.

12   The Scottish Conservatives withdraw their earlier call for a directly elected Scottish Assembly.

June

16   The Rooker-Wise amendments to the Finance Bill tie income tax reliefs to the cost of living.

24   The European Assemblies Bill is published, presenting the alternatives of the traditional electoral method and a form of proportional representation based on the regional list.

Violent demonstrations and mass pickets of the Grunwick processing works, North London, turn the strike of Indian and Pakistani workers there, dismissed because of demands for union recognition, into a symbol of trade union and anti-racist struggle.

July

6	The TGWU conference votes for a return to unrestricted pay bargaining, against the leadership's advice.
7	The European Assemblies Bill is given a second reading on a free vote by 394 to 147 votes, with six Cabinet ministers and 26 junior ministers in the minority.
9	The Royal Commission on the Press rejects all forms of state control or aid as a threat to freedom of the press, and recommends a strengthened Press Council to deal with complaints.
11	The magazine, *Gay News*, is fined £1,000 for blasphemous libel, the first such case for 56 years.
12-13	The TUC economic committee tells Callaghan and Healey that a third year of pay restraint is not possible in the face of rank and file opposition.
15	Healey, in a Commons statement, tells employers that pay settlements of more than 10 per cent would incur financial penalties, and halves the tax cuts given by the government.
25	Maudling is finally cleared of the accusations of corrupt dealings in his association with John Poulson, but John Cordle, the Conservative MP for Bournemouth East, resigns from the Commons after he is accused of contempt of the House in his dealings with Poulson.
27	Callaghan and Len Murray renew the Social Contract by endorsing *The Next Three Years and into the Eighties*; a growth rate of 3 per cent and the creation of 1,000,000 jobs by planning agreements is promised.
28	Callaghan and Steel renew the Lib-Lab pact for the next parliamentary session.

August

13 A demonstration against the National Front at Lewisham becomes a major riot as anti-racists clash with police and National Front activists; 202 people are arrested, while 56 police and many demonstrators are injured.

26 The Scarman Report on the Grunwick strike recommends the reinstatement of strikers, but this is rejected by the employer.

September

1 A government White Paper on Rhodesia calls for an immediate return to legality by the appointment of Field-Marshal Lord Carver as a resident British Commissioner, the adoption of a democratic constitution and the incorporation of the African guerrilla forces into the army; Smith calls the proposals 'insane'.

5-9 The TUC Annual Congress, Blackpool, votes to return to free collective bargaining but accepts that wage rises would need to be within single figures for the next 12 months; Scanlon casts the AUEW vote for the motion against the wishes of his left-wing delegation; delegates call for an 'alternative economic strategy' of redistribution of wealth, public ownership and controls on capital outflows.

15 A Commons report on the Civil Service, the first since 1874, recommends that its powers be checked.

18 Thatcher, in a television interview, suggests that a referendum may be the best way for a future Conservative government to meet the sort of trade union challenge which toppled Heath in 1974.

26-Oct 1 The Liberal Party Assembly, Brighton, approves the Lib-Lab pact by a large majority; Cyril Smith resigns as Liberal Employment spokesman in protest and refuses to campaign for the party nationally.

October

3-7 The Labour Party annual conference, meeting in a pre-election atmosphere in Brighton, supports the government's economic policy by a large majority.

8   Reg Prentice joins the Conservatives to prevent 'a further lurch down the Marxist road'.

11-14   At the Conservative Party annual conference, Blackpool, Thatcher denounces state controls and restrictions, but insists that a Conservative government would be 'a truly moderate government' which would seek to avoid confrontation with the unions.

26   Healey's mini-budget, providing a modest reflation as a reward for the TUCs acceptance of pay restraint, allows an increase in personal allowances and a reward of a £10 Christmas bonus for pensioners.

British Leyland (BL) workers vote, against left-wing opposition, to support the company's plans to rationalise the wage structure through a single, all-union and nationwide annual negotiation.

November

7   In the mass picket at Grunwick, 42 police and scores of demonstrators are hurt as violence breaks out.

14   A national firemen's strike begins in a call for higher pay and shorter hours; troops are drafted to fight fires.

The Grunwick strike committee calls off mass pickets.

The Scotland Bill, providing for a Scottish Assembly, obtains its second reading by 307 to 263 votes; the Wales Bill, a separate devolution measure, passes its second reading by 295 to 264 votes.

16   A guillotine procedure is imposed successfully on both the Scotland and Wales Bills to ensure their passage.

December

2   The TUC General Purposes Committee opposes the firemen's strike as a breach of the 12-month rule.

13   In a severe blow to the Lib-Lab pact, proportional representation for the European elections is defeated in the Commons by 319 to 222 votes; 114 Labour MPs, including four Cabinet ministers, vote with the majority.

14   The Parliamentary Liberal Party upholds the Lib-Lab

pact despite this defeat, but a special assembly is called for January to pronounce its verdict on the pact.

In a ruling on the Grunwick strike, the Lords uphold the employer's right to dismiss his workforce.

1978

January

16   The firemen return to work after a bitter defeat.

17   The government tells its European partners that it is unable to take part in European elections until 1979.

18   Britain is convicted by the European Court of Human Rights of 'inhuman and degrading conduct', though not torture, of its detainees in Northern Ireland.

21   The special Liberal Party Assembly gives Steel the authority to continue the Lib-Lab pact by 1,727 to 520 votes; Lord Byers tells delegates that 'if you want proportional representation, you want alliance politics'.

25   An amendment to the Scotland Bill, providing for the repeal of the measure if 40 per cent of the registered electorate does not agree to devolution in a referendum, is passed against government wishes by 166 to 151 votes.

30   Thatcher, in a television interview, says that people are worried that they may be 'rather swamped' by an influx of people with a different culture, and calls for a halt to immigration for all but compassionate cases.

February

8   The NUM accepts a 10 per cent pay settlement after initially seeking 90 per cent.

14   Michael Edwardes, the Chairman of BL, announces redundancies for 12,500 workers and meets only a muted reaction from a once militant labour force.

17   In a fire-bomb attack, the Provisional IRA incinerates twelve people in the La Mon Hotel in County Down; the Provisionals are forced to accept condemnation and criticism from their own supporters.

22   The Scotland Bill is given a third reading by 297 to 257 votes.

March

3   David Owen is lukewarm to an internal Rhodesian settlement whereby moderate African nationalists led by Bishop Muzorewa are brought into the Smith government.

21   A Commons select committee unanimously calls for tighter immigration controls.

In Rhodesia, three blacks are appointed to the Cabinet after 88 years of white rule.

29   Moss Evans becomes TGWU General Secretary on the retirement of Jack Jones.

April

3   Regular radio reports of the House of Commons proceedings begins.

4   The Lords pass an amendment to the Scotland Bill providing for proportional representation by 155 to 64 votes.

11   Healey's budget is designed 'to increase the incentive for greater effort and to promote social justice'; it raises income tax thresholds and reintroduces free school milk for seven to eleven year-olds.

12   Steel expresses the Liberal disappointment at the failure to cut income tax.

13   The Liberal attempt to introduce proportional representation into the European Assembly Elections Bill fails by 123 to 68 votes.

May

2   Terry Duffy is elected President of the AUEW, ending left-wing control of the union.

5   The European Assemblies Bill is enacted.

8   In an unprecedented move, Callaghan refuses to resign after the government is defeated by 312 to 304 votes on an opposition amendment to the Finance Bill reducing income tax by 1p.

9   The Wales Bill passes its third reading by 292 to 264 votes, with the amendment providing for agreement by 40 per cent of the Welsh electorate in a referendum.

10	The government is again defeated on the Finance Bill, this time by 288 to 286 votes on an amendment raising the threshold for the 40 per cent tax from £7,000 to £8,000.
13	Steel declares that minority government is not only tolerable, but desirable.
25	Steel announces the end of the Lib-Lab pact at the end of the session as it had achieved its main objective of providing political stability.
31	The SNP does badly in the by-election at Hamilton, which it had captured in 1967.

June

8	Healey presents a new economic package which increases MLR, restricts bank lending and raises employers' national insurance contributions.
14	A Conservative motion to cut the Chancellor's salary in protest at his new measures is defeated by only 287 to 282 votes.
25	A dozen British missionaries and children are murdered at Umtali, Rhodesia, in the increasingly vicious war there.
30	Callaghan warns the Confederation of Shipbuilding and Engineering Unions (CSEU) that the wage guidelines would be reduced in the coming year, despite union discontent at the policy.

July

6	The Commons throws out the Lords amendment introducing proportional representation in the Scotland Bill by 363 to 155 votes.
6-7	The EEC summit in Bremen agrees to establish a European Monetary System (EMS), linking all EEC currencies within a narrowly defined margin of fluctuation.
14	The Grunwick workers abandon their strike after 591 days.
21	The government White Paper on incomes policy lays down a 5 per cent guideline for wage increases.
30	John Mackintosh, a Labour MP evolving a new social democratic doctrine, dies.

31   The Scotland Bill and the Wales Bill are enacted.

August

4   Thorpe and three others are charged with conspiracy to murder Norman Scott.

5   The North Devon Liberal Association expresses its full confidence in Thorpe and wishes to have him as a candidate at the next election.

14   The *Daily Mirror* calls for troops to be withdrawn from Northern Ireland.

27   The *Sunday Times* reveals that BP has been undertaking 'sanctions-busting' trading with Rhodesia.

September

4-8   At the TUC Annual Congress, Brighton, Callaghan teases the delegates about the possibility of an October election and warns of renewed inflation if the unions break the wage guidelines; the delegates support, by an overwhelming majority, a motion opposing arbitrary pay limits and reject a call to renew the Social Contract.

7   Callaghan announces that there will be no autumn election, a decision described by Steel as 'truly astounding' and by Thatcher as the act of 'a broken-backed government'.

12-16   At the Liberal Party Assembly, Southport, Thorpe appears to a cool reception despite being urged to stay away by colleagues.

19   The Bingham Report reveals that BP and Shell have been engaged in a major avoidance of sanctions on trade with Rhodesia.

**21-
Nov 2**   Ford workers strike successfully for wages above the 5 per cent pay guidelines.

October

2-6   The Labour Party annual conference, Blackpool, rejects all pay restraint policies, specifically the government's 5 per cent pay guidelines, by 4 million to 1.9 million votes;

Callaghan insists that the government must control the economy.

10-14   At the Conservative Party annual conference, Brighton, Heath demands support for the government's incomes policy in contrast to the calls for free wage bargaining by Thatcher, Joseph and Howe; Whitelaw promises that there will be a free vote in the Commons on capital punishment on the return of a Conservative government.

The Gallup poll shows 47 per cent Labour, 42 per cent Conservative and 7 per cent Liberal support.

November

1   The Queen's Speech promises five more seats for Ulster, reflecting Callaghan's desire to win Ulster Unionist support.

Callaghan tells the Commons that referendums on the Scotland and Wales Bills will take place on *1 March 1979*.

8   In the renewal of sanctions on Rhodesia, 114 Conservative backbenchers rebel against their leaders' decision to abstain.

13   Callaghan, in his Guildhall speech, attacks the Common Agricultural Policy (CAP) as irrational and calls for an end to the imbalance in Britain's contribution to the EEC budget.

15   Francis Pym is appointed the Conservative Foreign Affairs spokesman after Davies undergoes a brain operation.

24   In a Green Paper on the proposed EMS, strong doubts are expressed on British entry.

28   Healey announces discretionary action against Ford for reaching a 16½ per cent pay settlement of its strike which breaks the pay guidelines.

30   The *Times* and *Sunday Times* suspend publication because of continuing labour troubles.

December

5   Callaghan announces that Britain will not take part in the EMS for the time being.

12   Unions representing 1,000,000 workers in the NHS and local authorities reject their 5 per cent pay offer and call a programme of industrial action for the New Year.

13   The Commons refuses, by 285 to 283 votes, to allow the government to impose sanctions on Ford for breaking the 5 per cent pay guideline; Callaghan, indicating that sanctions on the private sector would no longer be used, calls a vote of confidence, threatening that the government would resign if it lost.

Thorpe is committed for trial at the Old Bailey.

14   The government survives its vote of confidence by 300 to 290 votes.

General

Inflation is at an annual 8.4 per cent.

Eric Hobsbawm, a Communist historian, argues in a lecture to the Marx Memorial Library called 'The Forward March of Labour Halted' that the labour movement must build a broad-based movement if it is not to decline irrevocably.

1979

January

3   Lorry drivers begin a national strike for a 25 per cent pay rise, opening the 'winter of discontent' as abnormally severe weather conditions grip Britain.

4-6   An informal summit meeting of the United States, British, French and West German leaders at Guadeloupe discuss political and security concerns, especially the negotiations for SALT II disarmament talks with the Soviet Union.

10   Callaghan, after his return from the Guadeloupe summit and a holiday in Barbados, questions whether there is a crisis in Britain.

14   Thatcher asks for all-party agreement against secondary picketing (i.e. at places of work not directly connected with a dispute) and for no-strike agreements in essential services, both of them areas of particular significance in the winter strikes.

16   Callaghan offers a relaxation of the pay guidelines for lower-paid workers as regional strikes by ambulance drivers, water and sewage workers, dustmen and grave-diggers disrupt social life.

19   The government renounces the pay guideline policy, and the lorry drivers' strike ends through local settlements over the next three weeks.

22   A programme of industrial action by 1½ million public service workers begins with a 24-hour strike.

February

14   A joint TUC-government statement issues guidance on the conduct of strikes, particularly with regard to secondary picketing, but it is described by Thatcher as a 'boneless wonder'.

The water and sewage workers accept a 16 per cent pay offer.

23   The civil servants' union, the Civil and Public Services Association (CPSA), strikes in protest at low pay; David

Owen expresses pleasure at crossing their picket-line.

March

1   Scotland votes to accept the devolution proposals in its referendum, but only by 32.9 per cent of the electorate (1,230,937 votes) with 30.8 per cent (1,153,502 votes) against and 36.4 per cent abstaining.

Wales votes heavily against the devolution proposals in its referendum by 46.9 per cent (956,330 votes) to 11.9 per cent (243,048 votes) for devolution and 41.2 per cent abstention.

13   The EMS comes into operation, but without British membership.

22   Callaghan announces that the repeal of the Scotland Bill will be laid before Parliament without delay.

The House of Commons (Redistribution of Seats) Bill, increasing the Ulster constituencies from twelve to 17, is enacted, but it is postponed until after the Boundary Commissions fix the new constituency boundaries for the whole country.

28   The government is defeated on a motion of no-confidence by 311 to 310 votes; the government is forced into an election.

29   A general election is announced for *3 May*.

The Liberals win the Liverpool Edge Hill by-election, turning a Labour majority of 6,171 into a Liberal majority of 8,133.

The public service workers end their industrial action.

30   Airey Neave, the Conservative Northern Ireland spokesman, is killed in the Commons car park by a bomb planted by the Irish National Liberation Army (INLA), a republican socialist paramilitary group.

April

3   In lieu of a budget, the Finance Bill is agreed with minimum changes to the tax structure.

Thorpe and his colleagues are found not guilty of conspiracy to murder Norman Scott because of the unreliability of the evidence.

6   Labour's manifesto, *The Labour Way is the Better Way*, calls for greater powers for the Prices Commission to bring inflation down to 5 per cent by 1982; it is a moderate document after Callaghan had defeated left-wing policy proposals.

7   Parliament is dissolved.

10   The Liberal manifesto, *The Real Fight is for Britain*, identifies electoral reform as the key to the social and economic measures needed to revive Britain.

11   *The Conservative manifesto, 1979*, is a radical document proposing to control inflation by a strict control of the money supply and a general reduction in public expenditure; it proposes to limit secondary picketing by unions and to provide money to finance postal ballots.

In a major riot at a National Front electoral meeting in Southall, Blair Peach, an anti-racist, is killed and 300 people are arrested.

May

3   Polling day, with a turnout of 76.0 per cent (31,221, 361 votes); the Conservatives win with an overall majority of 43, as 339 Conservative MPs, 268 Labour, eleven Liberals, ten various Ulster Unionists, two Plaid Cymru, two SNP, one Irish SDLP, one Irish Republican and the Speaker are elected; the Conservatives obtain 13,697,923 votes (43.9 per cent) Labour 11,532,218 votes (37.0 per cent), the Liberals 4,313,804 votes (13.8 per cent) and the National Front only 191,719 votes (0.6 per cent).

4   Thatcher becomes Conservative Prime Minister, with Sir Geoffrey Howe as Chancellor of the Exchequer, William Whitelaw as Home Secretary, and Lord Carrington as Foreign Secretary; Heath remains on the back benches, having been refused the Foreign Office and rejecting any other appointment.

10   Tony Benn refuses to stand for the 'shadow Cabinet' elections, preferring the freedom of the back benches, and begins a campaign to rally the left and to change the Labour constitution.

15   Sir Keith Joseph, the Industry Secretary, announces that the Price Commission is to be abolished.

June

1   Bishop Muzorewa, a moderate African nationalist, becomes Prime Minister of Zimbabwe-Rhodesia.

7   Only a third of the British electorate vote in the first direct elections to the European Parliament; 60 Conservatives, 17 Labour, two Ulster Unionists, one SNP and one Irish SDLP are elected, to Liberal cries of outrage at the unfairness of the electoral system.

12   Howe's budget reduces income tax by 3p in the pound and cuts public spending by £4,000 million, but also increases VAT to 15 per cent in a move which boosts inflation; Howe tells the Commons that 'we cannot go on avoiding difficult choices'.

14   The 'shadow Cabinet' is elected; Peter Shore becomes Labour Foreign Affairs spokesman, with David Owen demoted.

19   Thatcher rejects any incomes policy, but tells the Commons that only increased unemployment can be the result of high wage claims.

20   The Scotland Act is repealed.

25   On a free vote of 248 to twelve, the Commons sets up a new system of 14 permanent Select Committees to examine expenditure, administration and policy of the Departments of State.

26   The Wales Act is repealed.

July

6   Thatcher warns that the government will not print money to finance 'irresponsible' pay settlements.

9   James Prior, the Employment Secretary, presents a consultative document on trade union law, ending the closed shop, banning secondary picketing and providing funds for the election of union officers by post; the TUC rejects it as 'a major challenge to the rights of workers'.

11   The TGWU conference votes for the maximum action against the trade union proposals.

17   Joseph cuts regional aid by £233 million over a three-year period.

19   Joseph announces that the NEB is to be run down, starting with the sale of £100 million of assets in 1979–80.

In a free vote, the Commons votes to reject the reintroduction of capital punishment by 362 to 243 votes.

20   John Nott, the Trade Secretary, announces that the government is to sell its minority shareholding in British Airways.

23   Joseph announces that British Aerospace is to be 'privatised', becoming a public limited company.

26   The Education Bill, removing the compulsion on local authorities and the governors of independent schools to reorganise education on comprehensive lines, is enacted.

David Howell, the Energy Secretary, announces proposals to reduce the role of BNOC in the production of North Sea oil.

30   The Lewisham Area Health Authority is suspended by Patrick Jenkin, the Health and Social Services Secretary, after it refuses to implement a £5 million cut in its budget.

31   Nigeria nationalises the assets of BP in a gesture to protest at British inactivity over Rhodesia.

August

1-8   The Commonwealth Prime Ministers' conference at Lusaka places the responsibility for action to end the Rhodesian crisis on Britain.

14   Lord Carrington, the Foreign Secretary, issues invitations to both sides in the Rhodesian War to a constitutional conference in London.

22   Terry Duffy, the AUEW President, attacks those Labour NEC members who wish 'to subvert the traditions and values' of the British Labour movement.

27   Lord Mountbatten and three others are killed by an IRA bomb on their fishing boat off Sligo, while 18 British soldiers are killed in an IRA ambush in South Armagh.

September

3-7   The TUC Annual Congress, Blackpool, unanimously agrees to campaign against the trade union legislation, but a call for mass demonstrations and resistance to the Prior proposals is narrowly defeated.

10   The talks between the Rhodesian government and the African nationalist guerrilla forces open at Lancaster House, London.

Michael Edwardes informs the BL workforce that 13 plants are to be closed with the loss of 25,000 jobs.

12   Joseph announces that the (profitable) telecommunications section of the Post Office is to become a separate corporation.

28-9   The Liberal Party Assembly is held at Margate.

October

1-5   The Labour Party annual conference, Brighton, votes to make the mandatory reselection of MPs part of the party constitution and calls on the NEC to submit plans to control the election manifesto.

4   An agreement by the AUEW and the engineering employers to cut the working week by one hour is hailed by the union as 'an historic breakthrough'.

5   Muzorewa accepts the new Rhodesian constitution negotiated at Lancaster House, despite Smith's opposition.

13-16   At the Conservative Party annual conference, Blackpool, Thatcher is adamant on the need for union reform and calls for Britain to take a new direction; Howell confirms that BNOC revenue bonds are to be put on sale.

18   The African nationalist guerrillas accept the Lancaster House constitution.

23   Howe announces the abolition of all remaining exchange controls, after a major liberalisation on *12 June* and *18 July*, creating a market environment for the export and import of capital.

24   Callaghan describes the meetings of the Labour NEC as 'visits to purgatory' after his demand for PLP representation on the NEC committee investigating the structure of the party is rejected.

November

1   The White Paper on public expenditure foreshadows a

cut of £3,500 million in 1980/1, with exemptions only for defence, the police and the social services.

A ballot organised by BL management shows an overwhelming acceptance of the company's reorganisation, defeating union attempts to resist the plans.

7   Sanctions against Rhodesia are not renewed.

8   The British Aerospace Bill, privatising the industry, is introduced.

13   The *Times* and the *Sunday Times* reappear after a year's suspension.

16   MLR is raised from 14 per cent to an unprecedented 17 per cent in order to control the money supply, a move which startles industry.

20   The entire NEB membership resign after Joseph announces that Rolls Royce is to be taken from the NEB and placed under his control; the trade unions refuse to serve on the reconstituted Board.

22   Roy Jenkins calls for a 'politics of the centre' and electoral reform in his Dimbleby Lecture.

29-30   The EEC summit at Dublin fails to reach any agreement over the British demand for a £1,000 million budget relief.

December

4   The government amends the immigration rules by removing the right of entry to husbands and fiancés of women not born in Britain; 19 Conservative MPs abstain.

5   A ceasefire is agreed in principle between the two warring sides in Rhodesia.

An NUM pithead ballot rejects industrial action by 51.2 per cent to 48.8 per cent, a major blow to the left.

7   The Employment Bill incorporating the Prior proposals is introduced, as the Labour-TUC liaison committee pledge the repeal of the legislation by the next Labour government.

Lord Soames is appointed the new British Governor of Rhodesia.

8   The National Health Service Bill, giving the Secretary of State the power to restructure the Service and to reverse the Labour policy of phasing out private beds, is introduced.

The Local Government Bill, to repeal the Community Land Act, is introduced.

10   The Rhodesian Parliament formally ends the rebellion against Britain.

12   Lord Soames arrives in Salisbury, the Rhodesian capital.

21   A settlement is signed between the Rhodesian government and the guerrillas.

25   The Soviet Union invades Afghanistan.

General

Inflation reaches an annual 17.2 per cent.
Labour Party membership is 7,236,000.

1980

January

2 The steel workers strike, after Joseph refuses to intervene in the mediation process.

6 Eric Heffer calls for Labour to become a genuinely socialist party rather than a mildly reformist party propping up capitalism.

7- A constitutional conference on Ulster fails to reach agree-
Mar 24 ment on the role of the Roman Catholic minority.

24 Carrington announces the cancellation of military links with the Soviet Union and refuses to renew the Anglo-Soviet trade agreement, in protest at the Soviet occupation of Afghanistan.

26 After violent incidents in the steel strike, the Court of Appeal orders the steelworkers union, the Iron and Steel Trades Confederation (ISTC), not to picket private companies; the union obeys, but reimposes the picket after the Lords overrules the Appeal Court.

February

14 Thatcher calls for a boycott of the Olympic Games because they are to be held in Moscow.

Polling for 20 white seats takes place in Rhodesia; Ian Smith's party, the Rhodesia Front, emerges as the victor.

27 The TUC General Council rejects a proposal to consider state finance for secret ballots by 35 to three votes.

Polling for 80 black seats takes place in Rhodesia, with Robert Mugabe's Marxist ZANU-PF party emerging as the victor.

March

4 Lord Soames, the Governor of Rhodesia, invites Robert Mugabe, the leader of the ZANU guerrilla forces, to become Prime Minister of an independent Zimbabwe after his party's election victory, monitored by a force of 1,300 men.

The TUC breaks off discussions with Prior on his Employment Bill.

17   The Commons votes to recommend a boycott of the Moscow Olympics by 315 to 147 votes.

20   A report by Lord Underhill gives detailed evidence of infiltration of the Labour Party by the Trotskyist *Militant* group.

21   The British Steel Corporation (BSC) and the steel unions agree to a committee of inquiry under Lord Lever into their pay dispute.

25   The British Olympic Association defies the government in deciding to participate in the Moscow Olympics.

26   Howe's budget sets the Public Sector Borrowing Requirement (PSBR) at £8,500 million and cuts government spending by £1,275 million, especially in education; prescription charges and indirect taxes are raised, but there is to be more spending on the police, defence and pensions. Callaghan describes the budget as 'the meanest since 1931'.

31   The Lever Committee issues a compromise pay offer of 11 per cent in the steel dispute (the employers had offered 10 per cent).

April

1   Zimbabwe becomes independent.

2   Riots break out in Bristol, led by unemployed youths.

A White Paper says that Britain is giving consideration to the development of chemical weapons.

3   The steel strike ends after the Lever Report is accepted by both sides; BSC claims that there has been a permanent loss of 10 per cent of the steel market.

The Competition Bill, abolishing the Prices Commission, is enacted.

8   A BL decision to pay its original wage offer, after negotiations with the union break down, succeeds in gaining acceptance by the workforce, despite union outrage.

10   An ITV programme, *Death of a Princess*, reconstructing the execution of a Saudi princess for adultery, causes fury in Saudi Arabia.

23   The British Ambassador to Saudi Arabia is ordered to leave.

John Methven, the Director-General of the CBI, dies.

30   A group of six dissident Iranians seize the Iranian Embassy in London.

May

1   Labour makes gains in the local elections.

The British Aerospace Bill is enacted, privatising the industry.

2   Joseph reveals that the government has agreed to pay a sum of £675,000 plus an additional amount of up to £1.15 million for Ian McGregor to take over as BSC Chairman from the end of June.

5   After two of the hostages in the Iranian Embassy siege are shot, an SAS detachment storms the embassy and kills five of the dissidents; a cult immediately grows around the SAS.

14   The TUC holds a 'Day of Action' against the government's economic and industrial policies, but it draws an uneven response, with the CBI claiming 90 per cent of the workforce reporting normally.

30   The EEC foreign ministers reach a settlement to reduce Britain's budget contributions.

31   A special Labour Party conference in London approves *Peace, Jobs and Freedom*, an attempt to reconcile the different wings of the party, but Benn draws applause when he calls for the abolition of the Lords, a major extension of public ownership and no compensation for renationalised industries.

Inflation reaches an annual 21.9 per cent.

June

2   The Cabinet agrees to the EEC budgetary settlement.

8   Shirley Williams rejects the idea of setting up a new centre party as it would have 'no roots, no principles, no philosophy and no values'.

17   Francis Pym, the Defence Secretary, names sites in Greenham Common and Molesworth to store 160 United States Cruise missiles.

25 The Wilson Committee investigating the City, reports that there is no case to support the charge that British industry is starved of investment funds by the financial system.

30 The Industry Bill is enacted, abolishing the NEBs statutory function to extend public ownership into profitable areas of manufacturing and giving it a new function to encourage private enterprise.

  The Transport Bill is enacted, reconstructing the National Freight Corporation as a public limited company, and instituting a major reform of the bus licensing system.

July

2 Humphrey Atkins, the Northern Ireland Secretary, proposes a new assembly for Ulster, but this is rejected by the Unionists and the SDLP.

10 The Labour NEC draft manifesto bears a 'Bennite' stamp, with commitments to unilateral nuclear disarmament and the abolition of the Lords.

15 Pym announces the replacement of Polaris by Trident in the mid-1980s.

19 The Olympic Games open in Moscow, with the United States team boycotting and the British team taking part.

28 Saudi Arabia restores relations with Britain after Carrington apologises for the screening of the *Death of a Princess* programme.

  MLR is reduced to 16 per cent.

August

1 The Employment Bill, directed against the closed shop and secondary picketing, is enacted.

4 Thatcher orders the Clegg Commission on public sector pay wound up at the end of the year after it grants big pay rises to teachers, nurses and NHS staff; she states that pay comparability is no longer to be used to judge public sector wage increases.

8 The Housing Bill, giving local authority tenants the right to buy their homes, is enacted.

31   The Gdansk agreements in Poland recognise the Solidarity trade union.

September

1-5   The TUC Annual Congress, Brighton, votes for a campaign of non-cooperation with the government, including the use of industrial action.

8-13   At the Liberal Party Assembly, Blackpool, Steel criticises the talk of a new centre party as the Liberals are already the centre party, and calls instead for a Liberal-led government of reconciliation; the delegates vote against a unilateralist defence resolution and call for a £2,750 million job creation programme.

13   The steel works at Consett, County Durham, are closed with the loss of 3,400 jobs; the workers accept the loss with protest, as the plant is the chief means of livelihood for the town.

21   A CND rally is held at the proposed Greenham Common missile base.

29-Oct 3   The Labour Party annual conference, Blackpool, votes for a new leadership election procedure to be drawn up by a majority of 457,000 and for the mandatory re-selection of MPs by a majority of 98,000, but it votes against the NEC having final control over the election manifesto by a majority of 117,000; a special conference is to be held in January to decide the mode of electing the party leader.

October

1   Sir Terence Beckett is appointed the new Director General of the CBI.

11-15   At the Conservative Party annual conference, Brighton, Thatcher strongly reaffirms her determination to maintain the government's economic strategy despite the rise in unemployment, declaring that 'the lady's not for turning'.

14   Harold Macmillan criticises the government's harsh monetary policies and calls for an 'industrial parliament' to enhance co-operation between capital and labour.

15   Callaghan resigns as Labour leader in a move widely believed to be a tactical manoeuvre to prevent Benn taking advantage of the new election procedure.

20   Foot enters the Labour leadership contest reluctantly, with the aim of reunifying the party; a left-wing move to postpone the election until the new procedure could be decided upon is defeated in the PLP by 165 to 77 votes.

26   The revival of CND is marked by a march of over 50,000 in Trafalgar Square.

27   Seven Provisional IRA prisoners begin a hunger strike in the H-Block internment camps in Northern Ireland, in a demand for political status.

30   Shirley Williams, in an article in the *Times*, says that the division between left and right in the Labour party 'is becoming explicitly . . . unbridgeable'.

November

4   Healey leads the first ballot for the Labour leadership with 112 votes, against 83 for Foot, 38 for John Silkin and 32 for Peter Shore; Silkin and Shore are defeated.

6   Michael Heseltine, the Environment Secretary, announces that the rate support grant will be based on a maximum 6 per cent pay rise, forcing local authorities to meet any extra pay increases from rate rises or dismissing parts of their workforce.

10   Foot is elected Labour leader with 139 votes on the second ballot, against Healey's 129.

11   At the CBI conference, Sir Terence Beckett calls for 'a bare-knuckle fight' against restrictionist economic policies, causing some companies to resign in protest.

13   Healey is elected Labour deputy leader.

The Local Government Planning and Land Bill is enacted, replacing the existing rate support grant system by a single block grant, and imposing ceilings on capital expenditure by local authorities.

The Civil Aviation Bill is enacted, privatising British Airways.

Labour MPs prevent Black Rod from entering the Commons and force a suspension of proceedings after the government announcement of a rise in rents for local authority houses without a chance for debate.

21   David Owen, increasingly disillusioned with Labour's swing to the left, refuses to stand for the 'shadow Cabinet'.

The Industry Bill is introduced, authorising increased borrowing from the Exchequer fund by nationalised industries and injecting a large amount of capital into BL and Rolls Royce.

24   Howe announces a new economic package to cut public expenditure and increase taxation by a total of £3,000 million, while MLR is brought down to 14 per cent.

27   Heath intervenes in a Commons debate to warn that the government's economic policies are leading to disaster.

28   The Conservative 1922 Committee rebuffs Heath by giving its full support to the government.

December

4   Benn fails to be elected to the 'shadow Cabinet', and Heffer warns that the PLP majority 'does not really reflect the new spirit and views of the party in the country'.

8   Thatcher meets the Irish Prime Minister, Haughey, in Dublin, and they agree to establish joint studies on a range of key issues.

15   Local authorities reduce their housing expenditure by 4 per cent.

16   The government reduces the rate support grant by 1 per cent, shifting the burden of the reduction on to the inner city areas; the Association of Metropolitan Authorities chairman describes it as 'the most unjust settlement I have known'.

18   The IRA hunger strike in the H-Block camps is ended after 53 days on hints that the British government may seek a compromise on political status.

Inflation falls to an annual 15.1 per cent.

Unemployment is 2,133,000 (or 8.8 per cent).

Manufacturing output has fallen by 9 per cent, a sharper fall than the 1929–31 period.

General

Britain is experiencing its worst recession for 50 years,

with sharply falling output, high inflation and rising unemployment.

TUC membership is 12,173,000.

E.P. Thompson and Dan Smith write *Protest and Survive*, signifying the revival of CND.

1981

January

5   Norman St John Stevas is dismissed as Leader of the Commons after a series of Cabinet 'leaks' to the press; Pym succeeds him as Leader, while John Nott becomes Defence Secretary.

14   The British Nationality Bill is introduced, restricting the right to live in Britain to British citizens, while denying that right to the citizens of British dependent territories and British overseas citizens.

20   Ronald Reagan is inaugurated as United States President.

22   Rupert Murdoch's bid for the *Times* and the *Sunday Times* is accepted.

24   The special Labour Party conference at Wembley agrees to elect Labour leaders by an electoral college system, with the unions having 40 per cent of the vote, the PLP and the constituencies having 30 per cent each.

25   Roy Jenkins, David Owen, Shirley Williams and William Rodgers set up the Council for Social Democracy, with the aim of eventually setting up a new party.

27   Rodgers resigns from the 'shadow Cabinet' and Benn takes his place.

Unemployment reaches 2,419,000 (or 8.8 per cent).

The Gallup poll shows 40 per cent Labour, 33 per cent Conservative and 18 per cent Liberal support.

February

9   Shirley Williams resigns from the Labour NEC, declaring that the party she knew and cared for no longer exists.

10   The NCB announces a programme of pit closures which provokes an unofficial strike by miners.

17   The Labour Solidarity Campaign is set up by 100 Labour MPs, with Roy Hattersley in the chair, in order to counter the growing influence of the left.

18   The government announces that the NCB is withdrawing its pit closure programme, thereby ending the unofficial miners' strike.

22   John Biffen, the Trade Secretary, explains the government surrender to the miners on a television programme by saying that he did not enter politics as a *kamikaze* pilot.

25   Lonhro, an international trading and investment group, buys the *Observer*.

March

1   Bobby Sands, an IRA prisoner, begins a hunger strike which is gradually joined by other prisoners.

2   Owen, Rodgers and ten other MPs renounce the Labour Whip, but refuse to resign their seats; a Social Democratic parliamentary committee is formed under Owen to co-ordinate with the Liberals.

9   The Civil Service holds a one-day strike for higher pay.

10   Howe, arguing that 'to change course now would be disastrous', presents a harsh budget, increasing excise duties, imposing new taxes on bank profits and North Sea oil, and reducing public spending by £3,290 million; Foot describes it as 'a no-hope budget produced by a no-hope Chancellor'.

16   The government majority falls to 14 when eight Conservatives vote against and 25 abstain on the increase in petrol tax in the Finance Bill.

        Christopher Brocklebank-Fowler becomes the only Conservative to join the Social Democrats.

26   The Social Democratic Party (SDP) is formed, advocating proportional representation, a mixed economy, a fair distribution of wealth and positive membership of the EEC.

29   Wilson confirms a *Sunday Times* report that a *coup* had been planned against his government in the late 1960s, but denies that Mountbatten had been involved.

30   A memorial by 364 academic economists is published, attacking deflationary economic policies.

April

2   Benn announces that he will stand for the deputy

leadership, despite an appeal by Foot to withdraw in the interests of party unity.

9   Bobby Sands is elected anti-H Block MP in the Fermanagh and South Tyrone by-election with a majority of 1,446.

11-13   Unemployed black and white youths riot in Brixton, gutting several streets with petrol bombs and forcing the police to retreat; 114 police and 192 civilians are hurt.

13   Whitelaw announces an inquiry into the riot, under Lord Scarman.

30   Howe halves the petrol duty in the Finance Bill under backbench pressure from rural constituencies.

The Gallup Poll shows 34 per cent Labour, 33 per cent Liberal/SDP, and 30 per cent Conservative support.

May

5   Bobby Sands, the MP for Fermanagh and South Tyrone, dies of hunger in the Maze prison camp after 66 days of his fast.

7   Labour captures the GLC (50 Labour, 41 Conservatives and one Liberal councillor are elected) and make big gains in the local elections.

8   Ken Livingstone is elected GLC leader after the left assert their numerical superiority in the Labour delegation.

18   Keith Speed is dismissed as a junior Navy Minister after publicly appealing to the government not to make any further cuts in the Royal Navy.

19   Five soldiers are killed by a 1,000 pound bomb in South Armagh as the Provisional IRA avenge the death of Bobby Sands.

20   In defiance of the leadership, 71 Labour MPs, including Benn, vote against the Government Defence White Paper.

June

12   The Representation of the People Bill is introduced, disqualifying convicted prisoners from standing for election, thereby preventing a repeat of the Bobby Sands episode.

16   The Liberals and SDP conclude a political and electoral

Alliance, marked by the issue of a joint policy statement, *A Fresh Start for Britain*.

July

2   The Representation of the People Bill is enacted against Labour opposition.

3   A National Front demonstration in Southall provokes a major riot.

4-8   Ferocious rioting in the Toxteth area of Liverpool, where shops and offices are burnt and CS gas is used for the first time on the British mainland, is followed by rioting in the Moss Side area of Manchester, where the police station is attacked; the government and the opposition charge the riots to criminal hooliganism, though Labour says that the root cause is unemployment.

16   Roy Jenkins, standing as an SDP candidate, is defeated at the Warrington by-election, but reduces the Labour majority from 10,274 to 1,759 and pushes the Conservatives into third place.

     Heseltine is charged with an investigation of the problems of Merseyside.

27   Thatcher announces a £500 million programme to defeat unemployment.

     The British Telecom Bill is enacted, dividing the Post Office into two separate public corporations by hiving off the profitable British Telecom to deal with telecommunications and data processing.

28   In new Toxteth riots, a man is killed by a police car charging crowds.

30   The civil service industrial action is called off after the 7 per cent pay offer is accepted.

     Howe states that 'we have come to the end of the recession', referring to the end of the sharp drop in output since 1979.

August

20   Owen Carron, Bobby Sands's election agent, is elected anti-H Block MP for Fermanagh and South Tyrone in the

by-election caused by Sands's death.

31   Edward Heath, in a speech in Johannesburg, says that South Africa should not assume that the West would support her as long as apartheid remains.

September

3   Heseltine reduces the rate support grant by £300 million for high spending local authorities.

7-11   The TUC Annual Congress, Blackpool, calls for an early repeal of the Employment Act.

14   In a Cabinet reshuffle, Norman Tebbit becomes Employment Secretary and James Prior a reluctant Northern Ireland Secretary; Sir Ian Gilmour leaves the Cabinet after political arguments against the deflationary economic policies; Cecil Parkinson becomes Conservative Party Chairman.

14-19   The Liberal Party Assembly, Llandudno, votes overwhelmingly for the alliance with the SDP, but also votes to ban the entry of Cruise missiles; Steel appeals to delegates to discard the Liberal role of eternal opposition.

15   The Treasury announces a limit of 4 per cent for public service wage rises.

22   The SDP outline constitution sets up a Council of Social Democracy, to be composed half of women and only a quarter of MPs, as the parliament of the party.

27-
Oct 2   At the Labour party annual conference, Brighton, Benn fails to dislodge Healey from the deputy leadership, obtaining 49.6 per cent to Healey's 50.4 per cent of the vote; a unilateralist defence motion is carried by an overwhelming majority, but the 'hard left' loses its majority on the NEC and delegates vote by 5.3 million to 1.3 million votes to refer back a proposal to nationalise banks and insurance.

October

3   The hunger strike in the H-Block camps is ended after 203 days and the death of ten prisoners.

4-10   The SDP conference is held in Perth, Bradford and London on successive days; no votes or policies are adopted, but the adhesion of four more Labour MPs gives the SDP a total parliamentary strength of 21.

Heath, in a speech at Manchester, launches a severe attack on Thatcher's policies, asking how many millions more must become unemployed to get inflation down.

13-16   At the Conservative Party annual conference, Blackpool, Thatcher reaffirms her determination not to change policies merely to court popularity, partly in response to the Heath attack.

14   The CND conference approves the policy of setting up peace camps at Greenham Common and Molesworth.

16   After a mass meeting of BL workers votes to strike in November for higher pay, Edwardes threatens to dismiss all strikers.

19   David Howell, the Transport Secretary, announces the sale of the National Freight Corporation.

Nigel Lawson, the Energy Secretary, announces the sale of BNOC.

20   In the Lords debate on the British Nationality Bill, the Archbishop of Canterbury denounces the measure as morally questionable.

24   A CND rally in London draws 150,000 as massive anti-nuclear demonstrations take place in European cities.

30   The British Nationality Bill is enacted.

Cable and Wireless sells half its shares on the Stock Exchange.

The Gallup Poll shows 40 per cent Alliance, 29 per cent Conservative and 28 per cent Labour support.

November

10   Benn calls for no compensation over oil nationalisation in a Commons speech from the Labour front bench; Foot renounces the speech and says that he will not be voting for Benn in the 'shadow Cabinet' elections.

12   Thatcher announces the abolition of the Civil Service Department and the reallocation of responsibility for the service from the Prime Minister to the Treasury.

14   Robert Bradford, a Unionist MP for South Belfast, is killed by the IRA.

19   Benn is voted off the 'shadow Cabinet'.

25   The Scarman Report on the inner city riots points to

the acute deprivation of the areas involved and calls for a policy of positive discrimination in employing black and Asian youths.

26   Shirley Williams wins the Crosby by-election, turning a Conservative majority of 19,272 into an SDP majority of 5,289.

December

2   Howe announces a package of economic measures, including higher rents, rates and prescription charges.

3   Foot, in a Commons remark, denounces Peter Tatchell, a prospective Labour parliamentary candidate in Bermondsey, for his left-wing views.

8   Arthur Scargill is elected NUM President with 70 per cent of the vote.

10   Whitelaw announces more recruitment of blacks and Asians to the police force.

13   General Jaruzelski, the Polish Premier, imposes martial law, effectively destroying the Solidarity trade union as a legal force.

15   Tebbit announces the Youth Opportunities Scheme (YOPS), a year's training for all school-leavers without jobs.

Jim Mortimer is appointed Labour Party General Secretary.

16   The Labour NEC, by a vote of 15 to 14, bars Peter Tatchell from becoming Labour candidate for Bermondsey.

Heseltine abandons the Bill to increase government powers over local authorities and substitutes a Bill to enforce a single annual rate demand.

17   Lawson introduces a Bill to sell off the production interests of BNOC and British Gas.

The Law Lords uphold Bromley Council in forcing the GLC to end their cheap transport fares policy, on the grounds that London Transport was meant to be a commercial business rather than a social service.

1982

January

2   The Liberals and SDP suspend negotiations over the division of seats in their electoral alliance.

5   A Labour Party-TUC meeting at Bishop's Stortford proclaims party unity after the recent strife, but Benn later stresses that the unity must be around conference policies.

8   Spain agrees to end the Gibralter blockade.

21   After Gormley publicly opposes his Executive's call for industrial action for higher pay, a pithead ballot of NUM members defeats the strike proposal by 55 to 45 per cent.

26   Unemployment is 3,071,000 (or 11.7 per cent).

February

8   In the second reading of the Employment Bill, the SDP splits in its voting, with 17 voting for the Bill and five voting against.

13-14   A special SDP conference in London proposes that the leadership of the party be elected by all the members; this is sent out to the membership to be voted upon.

March

9   Howe's budget increases indirect taxes and reduces the PSBR by £1,000 million.

18   The government majority falls to 30 when 13 Conservatives vote to restore the reduction in the value of unemployment benefits.

21   At Greenham Common, 200 women hold a chained protest against Cruise missiles.

23   Roy Jenkins wins the Glasgow Hillhead by-election, turning a Conservative majority of 2,002 into an SDP majority of 2,038.

     The Gallup poll shows 33 per cent Alliance, 33 per cent Labour and 31 per cent Conservative support.

April

2   Argentina's armed forces seize the Falkland Islands and South Georgia, claiming them as Argentine territory.

3   In an emergency session of the Commons, the government's lack of military preparation comes under severe attack by Foot and by Conservative MPs; Foot makes a particularly effective speech in which he calls for resistance to a naked act of aggression; John Nott offers his resignation as Defence Secretary, but it is refused.

5   Lord Carrington insists on resigning as Foreign Secretary, as do Humphrey Atkins and Richard Luce, two Foreign Office Ministers; Francis Pym is appointed Foreign Secretary by Thatcher.

A naval task force sets out for the Falklands.

A TUC conference of trade union executives agrees to campaign against the Employment Bill and refuses to accept state funds for union elections.

7   A 200-mile exclusion zone around the Falklands is declared by the British government.

Benn stands out in the Commons by denouncing the British expedition and calling for a UN force to be sent instead.

25   South Georgia is recaptured by the British forces without any casualties; Thatcher asks the nation to 'Rejoice! Rejoice!'

May

2   The Argentinian battlecruiser, *General Belgrano*, is sunk by a British submarine outside the 200-mile exclusion zone; 368 Argentinian sailors are drowned.

3   The *Sun*, the most chauvinistic of a highly patriotic press, describes the sinking of the *Belgrano* with the headline 'Gotcha!', the most extreme example of the treatment of the war as a distant game.

4   Port Stanley, the Falklands capital, is bombed by the RAF; HMS *Sheffield* is sunk by an Exocet missile with the loss of 20 British lives.

6   The Conservatives, boosted by 'the Falklands factor', make big gains in the local elections.

9   A ballot of SDP members agrees with the proposal to elect a leader by a secret postal vote of the whole membership.

10   The Health Service unions begin a campaign in support of their 12 per cent pay claim.

21   The British land soldiers and marines in the Falklands at San Carlos Bay; HMS *Ardent* is sunk with 22 sailors lost.

26   HMS *Coventry* is sunk with the loss of 24 lives, while the *Atlantic Conveyor* container ship is sunk with nine lives lost.

28   British troops capture Port Darwin and Goose Green, capturing 1,400 Argentines.

June

3   The Conservatives win the Mitcham and Morden by-election through the split in the opposition after Bruce Douglas-Mann had resigned the seat to fight as an SDP candidate; a Labour majority of 618 is turned into a Conservative majority of 4,274.

6   A CND demonstration in London attracts 230,000.

7   Foot warns Labour's senior leaders to end their internal feuding if Labour is to have any chance at the next election.

8   An Argentinian airforce attack on British troops at Bluff Cove leaves 50 dead and 55 wounded, many of them hideously.

14   British forces capture Port Stanley and the Falklands War is effectively over.

16   The Labour NEC adopts a plan by 16 to ten votes for a register of acceptable non-affiliated organisations in order to isolate Trotskyist groups working within the Labour Party.

17   General Galtieri, the Argentine dictator, resigns after the defeat in the Falklands.

19   An internal Labour party report into the Militant group concludes that it is 'a well-organised caucus, centrally controlled'.

July

2   Roy Jenkins is elected SDP leader with 26,256 votes to 20,864 votes for David Owen.

20   IRA bombs at Regents Park and Hyde Park in London kill ten soldiers and injure 53 people.

26   Thatcher is infuriated at the St Paul's Thanksgiving service because the Church prays for the bereaved of both sides in the Falklands War instead of celebrating the British victory.

28   The Labour NEC orders a re-selection of a candidate for Bermondsey because of its choice of Peter Tatchell.

The Gallup poll shows 45 per cent Conservative, 26 per cent Labour and 26 per cent Alliance support.

August

2   Bob Mellish, the Labour MP for Bermondsey, resigns from the Labour Party after having given his support to an independent candidate against Labour.

A five-day strike by NHS workers closes hundreds of hospitals for all but emergency cases.

September

6-10   The TUC Annual Congress, Brighton, pledges co-ordinated action against the Employment Bill; Terry Duffy says that the unions are being pushed into a battle they do not want.

18   A Central Policy Review Staff document calling for a virtual end to the Welfare State is leaked.

20-5   The Liberal Party Assembly, Bournemouth, supports a unilateralist defence motion; Steel and Jenkins announce that they have virtually settled the SDP/Liberal dispute over the division of constituencies, with the Liberals having the larger quota of winnable seats; delegates endorse the Alliance document, *Back to Work*, which calls for a prices and incomes policy, with a large injection of government investment in capital works.

22   The TUC Day of Action in support of the Health Service workers draws an uneven response, with support greatest among miners and dockers, printworkers and transport workers.

27-   The Labour Party Annual conference, Blackpool, again
Oct 1   votes by a large majority for a unilateralist defence policy,

but votes narrowly against the nationalisation of the banks; Foot's position is strengthened by the NEC elections which further weaken the 'hard left', and Benn is forced off the key home policy committee.

October

5-8   At the Conservative annual conference, Brighton, Thatcher affirms her belief in the Health Service in a repudiation of the document leaked to the press on *18 September*.

11-14   The SDP conference is held in Cardiff, Derby and Great Yarmouth on successive days; the Council for Social Democracy rejects the statutory income policy favoured by Jenkins in favour of the flexible policy favoured by Owen.

20   In elections for the Northern Ireland Assembly, Provisional Sinn Fein, the political wing of the IRA, gains five seats.

27   The Labour NEC votes Benn off the powerful Labour-TUC liaison committee.

28   The Employment Bill is enacted, providing penalties for unions involved in 'unlawful industrial action', recognises the employer's right to dismiss strikers selectively, and provides state aid for strike ballots.

The Transport Bill is enacted, introducing private capital into the National Bus Company.

Labour narrowly wins the Birmingham Northfield by-election, turning a Conservative majority of 204 into a Labour majority of 289.

Foot is refused a High Court injunction staying the Boundary Commission report — the new boundaries give the Conservatives 20 seats as it is weighted to the suburbs and new residential areas.

November

1   Bob Mellish resigns from Parliament, forcing a by-election in Bermondsey where Labour has yet to re-select a candidate.

2   The miners vote against Scargill's call for a strike to fight pit closures and for higher pay by 61 to 39 per cent.

8   A one-day transport strike in support of the Health Service workers is called off after signs of a poor response.

10   President Leonid Brezhnev of the Soviet Union dies; he is succeeded by Yuri Andropov, who is expected to inaugurate reforms.

Lawson announces the sale of 51 per cent of the shares of Britoil, the marketing company for BNOC and British Gas.

11   The SDLP and Provisional Sinn Fein boycott the opening of the new Northern Ireland Assembly.

17   The Telecommunications Bill is introduced to privatise British Telecom (but it is not passed because of the election).

December

13   John Nott presents the Defence White Paper, with spending of £1,000 million on equipment to make up for losses from the Falklands War.

14   The health workers' union, the Confederation of Health Service Employees (COHSE), accepts the government's pay offer at its delegate conference after rejecting the alternative of an all-out strike, thereby bringing the dispute to an end.

15   The government is defeated by 290 to 272 votes (with 23 Conservatives voting against) on new immigration regulations governing the rights of entry of husbands and fiancés of women living in Britain.

21   The High Court declares that the Boundary Commission has not wrongly exercised its discretion nor misdirected itself, as claimed by Labour, but an appeal is made against the ruling.

General

Conservative Party membership is about 1.2 million.

Channel 4, a new ITV station, is launched to cater for minority interests, but finds it difficult to raise advertising revenue.

1983

January

6   In a Cabinet reshuffle, Heseltine becomes Defence Secretary and Tom King becomes Environment Secretary.

9   Peter Tatchell is finally selected as the Labour candidate for the Bermondsey by-election, with Foot's full support.

11   A Green Paper on the unions proposes compulsory secret ballots for strikes and the election of union officers.

18   The Franks Committee absolves the government of any blame for the Argentine seizure of the Falklands.

23-4   Water and sewage workers strike successfully for an increased pay offer.

26   The TUC General Council votes to boycott any talks with the government over trade union legislation.

February

1   The Public Expenditure White Paper estimates a further reduction of £500 million in government spending.

7   Labour withdraws 30,000 election leaflets in its disastrous Bermondsey campaign because they were printed by the same firm which prints *Militant*.

11   The Law Lords refuse to give the Labour leader leave to take the case of the Boundary Commission report to the High Court; this decision confirms that the next election would be fought on the new constituencies.

23   The Labour NEC votes to expel five members of the *Militant* editorial board.

24   Labour loses the Bermondsey by-election to the Liberals after a vicious campaign against Tatchell's homosexuality and his left-wing politics; a Labour majority of 11,756 is turned into a Liberal majority of 9,319.

28   South Wales miners strike over new pit closure plans and call for support.

March

10   In a pithead ballot NUM members refuses to support the South Wales miners by 61 to 39 per cent, and the strike in South Wales ends.

15   Howe's budget raises tax allowances by 14 per cent and improves social security after the PSBR had fallen £2,000 million more than projected.

21   Labour and the TUC issue a joint statement, *Partners in Rebuilding Britain*, in which a statutory incomes policy is rejected in favour of annual talks to assess incomes by the government, employers and unions.

23   President Reagan announces the Strategic Defence Initiative, a programme of space defence dubbed 'Star Wars'.

28   Shirley Williams angers Liberals by saying that Roy Jenkins is the obvious choice for prime minister of an Alliance government, though Steel later confirms her claim.

        Ian McGregor, having reduced manpower in the steel industry, is appointed NCB Chairman.

29   Labour's campaign document, *New Hope for Britain*, pledges a massive reflation programme and the removal of United States nuclear bases from Britain.

April

1   CND estimates that up to 100,000 people link arms between the Cruise missile base at Greenham Common and the Royal Ordnance factory 14 miles away.

May

5   The Conservatives generally maintain their position in the local elections.

9   A general election is announced for *9 June*.

        The British Shipbuilders Bill is enacted, changing the statutory framework of the industry to allow privatisation.

12   The Alliance manifesto, *Working Together for Britain*, promises to reduce unemployment by one million over two years through more public investment and greater government borrowing.

13   Parliament is dissolved.

16   The Labour manifesto, *New Hope for Britain*, promises to end the recession by spending which would create 2.5 million jobs within five years; it is denounced by Thatcher as 'the most extreme manifesto that has ever yet been put before the British people'.

18   The Conservative manifesto mainly defends the government's record, but promises further trade union reform.

20   Thatcher publicly rebukes Francis Pym for saying on television that it was undesirable for the government to have too large a majority.

28   An Alliance 'summit' at Ettrick Bridge fails to persuade Jenkins to step down as Prime Minister-designate in favour of Steel.

30   The New Ireland Forum holds its inaugural meeting in Dublin to draw up proposals to overcome the problems thwarting a united Ireland.

June

1   Healey, in a speech at Birmingham, causes a furore by saying that Thatcher was 'glorying in slaughter', for which he later apologises.

6   Neil Kinnock, Labour's Education spokesman, criticises Thatcher's militarism in the Falklands War by inferring that her courage was based on other people's deaths, causing another furore.

10   Polling day, with a turnout of 72.7 per cent (30,671,136 votes cast); the Conservatives win with a landslide majority of 144, while Labour suffers a disaster as it only narrowly obtains more votes than the Alliance, which is grossly under-represented in seats; Tony Benn and Shirley Williams are among the defeated; 397 Conservatives, 209 Labour, 23 Alliance (17 Liberals, six SDP), 15 various Ulster Unionists, two Plaid Cymru, two SNP, one Irish SDLP and one Provisional Sinn Fein are elected; the Conservatives obtain 13,012,315 votes (42.4 per cent), Labour 8,456,934 votes (27.6 per cent) and the Alliance 7,780,949 votes (25.4 per cent).

11   Thatcher re-forms her government, with Nigel Lawson as Chancellor of the Exchequer, Leon Brittan as Home

Secretary and Sir Geoffrey Howe as Foreign Secretary; Pym is left out of the government.

12   Clive Jenkins, leader of the white collar union ASTMS, states that Foot has declined to accept the union's nomination for the Labour leadership.

13   Roy Jenkins resigns as SDP leader ostensibly to make way for a younger man.

14   Steel says that he is not committed to leading the Liberals at the next election and takes a two-month holiday to decide his future.

15   Bernard Weatherill is elected Speaker of the Commons.
Foot formally resigns as Labour leader, with effect from the party conference.

16   It is announced that the Central Policy Review Staff is to be disbanded at the end of July.

21   David Owen is elected SDP leader without opposition.

July

6   The government Defence White Paper reaffirms the commitment to deploy Cruise missiles at Greenham Common and Molesworth if no agreement with the Soviet Union can be reached.

7   Lawson announces a total of £500 million in public expenditure, half in the NHS.

13   The Commons votes, by 344 to 263, not to reintroduce the death penalty for the murderers of police officers.

28   The Penrith and Border by-election shows the peculiar volatility of electoral patterns, as a Conservative majority of 15,421 falls to 552, with the Alliance second and Labour losing its deposit.

August

1   A government White Paper promises legislation to fix maximum expenditure levels and to impose ceilings on the rates for all local authorities in England and Wales.

5-9   The TUC Annual Congress, Blackpool, sees a victory for 'the new realism', Len Murray's term for a more pragmatic accommodation with the government, as delegates vote by 6.9 million to 3.6 million to resume discussions on proposed trade union legislation.

11-14   At the SDP conference, Salford, delegates vote against a merger of the two Alliance parties and for maintaining a separate political identity; they reject a joint selection of candidates for the European elections in favour of local consultation.

14   John Selwyn Gummer becomes Conservative Party Chairman.

16   The government sells its remaining shares in BP, raising £540 million.

19-24   The Liberal Party Assembly, Harrogate, sees Steel return to the fray; delegates vote for a United Ireland, the rejection of United States Cruise missiles and call for a halt to the government's privatisation policy; delegates also vote to give the leader final control of the manifesto and attempt to tighten up the Alliance by joint selection of candidates.

29   The TUC begins discussions with the government on the proposed union legislation.

October

2-7   The Labour Party annual conference, Brighton, elects Neil Kinnock Labour leader with 71.3 per cent of the vote, against 19.3 per cent for Roy Hattersley, 6.3 per cent for Eric Heffer and 3.1 per cent for Peter Shore; Hattersley is elected deputy leader with 67.3 per cent of the vote, against 27.9 per cent for Michael Meacher, 3.5 per cent for Denzil Davies and 1.3 per cent for Gwyneth Dunwoody; delegates reaffirm their unilateralism but defeat a motion which would reject the sale of council houses.

5   Cecil Parkinson, the Trade and Industry Secretary, admits having had an affair with his secretary, Sara Keays, who is expecting his baby.

9   A report that extremist and racist forces are infiltrating the Young Conservatives is leaked to the press.

11-14   At the Conservative party annual conference, Blackpool, Thatcher claims that the other parties are gradually moving on to the consensus created by her government.

14   Parkinson resigns after Keays tells the *Times* that he had broken his promise to marry her; Tebbit becomes Industry

Secretary and Tom King Employment Secretary

19   Owen calls for the deployment of United States Cruise missiles, thereby widening the divisions within the Alliance.

25-7   United States marines invade Grenada to overthrow a left-wing regime there; Thatcher's attempts to dissuade President Reagan are ignored, despite the island's membership of the British Commonwealth.

26   The Trade Union Bill is introduced, compelling secret ballots for strikes, union elections and political funds.

30   Pym, in a speech at Oxford, expresses dismay at the government's commitment to tax-cuts at a time of such high unemployment.

31   After the 'shadow Cabinet' elections, Hattersley becomes Labour Treasury spokesman.

The NUM imposes an overtime ban after it rejects a 5.2 per cent pay offer.

November

1   Heseltine warns that CND demonstrators would be shot if they got near the Cruise bunkers at Greenham Common.

12   Gerry Adams is elected Provisional Sinn Fein President; a strategy based on seeking electoral support as well as military action against the British is adopted.

13   Heseltine announces that United States Cruise missiles had arrived at Greenham.

15   In violent demonstrations outside the Greenham base, 141 CND demonstrators are arrested.

17   Lawson holds the PSBR at £8,000 million and warns of possible tax increases.

18   The NGA print union is charged £10,000 over its refusal to lift mass picketing of Eddy Shah's print works at Warrington.

25-6   A two-day strike halts Fleet Street newspapers in protest at the NGA fine, and violent clashes between pickets and police occur outside Shah's printworks.

28   The government offers 100 million shares in Cable and Wireless for sale.

30   The Court of Appeal orders the seizure of £10 million of the NGA's assets for contempt of court in not lifting the mass picketing at Warrington, and grants an injunction against further sympathy action in Fleet Street.

December

8	The Lords votes to have its proceedings televised.
9	Lord Carrington is appointed NATO Secretary-General.

The NGA is fined £525,000 for serious contempt of court over the Warrington dispute.

13 Len Murray publicly repudiates the TUC employment committee when it votes to support a 24-hour strike in sympathy with the NGA.

14 The TUC General Council supports Murray over the proposed NGA strike by 29 to 21 votes and the strike is called off.

17 An IRA car bomb outside Harrods department store in London kills six and injures 90 people.

20 Patrick Jenkin, the Environment Secretary, introduces the Rates Bill to fix a ceiling on the rates set by high-spending councils.

29 Peter Walker, the Energy Secretary, pleads for policies to reduce unemployment and promote economic expansion in an address to the Tory Reform Group.

General

Labour Party membership is 6,454,000.

Boris Sarlvik and Ivor Crewe, in *Decade of Dealignment*, argue that partisan voting is no longer so closely tied to social class.

1984

January

25   In a major blow to the TUC's 'new realism' policy, Howe bans trade unions at the Government Communications Headquarters (GCHQ) at Cheltenham, provoking union outrage.

February

9   President Yuri Andropov of the Soviet Union dies and is succeeded by Konstantin Chernenko.

10   Harold Macmillan becomes Earl of Stockton on his 90th birthday.

21   Thatcher rejects the report of a Commons Select Committee by insisting that union membership at GCHQ involves an inherent conflict with the national interest.

Scottish miners strike over the closure of Polmaise Colliery.

28   There is a half-day stoppage in much of the Civil Service in protest at the GCHQ ban on unions.

29   The TUC withdraws from the NEDC in protest at the GCHQ ban.

March

1   Tony Benn returns to the Commons after winning the Chesterfield by-election.

5   Yorkshire miners strike in protest at the proposed closure of Cortonwood Colliery, setting off a national miners' strike.

6   The NCB confirms that it will close 20 high-cost pits.

8   The NUM Executive gives official support to regional strike action by 21 to three votes; the strike spreads through 'flying pickets' as a ballot is not called.

13   Lawson's budget reduces corporation tax and increases income tax allowances, taking 850,000 people out of the tax system.

14   A picket is killed in fighting between pro- and anti-strike miners at Ollerton Colliery in Nottinghamshire.

15   As a result of the miners' basic appeal to solidarity through the use of picketing, 140 pits are stopped within a week of the strike's start, but the Nottinghamshire pits vote to defy union solidarity and remain at work.

18   Police stop Kent miners from crossing the Dartford and Blackwall tunnels to prevent them picketing, a move denounced by Labour as a clear infringement of personal liberty.

19   British Rail announces that the Sealink ferry service is to be sold.

23   Sarah Tisdall, a junior employee at the Ministry of Defence, is sentenced to six months' imprisonment for giving a confidential document to the *Guardian*, a decision attacked by Labour Home Affairs spokesman, Gerald Kaufmann, as dangerous to freedom.

The Gallup poll shows 41 per cent Conservative, 38 per cent Labour and 19 per cent Alliance support.

April

2   Norman Fowler, the Health and Social Services Secretary, announces a fundamental re-examination of the NHS.

11   A one-day teachers' strike for higher pay begins a campaign of selective disruption in schools.

12   The Telecommunications Bill, providing for the transfer of British Telecom to private ownership, is enacted.

17   Yvonne Fletcher, a policewoman, is killed and eleven anti-Ghaddaffi demonstrators are hurt in London's Belgravia when shots are fired from the Libyan Embassy, which is immediately besieged by police.

20   An NUM delegate conference votes against holding a national ballot for strike action and resolves to spread the strike by all other means.

22   Britain breaks diplomatic relations with Libya.

28   The Libyan embassy is evacuated and its members deported.

May

3   Labour and the Alliance make big gains in the local elections, while the Alliance comes second in three by-elections at Stafford, South-west Surrey, and Cynon Valley.

4   Kinnock says that the miners' strike would have to be settled by a halt to pit closures.

6   Scargill claims that the miners are winning the dispute and that coal stocks are down to eight weeks.

11   As a compromise to save the threatened Ravenscraig steel works in Scotland, two trainloads of coal per day are allowed by the NUM.

15   Hattersley says that the claim that unemployment could be cured by a massive boost to demand was not really convincing.

29   A battle at the Orgreave Coke Works between miners and police leaves 64 injured and 84 arrested.

June

1   Kinnock condemns violence on the picket lines.

2   Thatcher entertains the South African Prime Minister, P.W. Botha, at Chequers, the first visit by a South African leader for 23 years; Tom King announces that the unions are to be deprived of legal immunity when strikes are called without a ballot under the new Trade Union Bill.

7-9   A summit of the West's leaders in London agrees to new proposals to meet the problems of international debt.

14   In the European Assembly elections, there is a low turnout of 32.4 per cent; 45 Conservatives, 32 Labour, two Ulster Unionists, one SNP and one Irish SDLP are elected.

     The SDP captures Portsmouth South, turning a Conservative majority of 12,335 into an SDP majority of 1,341.

18   Pitched battles between miners and police, the worst of the strike, occur at Orgreave, where police use cavalry charges and short-shield units to beat back the pickets; many miners, including Scargill, are injured.

23   A march of 10,000 miners and their supporters in London ends in violence outside the Houses of Parliament, while a rail strike called in sympathy draws uneven support.

25-6   The EEC summit at Fontainebleau resolves the problems of the British contribution to the Community budget, reducing it by half.

26   The Rate Bill, enabling the government to place a ceiling on rates, in effect rate-capping local authorities, is enacted.

28   Ron Todd is elected TGWU General Secretary, confirming the left's hold on the union.

The Lords reject, by 191 to 143 votes, a government plan to cancel the 1985 elections to the GLC.

July

2   The TUC Steel Committee pledges unanimously to maintain production with whatever coal comes in.

5   Thatcher announces an amendment to the Paving Bill to prolong the GLCs life by a year without the need for elections.

9-21   A national dock strike is called over the use of non-registered labour to unload imported coal at Scunthorpe, but it is called off after lorry drivers threaten to burn down the docks.

11   The NUM conference votes to adopt new disciplinary procedures in defiance of a High Court ruling forbidding the vote.

12   The Mirror Group of newspapers is sold to Robert Maxwell's Pergamon Press.

16   Justice Glidewell rules in the High Court that the decision to ban unions at GCHQ without consultation was contrary to natural justice, but the government appeals.

24   Patrick Jenkin rate-caps 18 local authorities, including the GLC.

25   The government orders British Shipbuilders to sell off its profitable warship yards by March 1986.

26   The Trade Union Bill is enacted, removing legal immunity for unions who hold a strike without a ballot, providing regular voting on the retention of political funds, and enforcing secret ballots for union officers.

31   Thatcher makes a savage attack on Kinnock in the Commons for refusing to oppose the coal strike, while Martin Flannery is suspended from the House after referring to 'tame Tory judges'.

August

6   The Appeal Court overrules the High Court decision on union recognition at GCHQ.

British Telecom becomes a public limited company.

22   After a pitched battle with miners in Armthorpe, a South Yorkshire village, riot police run through people's houses in search of pickets; the tension in many miners' villages in the area reaches a near-insurrectionary level.

23   Hattersley says that a political strike would not deserve to succeed, though he makes it clear that he does not see the coal dispute as political.

24   The TGWU calls a national dock strike again, in protest at steelworkers unloading coal that dockers had refused to touch.

September

2   Frank Chapple of the electricians' union, the Electrical, Electricians Trades and Plumbers Union (EETPU) warns that his workers in the power stations would cross miners' picket lines if necessary.

3-7   The TUC Annual Congress, Brighton, votes overwhelmingly for financial aid to the miners, and for a complete blockade of the movement of coal and coke.

4   Norman Willis is elected TUC General Secretary with 7.3 million votes to 2.7 million for David Lea.

10   Prior resigns as Northern Ireland Secretary to work for the GEC electrical company, claiming to have represented 'the politics of one nation' in the Cabinet; he is replaced by Douglas Hurd.

10-12   At the SDP conference at Buxton, Jenkins and Williams call for closer co-operation with the Liberals, differentiating themselves from Owen's calls for a clearer distinction between the two parties.

13   The SNP, in Inverness for its 50th conference, votes by 246 to 238 for a motion demanding a Scottish constitutional convention.

Hattersley claims that there is a need for a detailed and voluntary incomes policy.

17-22   The Liberal Party Assembly, Bournemouth, votes for

the removal of United States Cruise missiles by 611 to 556 votes.

18   The dock strike, never fully obeyed, is called off having won a partial success.

20   The TGWU directs its members not to transport fuel across miners' picket lines, though this direction is often disobeyed in face of the lucrative rewards of helping to break the strike.

21   The Bishop of Durham, Dr David Jenkins, preaches reconciliation and accuses the government and the NCB of indifference to poverty.

23   Hattersley, in a speech to the Socialist Economic Review Conference in London, calls for a conception of socialism as social ownership — where enterprises are owned by their employees and autonomous from the state — and calls on Labour to 'abandon the idea of a mixed economy'.

October

1-5   The Labour Party annual conference, Bournemouth, overwhelmingly passes a motion condemning the police for organised violence against the miners, and votes against the wishes of the NEC to keep the police out of future industrial disputes; Leon Brittan, the Home Secretary, accuses Labour of taking leave of its senses; despite the pleas of Callaghan and Healey, the delegates support a non-nuclear defence policy by an 80 per cent majority.

3   Leslie Curtis, the Police Federation President, attacks the Labour Party and raises doubts as to whether the police would serve under an extreme Labour government; he is rebuked for this speech by superior officers in the police force.

9   Clive Ponting is sent for trial over the leaking of government documents to Tam Dalyell, a Labour MP accusing the government of unnecessarily sinking the Argentine battlecruiser *General Belgrano*.

9-12   At the Conservative Party annual conference, Brighton, Leon Brittan declares that the coal strike is not an industrial dispute but an attack on the rule of law.

10   Scargill is fined £1,000 and the NUM £200,000 for contempt, in treating the miners' strike as official despite the lack of a ballot.

12   The Cabinet is nearly assassinated by an IRA bomb which explodes in the Grand Hotel, Brighton, during the Conservative Party conference, killing five and injuring 31; Tebbit is seriously injured and Thatcher narrowly escapes death.

15   Talks between the NUM and the NCB, under ACAS auspices, break down after two weeks due to fundamental differences in approach between the two sides.

17   The coal deputies union, the National Association of Collierymen, Overseers and Deputies (NACODS) armed with a vote of 82.5 per cent for industrial action against pit closures and the refusal of the NCB to pay deputies who cross picket lines, calls a strike for *25 October* which would close all pits immediately.

24   At the last minutes NACODS calls off its strike after the NCB agrees to pay deputies who refuse to cross picket lines and to set up a new procedure to consider pit closures.

25   The NUM assets are ordered to be seized by the High Court as the union refuses to pay fines, but most of the funds have been transferred to Dublin, Luxembourg and Switzerland.

28   It is revealed that an NUM delegation had been appealing for money from the Libyan trade unions.

November

6   President Reagan is triumphantly re-elected, beating his Democratic opponent, Walter Mondale, in the United States Presidential elections.

10-24   After the promise of deferred bonus payments 11,000 miners return to work, though the return slackens after the cut-off date for payment of the bonus.

12   Lawson, in his autumn statement, predicts that £1,500 million will be available for tax cuts in 1985.

13   Willis meets hostility at Aberavon when he denounces violence in the coal strike.

15   Edward du Cann is defeated by Cranley Onslow for the chair of the 1922 Committee in a victory for the Thatcher wing of the party.

18-19   Thatcher meets Dr Fitzgerald at Chequers, but tells a press conference that the proposals of the New Ireland

Forum were not under consideration because they impinged upon the constitutional status of Ulster.

22   The Law Lords finally uphold the government action in banning unions at GCHQ on the grounds that national security was involved.

The Local Government Bill, abolishing the GLC and the metropolitan counties, is introduced.

26   The TGWU is fined £200,000 for refusing to hold a ballot for the Austin Rover car strike; the fine is collected by the Queen's Remonstrator.

26-8   More than £8,000 million is raised from the sale of British Telecom, with a million individuals applying for small shares.

30   A taxi driver driving two strikebreakers to work in South Wales is killed by concrete posts thrown through his windscreen.

The High Court removes Scargill and four other trustees of the NUM as unfit to hold their posts, and appoints a Receiver in their stead to get the union funds back.

December

5   Sir Keith Joseph, the Education Secretary, withdraws radical changes in grants to students which would have increased parental contributions after facing backbench Conservative protests.

The TUC resumes its attendance at the NEDC, having failed to defeat the government on the GCHQ affair.

13   The Conservatives retain Enfield Southgate in the by-election, but their majority is cut from 15,799 to 4,711, with the Alliance second.

14   Scargill is fined £1,000 for obstruction at Orgreave in June and refuses to appeal because 'I have no faith in getting a fair trial'.

18   Patrick Jenkin announces a £300 million cut in local authorities' allowance for housing investment.

19   Thatcher signs an agreement in Peking transferring Hong Kong to China in 1997, while allowing the colony the freedom to maintain its political and economic lifestyle for 50 years.

20   The Nottingham NUM votes to delete from its area

constitution the rule giving precedence to national union rules, provoking the accusation that it is going to revive the 'Spencer' company union of the 1920s.

29   Peter Walker, the Energy Secretary, promises that there will be no power cuts in 1985, further demoralising the miners.

General

TUC membership is 10,082,000.

Francis Pym, in *The Politics of Consent*, accuses Thatcher of being more like a President than a Prime Minister, and says that her regime is inflexible and intolerant.

1985

January

8   The highest peak demand for electricity ever recorded occurs without any trouble, highlighting the miners' failure to affect power supplies.

14   The pound falls to US$1.1105 despite a rise in MLR.

22   In the Public Spending White Paper, the government proposes cuts in public spending in 1985/6 followed by a period of restraint.

23   The proceedings of the House of Lords are televised for the first time.

February

5-6 The army undergoes a major operation to remove peace protestors from Molesworth missile base.

7   The NCB claims that 50 per cent of the miners are now working, a claim denied by the NUM.

11   Clive Ponting is acquitted after the jury agrees that his leak of documents did not affect national security.

18   In the Commons debate on the sinking of the *Belgrano*, Heseltine accuses Ponting of duplicity.

20   The NUM rejects proposals for a settlement of the coal strike worked out by Willis, who then refuses to attend a miners' rally in London.

24   The NUM rally in London ends in violence as police fight marchers, many of them women and children, in Whitehall.

26   The teachers begin industrial action in schools in a campaign which lasts throughout the year.

March

3   The NUM delegate conference calls off the strike by 98 to 91 votes against the advice of Scargill; the NCB refuses an amnesty for the 700 miners dismissed during the dispute.

4   Kinnock says that an amnesty is impossible for those miners convicted of serious crimes.

5   The NUM returns to work a year after the strike began, though the Kent area makes a forlorn attempt for a few days to continue the strike.

6   Kinnock tells NATO officials in Brussels of his hostility to Reagan's 'Star Wars' policy, which creates the danger of a new arms race.

10   President Konstantin Chernenko of the Soviet Union dies and is succeeded as Communist Party leader by Mikhail Gorbachev.

The GLC votes to adopt a legal budget after the left calls for the rate-capping law to be ignored; Ken Livingstone breaks from the left on the issue.

15   Howe, at the Royal United Services Institute, urges the 'utmost deliberation' over Star Wars.

19   Lawson's budget raises indirect taxes but increases the income tax thresholds by more than the rate of inflation, taking 800,000 families out of the tax system, and allocates £1,000 million for special employment creating measures.

21   South African police at Uitenhage fire on a black demonstration mourning the 25th anniversary of the Sharpeville massacre, killing 18 and wounding 36; a virtual insurrection is set off in the black townships.

The Gallup poll shows 39.5 per cent Labour, 33 per cent Conservative and 25.5 per cent Alliance support.

April

2   The NUM delegate conference votes against Scargill's advice to lift the ban on overtime in force since October 1983.

6   Thatcher, in a visit to Malaysia, claims to have 'seen off the miners', while calling the NUM leaders 'the enemy within', causing uproar in Britain.

30   The Lords upholds the purpose of the Bill abolishing the GLC by only 213 to 209 votes in the committee stage when an amendment to establish a London Metropolitan Authority, similar to the GLC, is defeated.

May

1	Peter Walker, in a speech at Cambridge, calls on the government to review its priorities in order to reduce unemployment effectively.
2	The Conservatives suffer extensive losses in the county council elections.
10	The remaining government holdings in British Aerospace are sold.
14	Francis Pym defends the creation of Centre Forward, a Conservative group opposed to the leadership, but says that it will not act as a party within a party after being sharply criticised for disloyalty, and the group is virtually stillborn.
15	The Sealink subsidiary of British Rail is sold, despite protest strikes.
16	A government White Paper proposing greater police powers links strike picketing with football hooliganism.
18-20	At the British Communist Party Congress, the Eurocommunists, a group which seeks to distance the party from traditional working-class militancy, wins all 45 seats on the Executive and expels the *Morning Star* editor and his deputy; the *Morning Star* ceases to be the official Communist Party newspaper.
20	A 24-hour strike on the London Underground, called by the NUR without a ballot and in defiance of a court injunction, fails when most workers cross picket lines.

June

3	Norman Fowler, the Social Services Secretary, announces a major review of the Welfare State; it includes the phasing out of SERPs (State Earnings Related Pensions), the reform of housing benefit, the replacement of supplementary benefit by an income support grant, and the replacement of family income supplement by family credit paid through the wage packet; the scheme draws widespread condemnation from the CBI, the Labour Party and from various poverty action groups.
10	Larry Whitty becomes General Secretary of the Labour Party and proceeds to modernise its image and organisation.
15	Ron Todd is re-elected TGWU General Secretary after

a move is made to oust him by claims that his first ballot victory was the result of ballot-rigging.

16   Liverpool Council, strongly influenced by the Militant Tendency fixes an illegal rate in defiance of government rate-capping policies.

28   Liverpool councillors are served with notices of personal surcharges for setting an illegal rate.

July

3   Lambeth Council, controlled by Labour's 'hard left', surrenders to government pressure to set a legal rate, leaving Liverpool isolated in its resistance.

4   The Liberals win the Brecon and Radnor by-election, turning a Conservative majority of 8,784 into a Liberal majority of 559 and pushing the Conservatives into third place.

8   Howe lifts the ban on imports from Argentina.

13   The Live Aid rock concert, organised by Bob Geldof, raises £40 million worldwide in an attempt to alleviate starvation in East Africa; this highly popular event, signifying a 'responsible' rock music concerned with charity rather than rebellion, attracts the interest of political strategists seeking the support of youth.

16   The Local Government Bill, abolishing the GLC and the metropolitan authorities, is enacted.

    The Representation of the People Bill is enacted, raising the deposits paid by candidates for election from £150 to £1,000 in order to reduce the number of silly candidates, while reducing the amount of votes needed to avoid forfeiture of the deposit from 12½ per cent to 5 per cent.

26   Thatcher expresses her strong opposition to any showing of the BBC *Real Lives* programme containing an interview with a Sinn Fein leader.

29   Leon Brittan writes to the BBC asking it not to show the *Real Lives* programme because it enabled the IRA to 'advocate or justify the use of murder . . . before a huge public audience'.

30   The BBC Board of Governors, under great pressure from the government, cancels the *Real Lives* programme and agrees to show an edited version at a later date.

August

7   BBC and ITV journalists hold a one-day strike in protest at the cancellation of the *Real Lives* documentary.

Britoil's shares go on public sale and are over-subscribed by four times.

The High Court refuses to grant an injunction which would prevent Nottinghamshire miners from setting up their own union.

28   The NUR holds a ballot for strike action in support of guards threatened with redundancy over the introduction of driver-only trains, but the call for strike action is narrowly defeated.

The Labour-TUC document, *A New Partnership: A New Britain*, stresses the workers' right to a voice in company policies and calls for a gradual expansion of the economy.

September

2   In a Cabinet reshuffle, Douglas Hurd becomes Home Secretary in place of Leon Brittan, who becomes Trade Secretary; Norman Tebbit is appointed as the Conservative Party Chairman, with the novelist Jeffrey Archer as his deputy.

2-6   The TUC Annual Congress at Blackpool narrowly averts a major split when it decides not to expel the AUEW for accepting state funds for postal ballots.

6   A Liberal document is leaked blaming SDP divisions for hindering the Alliance's path to power, and causes new tensions within the Alliance.

8-11   At the SDP conference, Torquay, David Steel heals divisions within the Alliance by attacking the author of the leaked Liberal document, but both Steel and Owen reject calls for a single Alliance leader; delegates vote for a budgetary expansion of £5,000 million.

9-10   In serious rioting and arson in Birmingham's Handsworth district, two Asians are accidentally killed.

13   Britain expels 25 Soviet diplomats for espionage, provoking a series of retaliatory expulsions between London and Moscow.

16   An indefinite strike in Liverpool in support of the

council's defiance of the government has to be called off because of the poor response from workers in the city.

16-21   At the Liberal Party Assembly in Dundee, meeting in a mood of restrained optimism, Steel differentiates himself from Owen by saying that the largest party in any hung parliament must first attempt to form a government; delegates vote to modify their commitment to a United Ireland in order to align themselves more closely to the SDP.

19   Hattersley announces a plan for the repatriation of British capital from abroad to redirect it within Britain.

25   The Group of Five leading financial countries, meeting in New York, agree to co-ordinate intervention to prevent the overvalued dollar from depreciating too rapidly.

28   The accidental shooting of Mrs Cherry Groce by police during a search of her house leads to new rioting in Brixton.

29-   The Labour Party conference, Bournemouth, votes to
Oct 4   demand that a Labour government restore the NUM's legally mulcted funds, but Kinnock rejects any prior commitment to do so; Kinnock rallies majority support in the party when he attacks the Liverpool Militants for playing politics with jobs and services, but earns a bitter resentment from the 'hard left'; delegates overwhelmingly vote against the establishment of separate black sections.

October

6-7   In rioting at Broadwater Farm Estate in Tottenham, north London, caused by the death of a black woman during a police search, guns are fired and a policeman is killed by a mob wielding machetes; Sir Kenneth Newman, the Metropolitan Police Commissioner, warns Londoners that CS gas and plastic bullets may be used next time.

8-12   At the Conservative Party annual conference, Blackpool, Hurd promises that a Public Order Act would strengthen police powers, while Thatcher offers the police a 'blank cheque' for more equipment and recruits in order to enforce the law against street violence and riots.

15   Lord Aldington warns the Lords Select Committee on Overseas Trade that unless policies were changed the decline in British manufacturing could become irreversible.

16-23   At the Commonwealth Prime Ministers' conference in

Nassau, Thatcher strenuously opposes sanctions against South Africa and a compromise is reached whereby only minor sanctions are imposed pending the visit of an Eminent Persons Group from the Commonwealth to South Africa.

18   A majority of Nottinghamshire miners votes to form the Union of Democratic Mineworkers (UDM) as a rival to the NUM.

30   The Transport Bill is enacted, privatising the National Bus Company.

November

6   Lawson, in his autumn statement, says that he expects public expenditure to increase by £5,000 million over the next two years.

12   The government postpones the sale of the Trustee Savings Bank (TSB) after the Court of Session at Edinburgh rules that in Scotland the bank belongs to its depositors.

14   The sequestration order on the NUM is lifted after the union purges itself of contempt.

15   The Anglo-Irish Accord, whereby the Irish and British governments agree that any change in Northern Ireland's status must only be with the consent of the majority of its people, and the Irish Republic is given a consultative role in Ulster affairs through Intergovernmental Conferences, is signed at Hillsborough Castle near Belfast by Thatcher and Fitzgerald; Unionist reaction is furious.

Ian Gow resigns as Minister of State at the Treasury in protest at the Hillsborough Accord.

19-21   President Reagan meets Gorbachev in a summit at Geneva and, while nothing substantial is achieved, their general friendliness is widely marked as beginning an attempt to ease international tensions.

20   The Commons votes by 275 to 263 against the televising of its own proceedings.

22   Liverpool City Council, on the eve of bankruptcy, accepts a financial compromise which capitalises funds in its house repair account.

23   A huge Unionist protest rally against the Hillsborough Accord is held in Belfast.

27   The Labour NEC votes by 21 to five to suspend the

Liverpool District Labour Party while investigations of corruption and malpractice take place, and are accused by the 'hard left' of conducting a McCarthyite witch-hunt.

Heath attacks the government's policy of privatisation and warns that a national emergency is being created by unemployment.

29   An IRA threat to a building firm in Northern Ireland which is undertaking defence contracts leads to the withdrawal of many firms from contract work for the security forces.

December

3   A Church of England Commisson on Urban Priority Areas describes the government's policies as unacceptable and calls for emergency action to alleviate the plight of the inner cities; it is denounced by Conservatives as a Marxist document.

13   The Westland Helicopter Company, facing bankruptcy, rejects a takeover bid by a European consortium engineered by Heseltine, the Defence Secretary, in favour of a rescue deal by the United States Sikorsky company and the Italian firm, Fiat.

16   Leon Brittan, the Trade Secretary, says that Westland is free to choose whichever rescue bid is the most favourable and indicates his scepticism concerning the European bid favoured by Heseltine.

A government White Paper on the NHS decides to retain SERPs under pressure from the CBI.

17   All 15 Unionist MPs resign their seats in protest at the Hillsborough Accord and hope to turn the mass by-election campaign into a mini-referendum on the deal.

19   The Cabinet snubs Heseltine by affirming the freedom of Westland to choose the most favourable rescue bid.

29   Kinnock stressses that re-nationalisation of industries privatised by the government is not a top priority for a future Labour government.

General

Lawson admits that the coal strike cost the government and the NCB £4,600 million and other nationalised industries £2,750 million. The number of days lost in strikes in 1985, at 6.4 million, is the lowest since 1967 and sharply down on the 1984 total of 27.1 million.

Lord Blake, in *The Conservative Party from Peel to Thatcher*, argues that Thatcher succeeded where Heath failed because the intellectual atmosphere for pro-market ideas was created only in the 1970s.

1986

January

3 Heseltine makes public a letter to Sir David Horne, the financial adviser to the European consortium, warning Westland that if it accepts the Sikorsky/Fiat bid it may be prevented from participating in other military projects because of technical incompatibility.

6 Sir Patrick Mayhew, the Solicitor General, sends a private letter to Heseltine asking him to avoid 'material inaccuracies' in his warning to Westland; the letter is mysteriously leaked to the press.

8 The Westland company finally turns down the European consortium bid.

9 Heseltine walks out of a Cabinet meeting after accusing Thatcher of manipulating the issue and then resigns as Defence Secretary, to be replaced by George Younger.

13 The Public Order Bill, introducing the offence of disorderly conduct to be applied at football matches and strike pickets, is given a second reading in the Commons by 292 to 201 votes.

15 The White Paper on Expenditure projects a fall in public spending as a percentage of Gross National Product (GNP) from 46½ per cent in 1982/3 to 41 per cent by 1988/9.

22 Tam Dalyell names Colette Bow, the Head of Information at Leon Brittan's Department of Trade and Industry, as responsible for the leak of the Mayhew letter during a Commons debate.

23 The Unionists gain their massive endorsement in the Ulster by-elections, but the SDLP wins Newry and Armagh.

24 Brittan resigns from the government, accepting responsibility for leaking the Mayhew letter; Paul Channon succeeds him as Trade and Industry Secretary.

26-7 Rupert Murdoch moves his printing plant from central London to Wapping in east London after dismissing 5,000 employees who refused to sign a no-strike deal; the employees, members of the National Graphical Association (NGA) and Society of General and Allied Trades (SOGAT 82) print unions, strike while members of the EETPU electricians union undertake their printing work. SOGAT calls for a boycott of Murdoch's newspapers.

February

6   Thatcher is overruled by the Cabinet and is forced to veto a takeover bid for BL by Ford.

10   The £17 million assets of SOGAT are seized for contempt of court after the union refuses to lift the boycott of Murdoch's newspapers.

15-16   Police use riot shields at Wapping to break up a demonstration addressed by Tony Benn, who accuses them of launching an unprovoked attack.

17   A Single European Act is signed by Britain and other EEC countries tightening the cohesion of the Community in social and economic affairs.

March

3   Violence and intimidation mark a one-day Loyalist strike in Ulster against the Hillsborough Accord; much commercial and industrial life is brought to a standstill.

4   Eddie Shah launches a new colour newspaper, *Today*, run on low costs, and forces other Fleet Street papers to become more competitive.

5   The High Court dismisses appeals by Lambeth and Liverpool councillors against surcharges imposed on them as a punishment for refusing to set legal rates on time.

7   Channon gives his consent to the sale of Vickers Shipbuilding and Engineering, virtually completing the privatisation of the profitable warship yards.

18   Lawson's budget reduces income and corporation tax, abolishes capital transfer tax for gifts, and promises tax-free personal equity plans on capital gains in an attempt to encourage wider share ownership.

26   Kinnock is set back when the Labour NEC is unable to expel twelve Militants, the 'hard left' members having walked out to deny the meeting a quorum.

     The Local Government Bill is enacted, prohibiting political publicity and forcing local authorities to set a rate by the first day of the new financial year.

April

1   The GLC and the six metropolitan county councils cease to exist as the London borough councils and the metropolitan district councils take over their functions.

10   Labour gains Fulham in a by-election victory; the moderate candidate turns a Conservative majority of 4,789 into a Labour majority of 3,503.

15   Setting off from British bases, United States F-111 aircraft are launched in air strikes against Tripoli and Benghazi in Libya as retaliation for Ghaddafii's support of terrorism; about 130 people, mainly civilians and including Ghadaffi's baby daughter, are killed.

     The Shops Bill, which seeks to lift the ban on Sunday trading, is defeated by 296 to 282 votes as 68 Conservative MPs vote against the government.

17   Thatcher modifies her support for the United States air attack on Libya by saying that she could not envisage Britain being used as a base for any such future attacks.

     Three British hostages are killed in Beirut after the Libyan raids; Nezar Hindawi, a Jordanian, attempts unsuccessfully to use his pregnant, and unknowing, Irish girlfriend to place a bomb on an El Al aircraft at Heathrow.

22   Labour launches its Freedom and Fairness campaign, dropping its red flag logo in favour of the red rose of the European socialists, in an appeal to moderate working-class voters.

26   The world's worst ever nuclear accident occurs at Chernobyl in the Soviet Union, where fire burns down the nuclear reactor, releasing a major radioactive cloud across Europe.

29   Bill Jordan is elected AEU President, consolidating the anti-left-wing control of the union.

May

3   In renewed violence at Wapping, 150 demonstrators and 175 police are reported hurt in clashes.

8   The Liberals capture Ryedale from the Conservatives,

turning a Conservative majority of 16,142 into a Liberal majority of 4,940; the Conservative majority in West Derbyshire is reduced from 15,325 to only 100.

The Conservatives lose heavily in borough and district council elections to Labour and the Alliance.

SOGAT regains control of its assets after apologising to the Court for its contempt, but Brenda Dean, General Secretary of SOGAT, is severely criticised by the Wapping militants for doing so.

13   Hattersley, in a speech at Bournemouth, promises a tough framework for public spending and borrowing by a future Labour government if employment is to be created.

19   The Eminent Persons Group sent to South Africa by the Commonwealth ends its visit in disgust after six days when South African forces raid alleged African National Congress (ANC) targets in Zambia, Zimbabwe and Botswana.

21   Sir Keith Joseph retires from the government and is succeeded as Education Secretary by Kenneth Baker.

30   John Stalker, the Deputy Chief Constable of Manchester, under suspicion of consorting with criminal elements, is removed as the head of an inquiry into the alleged 'shoot to kill' policy of the Ulster police.

June

5   David Owen, in a speech in Bonn, reaffirms his belief that Polaris must be replaced by a more modern nuclear weapon like Trident, undermining attempts within the Alliance to heal divisions with the Liberals, who oppose Trident.

12   Tom King, the Northern Ireland Secretary, announces that the elections to the Northern Ireland Assembly are to be indefinitely postponed.

Derek Hatton, supporter of Militant and deputy leader of Liverpool council, is finally expelled from the Labour Party.

26-7   The EEC summit is prevented from imposing immediate sanctions on South Africa by Thatcher's opposition, and it is agreed that Howe should first visit southern Africa in a bid to begin conciliation.

30   Scargill, in a speech to the NUM conference at Tenby,

declares that industrial action is still necessary to resist NCB plans for pit closures, but he meets a cool response.

July

3   Nicholas Ridley, the Environment Secretary, postpones the privatisation of water until after the next election.

17   The United States Senate votes by 87 to ten to ratify an extradition treaty with Britain which removes political liability from offences involving violence, thereby opening the way for the extradition of IRA suspects.

Labour holds the seat at the Newcastle-under-Lyme by-election, but the moderate candidate is unable to prevent the Labour majority falling from 2,804 to 799.

20   The *Sunday Times* attributes to 'sources within the Palace' its report that the Queen is 'dismayed' at the possible break-up of the Commonwealth because of Thatcher's obduracy over South African sanctions; the report is denied as constitutional embarrassment results.

24   The Commonwealth Games open in Edinburgh, but are boycotted by 32 countries in protest at Thatcher's stand against sanctions.

Howe is publicly rebuked by Zambia's President Kaunda at Lusaka airport for his government's opposition to sanctions.

Partnership for Progress, the Alliance programme, modifies the earlier insistence that proportional representation is a prerequisite for any pact made with another party by saying that it is only a consideration.

A Commons Select Committee into the Westland affair censures five top civil servants, including two senior Downing Street aides, but Thatcher rejects their criticisms.

29   Botha, in a meeting with Howe, rejects the possibility of freeing the jailed nationalist Nelson Mandela or of recognising the ANC.

31   The High Court bans mass pickets at Wapping.

Inflation, at 2.4 per cent, is at its lowest since November 1967.

Unemployment, at 3,279,000, reaches a record level.

August

3-5   A mini-summit of Britain, Australia, Canada, India, Zambia, Zimbabwe and the Bahamas to discuss sanctions against South Africa fails, with Thatcher maintaining that any British sanctions would be voluntary.

7   Peter Robinson, the Democratic Unionist Party (DUP) deputy leader, leads a Loyalist group over the Irish border and is arrested after violent incidents at a police station.

14   A Loyalist demonstration in Dundalk, in the Irish Republic, when Peter Robinson makes a court appearance, is attacked with petrol bombs.

19   Harry Phibbs, the editor of the Young Conservative magazine *New Agenda*, is served an injunction from Norman Tebbit after he accuses Harold Macmillan of war crimes for handing over anti-Communist Russians to the Red Army in 1945; he is forced to withdraw the journal and apologises unreservedly.

22   John Stalker is reinstated after being found innocent of consorting with criminals in Manchester.

September

1-5   At the TUC Annual Congress, Brighton, print union pickets assault Eric Hammond, the EETPU leader, because of his role in the Wapping dispute; delegates endorse *People at Work: New Rights, New Responsibilities*, a joint Labour-TUC document providing for a new legal framework for unions, including ballots for strike action.

14-17   The SDP conference at Harrogate supports a tough defence policy statement calling for a European nuclear deterrent but, in an attempt to conciliate the Liberals, delegates do not rigidly insist on a replacement for Polaris.

16   EEC foreign ministers impose sanctions on South Africa, but Thatcher and West Germany's Chancellor Kohl distance themselves from the decision.

22   The Stockholm Security conference adopts an arms agreement setting limits on East-West military activity and establishing inspection systems to check that these limits are kept.

22-6   The Liberal Party Assembly at Eastbourne rejects Steel's bid for unity within the Alliance on defence by voting against a European nuclear deterrent by 652 to 625 votes; in order to maintain the Alliance and its electoral credibility, Steel defies the conference by pledging himself to maintain and update Polaris.

28- The Labour Party annual conference, Blackpool, is a suc-
Oct 3 cessful one for the leadership, with Kinnock reaffirming Labour's alliance with the United States by stressing that non-nuclear facilities essential to NATO security would be maintained, and with Hattersley's ideas of social ownership endorsed; delegates affirm the expulsion of the Militants by 6,146,000 to 325,000; however, a motion to phase out nuclear power within five years is carried by 4,213,000 to 2,143,000.

29 United States Defence Secretary Caspar Weinberger causes uproar when he says on the BBC *Panorama* programme that Labour defence policies would lead to the break-up of NATO.

October

7-10 The Conservative Party conference at Bournemouth is used by ministers to unveil a set of proposals for the next Conservative government, including an accelerated programme of privatisation and legislation to force local authorities to accept tenders from private contractors.

10 Tebbit lodges a complaint against the BBC alleging bias against the government in its reporting of the American raids on Libya.

11-12 Reagan breaks off negotiations with Gorbachev at the Reykjavik Summit in order to maintain his Star Wars policy, thereby aborting a wide-ranging arms control agreement.

22 The Labour NEC votes by 13 to nine to bar Les Huckfield, a left-wing Euro-MP, as a candidate for the pending Knowsley North by-election, and to impose the moderate, George Howarth; the constituency party refuses to work for Howarth in protest.

24 Britain breaks diplomatic relations with Syria after it is alleged that Nezar Hindawi, found guilty of attempting to plant a bomb on an El Al airliner in April, had links with the Syrian Embassy.

26   Jeffrey Archer resigns as Conservative Party Deputy Chairman because of his 'lack of judgement' in allowing his name to be associated with that of a call-girl.

November

5   A court in New South Wales, Australia, orders the British government to produce secret documents relating to the memoirs of Peter Wright, an ex-MI5 agent, whose publication it is attempting to prevent.

6   Lawson, in his autumn statement, reveals a major increase in public spending, with £10 billion extra expenditure on education, health, social security and housing.

12   President Reagan admits that the United States shipped military equipment to Iran in the hope of improving relations with a strategically vital country, arousing the strongest criticism of his presidency as it is revealed that money from the arms sales was illegally filtered to the 'Contras', a right-wing guerrilla group fighting the Nicaraguan government.

13   Labour retains the Knowsley north by-election, but its majority in a safe seat is reduced from 17,191 to 6,724.

27   Hattersley, in a speech to the Fabian Society in London, states that low inflation must be the first and overriding requirement for Labour's plans on the economy and employment.

28   Kinnock admits to having had contact with Peter Wright's Australian lawyers, and Thatcher temporarily considers withdrawing the usual consultations between the Prime Minister and the Leader of the Opposition on security and defence.

December

3   General Bernard Rogers, the NATO Supreme Commander, warns that a unilateralist non-nuclear defence policy would ultimately lead to United States troops pulling out of Europe.

8   British Gas is sold after a mass advertising campaign.

16   The government majority is reduced to 18 as the Commons votes by 211 to 193 to prevent unemployed homeowners claiming full benefit for mortgage relief.

18 The government announces its support of the United States AWACS (Airborne Warning and Control System) instead of the British Nimrod system, without any of the turmoil surrounding the Westland affair.

19 Soviet dissident Andrei Sakharov is released in a major move by the Soviet regime towards a more favourable international image.

22 David Penhaligon, a prominent Liberal spokesman, is killed in a car accident.

29 Harold Macmillan dies at the age of 92.

The Gallup poll shows 41 per cent Conservative, 32.5 per cent Labour and 23.5 per cent Alliance support.

1987

January

7-8 The Labour 'shadow cabinet', in a two-day strategy and policy making meeting in Bishop's Stortford, agrees on a £6 billion programme to create over a million jobs in two years.

8 The Alliance parties agree on a final division of seats for the election, with 327 Liberal and 303 SDP candidates.

11 Kinnock says that Labour will reverse any tax cuts made in Lawson's coming budget, a remark seen by Conservatives as electorally damaging to Labour.

12 The Alliance parties name 24 joint spokesmen, including non-MPs Shirley Williams and Bill Rodgers; Liberal discontent is expressed at the appointment of John Cartwright, the SDP Whip, as Defence spokesman.

14 The Government details plans adding £4.7 billion to public spending plans, with particular emphasis on health, education, and law and order.

A report from the Royal Institute of Public Administration rejects accusations that Thatcher chose top civil servants on the basis of their political beliefs, but it calls for less secrecy in their selection.

16 Hattersley, in a speech to the Chemical Industries Association in London, attempts to focus public concern on the growing number of unproductive mergers by attacking Britain's weak anti-monopoly legislation.

21 David Owen, in a speech to the Council of Foreign Relations in New York, attempts to heal Alliance differences over defence by claiming that Reagan's willingness to talk to Gorbachev on arms control would make the deployment of Trident a non-issue.

24 A demonstration to mark the anniversary of the Wapping dispute breaks into violence, with 162 police and over 300 demonstrators hurt.

February

4 A cross-party home affairs committee of the Commons

notes with alarm the increasing number of constituencies since 1950, and recommends a freeze at the present level of 650.

5   SOGAT 82, the main print union involved in the Wapping dispute, votes to end the strike, causing widespread anger and dismay among the strikers.

6   The Wapping dispute is officially ended as the NGA print union calls off the strike to avoid sequestration.

Kinnock tells a Labour Local Government conference at Leeds that a Labour government could not provide funds on a scale matching the government cuts of recent years.

11   Dealings in British Airways shares opens, with the £900 million offer for sale over-subscribed.

24   The government reveals plans for further legislation against the trade unions; the aim is to extend postal ballots for union offices, end the legal protection of the closed shop, and protect strikebreakers from union disciplinary measures.

26   In a spectacular victory at the Greenwich by-election, Rosie Barnes turns a Labour majority of 1,211 into an SDP majority of 6,611.

March

9   James Callaghan, during a Commons debate on arms control, goes against the party's defence policy by rejecting the unilateral abandonment of Trident; this intervention causes a furore in Labour's ranks.

10   Roy Jenkins, for the Alliance, proposes a reflationary programme to reduce unemployment by a million within three years.

12   The Alliance retains Truro in a by-election, with the Liberal majority increased from 10,480 to 14,617.

The House of Lords uphold the dismissal of 47 Labour Councillors in Liverpool for failing to set a rate for the city; the Liberals take over the city's administration.

16   John Banham becomes CBI Director General.

17   Lawson's budget, stressing caution and prudence, cuts income tax by 2p in the pound and reduces the public borrowing target by £3 billion.

21-2   The Conservative Central Council, a delegate conference, calls for an early election, in spite of the temporary advance of the Alliance to second place in opinion polls.

23   A strong attack on the Alliance by Tebbitt, which is felt to have the opposite effect to that intended, causes concern on the Conservative backbenches.

24   Labour launches *New Industrial Strength for Britain*, calling on the government to direct and encourage enterprise through a British Investment Bank.

26   Kinnock makes a disastrous trip to the United States, where his attempt to allay American fears about Labour defence policy fails, and a White House spokesman creates the impression of a sharp Presidential rebuff.

28-   Thatcher makes a successful trip to the Soviet Union,
Apr 2 where her relationship with Gorbachev and her 'walk-abouts' in the Moscow suburbs create an impression of statesmanship.

April

2   The Cabinet threatens to retaliate against Japanese trade imbalances, especially the exclusion of Cable and Wireless from Japanese markets, by refusing licences for new Japanese banks and insurance companies in London.

14   Gorbachev, in talks with US Secretary of State Schultz in Moscow, offers to dismantle Soviet short-range missiles in Europe.

15   Letter bombs are sent by the IRA to Thatcher's aides, Bernard Ingham and Brian Unwin.

21   John Edmonds, the GMBU Union General Secretary, warns the Scottish TUC Congress at Perth that Labour is in danger of being diverted from its main campaign themes by internal disputes.

24   Kinnock, in a speech to Labour candidates at Northampton, warns against the 'fruit machine' politics of tactical voting for the Alliance to defeat Thatcher.

26   *News on Sunday*, a left-of-centre paper, is launched.

27   The *Independent* publishes long extracts from Peter Wright's memoirs, claiming that 30 MI5 officers were engaged in a plot to overthrow the Wilson Government in 1974.

29   The Labour NEC suspends Ms Sharon Atkin as Labour

candidate for Nottingham East after a speech in which she allegedly described Labour as a racist party for its opposition to black sections.

May

3   A quarter of a million people, less than expected, form a human chain from Liverpool to London to protest at unemployment.

6   Thatcher rejects a call from James Callaghan, a former prime minister, to investigate the MI5 plot to overthrow Wilson alleged by Peter Wright.

7   Local elections in England and Wales provide a filip to Conservative morale; Tories and the Alliance make gains at Labour's expense, though Liverpool is recaptured by Labour despite the Militant controversy.

8   In the greatest loss of IRA life in a single incident for 60 years, eight guerrillas and one civilian are killed at Loughgall, Co. Armagh.

11   A general election is announced for *11 June*.

14   George Younger, the Defence Secretary, speaking at a meeting of NATO defence ministers at Stavanger, Norway, says that Britain may offer itself as a base for US submarine launched Cruise missiles to compensate NATO for the loss of any missiles in the forthcoming arms control talks.

18   Parliament is dissolved.

The Alliance election manifesto, *Britain United*, proposes a wide-ranging programme of constitutional reform, notably proportional representation, together with changes to the tax and social security systems in order to reduce poverty; further privatisation, including British Steel, is promised.

19   The Conservative manifesto, *The Next Moves Forward*, proposes radical changes in housing and education, involving a reduction in the scope and power of local authorities, coupled with further privatisation and tax cuts.

The Labour manifesto, *Britain Will Win*, stresses the need to reduce unemployment, together with an anti-poverty programme to help the pensioners and the long-term unemployed.

28   Kinnock claims at a press conference that Polaris submarines would be recalled from patrol duties as soon as a

Labour government was elected.

Owen and Steel refuse to change strategy in the face of the failure of the Alliance to advance in opinion polls.

June

2   Lawson promises at a press conference that the Conservatives, if re-elected, would privatise further industries, specifically airports, water and electricity.

3   A public conflict between the Alliance leaders, after Steel says that he would not support a Thatcher government in a hung parliament, is quickly healed after Steel partially withdraws his statement.

The Militant-led Broad Left win control of the CPSA civil servants union.

8   Lawson claims in a radio interview that Hattersley 'is lying through his teeth' over tax policies and points to hidden Labour commitments, including the abolition of married man's allowances.

8-10   The Venice economic summit of world leaders fails to propose any policies to overcome world trade imbalances and the US budget deficit; Thatcher visits the summit for one day.

11   Polling day with a turnout of 75.4 per cent (32,529,423 votes cast); despite an impressive Labour media campaign, the Thatcher government is returned for a third time, with a Conservative overall majority of 101; Labour does particularly well in the North, especially Scotland, while the Conservatives dominate the South; Enoch Powell, Roy Jenkins and the Scottish Nationalist leader, Gordon Wilson, are among the defeated; 375 Conservatives, 229 Labour, 22 Alliance (17 Liberals, five SDP), three Plaid Cyrmru, three SNP, 13 Various Ulster Unionists, three SDLP, one Provisional Sinn Fein and the Speaker are elected; the Conservatives obtain 13,736,747 votes (42.2 per cent), Labour 10,029,270 (30.8 per cent), and the Alliance 7,341,275 (22.6 per cent).

13   In a Cabinet reshuffle, Cecil Parkinson is brought back as Energy Secretary, John Wakeham replaces the independent-minded John Biffen as Leader of the Commons and Lord Hailsham retires as Lord Chancellor.

14   David Steel calls for a 'democratic fusion' of the two

Alliance parties after the disappointing election result, with the joint leadership issue and his own position as Liberal leader being resolved later; dissension within the SDP results, with Owen opposed to a merger against Roy Jenkins and Shirley Williams.

15 The SDP ends the system of joint spokesmen with the Liberals operated during the election campaign.

18 Unemployment falls by 64,300, the largest fall since 1948, to 2.954 million.

25 Parliament is opened by the Queen's Speech, outlining a programme of far-reaching changes in education, rates reform, housing and trade unions.

29 The SDP national committee votes by 18 to 13 to support Owen in rejecting pressure for an immediate merger; a ballot on the issue is to put to the party rank and file.